FISCAL POLICY,
ECONOMIC
ADJUSTMENT,
AND
FINANCIAL
MARKETS

FISCAL POLICY, ECONOMIC ADJUSTMENT, AND FINANCIAL MARKETS

*Edited
by
Mario Monti*

*Papers presented at a seminar sponsored by the
International Monetary Fund and Centro di
Economia monetaria e finanziaria, Università Bocconi,
held in Milan on
January 28-30, 1988*

International Monetary Fund, Washington, D.C.
Centro di Economia monetaria e finanziaria, Milan
1989

Library of Congress Cataloging-in-Publication Data

Fiscal policy, economic adjustment, and financial markets.

Includes bibliographical references.
ISBN 1-55775-118-8
  1. Fiscal policy. 2. Debts, Public. 3. Finance.
I. Monti, Mario. II. International Monetary Fund.
HJ236.F556   1989   336.3   89-19934

Price: US$16.00

Address orders to:
International Monetary Fund, Publication Services
700 19th Street, N.W., Washington, D.C. 20431, USA
Telephone: (202) 623-7430
Telefax: (202) 623-7491
Cable: Interfund

The following symbols have been used throughout this book:

... to indicate that data are not available;

— to indicate that the figure is zero or less than half the digit shown, or that the item does not exist;

– between years or months (e.g., 1988–89 or January–June) to indicate the years or months covered, including the beginning and ending years or months;

/ between years (e.g., 1987/88) to indicate a crop or fiscal (financial) year.

"Billion" means a thousand million.

Details may not add to totals shown because of rounding.

Foreword

As the papers presented here make clear, the three topics that served as the theme for this seminar—fiscal policy, economic adjustment, and financial markets—cannot be considered only in isolation; an understanding of the relationships between them, leading to an informed approach to policy coordination, is essential not only in the conduct of domestic economic policy, but in the coordination of international economic policy. This volume, which contains the proceedings of a seminar held in Milan in January 1988, includes papers on all three topics viewed from various perspectives: individual country studies; international policy coordination; and the role of the international financial institutions.

In the panel discussion that followed the formal presentation of the papers, these topics were examined in closer detail, in particular the coordination (and possible conflicts) between various policy tools—especially monetary and fiscal policy—in containing inflation and public expenditure.

This seminar, which was co-sponsored by the Centro di Economia monetaria e finanziaria of the Università Commerciale Luigi Bocconi, is one of several such seminars the Fund has helped to organize in an effort to widen the dialogue between academics, government officials, and professional economists and to provide a forum for an open exchange of views on economic adjustment and the role of international financial institutions in the adjustment process.

MICHEL CAMDESSUS
Managing Director
International Monetary Fund

Acknowledgments

The Centro di Economia monetaria e finanziaria of Università Commerciale Luigi Bocconi is honored to have had the opportunity to sponsor jointly with the International Monetary Fund this seminar on *Fiscal Policy, Economic Adjustment, and Financial Markets*. As director of the Centro and editor of this volume, I wish to express my appreciation to the Fund and, in particular, to Salvatore Zecchini, Vito Tanzi, and Manuel Guitián for their support and their active participation in the seminar. Special thanks are due to Hellmut Hartmann, coordinator of the seminar, who personally did so much for its success.

The Italian authorities also lent their support, and I wish to thank Giovanni Spadolini, President of the Senate and of Università Bocconi; Giuliano Amato, Deputy Prime Minister and Treasury Minister; and the Banca d'Italia for their valuable contributions to the proceedings.

Università Bocconi hosted the seminar, which was open to students—a welcome departure from the tradition of Fund seminars. The Rector, Luigi Guatri, opened the proceedings and was generous in encouraging this initiative from the beginning. Organization of the seminar was considerably smoothed by Mirka Giacoletto Papas and her colleagues of Bocconi Communicazione. Within the Centro di Economia monetaria e finanziaria, I owe a special acknowledgment to the Deputy Director, Angelo Porta. Marina Grandi and other members of the staff were generous in providing their assistance.

The greatest debt of an editor, of course, is to the contributors to the volume. This case is no exception, given the thorough and perceptive contributions provided by the authors, discussants, the chairmen of the various sessions, and the members of the concluding panel discussion.

Finally, I would like to thank Sara Kane of the Editorial Division of the International Monetary Fund for her valuable help in the editing of this volume. Thanks are also due to the Graphics Section of the International Monetary Fund, which was responsible for the production and design.

MARIO MONTI
Milan

Contents

Opening Remarks

Giovanni Spadolini

President of the Italian Senate and
President of Università Bocconi

Monetary and fiscal authorities, officials, and scholars from many countries are assembled here for three days to debate important and exacting issues. I wish them a pleasant stay and a successful outcome to the meeting, which will certainly produce rich results for scientific research and policies. Economic policies should never be devoid of or severed from the progress of research.

The topic of the conference is very important: the role of budgetary policies in macroeconomic equilibrium and their relation to the financial markets. It is a central issue for both the international economy and for the economy of each individual country. But I would like to stress that it is particularly important in the Italian case, where for many years the public sector deficit and debt have profoundly conditioned the real and financial development of the economy. May I say that few other problems commanded so much of my attention and concern when I served as Prime Minister in 1981–83.

In my present role as President of the Senate, I confront the same harsh and unyielding problem on the legislative front. I do so at a time when tensions and contradictions not intrinsic to constitutional questions are besieging the political institutions and when there is a great risk of confusing the need to change worn-out mechanisms with the carrying out of the many constitutional principles and imperatives that, so far, have been impeded or blocked. The two issues are connected, though different.

The role of Parliament becomes increasingly delicate and crucial in the drawing up of the government budget and in determining its level of consistency and rigor. This role will be reinforced and will become more reliable once parliamentary regulations and work procedures of the Houses are revised. The revision of Article 81 of the Italian Constitution is at the center of these institutional debates. The provisions of this article have been too often eluded or avoided, causing—in both recent and less recent times—a runaway, ever increasing public deficit.

I am thinking, in particular, about the last subsection of Article 81: "Every law issued which entails new and increased expenses must indicate the means with which these expenses are to be met." And I am also thinking about the constitutional provision that links the legislative function with the duty to impede the kinds of increases in public spending that would compromise the governance of the economy.

This last subsection originated at the Constituent Assembly, thanks to the courageous initiative of Luigi Einaudi, the future President of the Republic. The initiative was undertaken to prevent members of Parliament—whose object was "becoming popular," in the words of Einaudi—from proposing expenditures "without even considering the necessary means to meet them."

Now, forty years after the drafting of the Republican Constitution, fulfilling and applying the provisions of Article 81 mean recovering that sense of the state and that consciousness of public duties that have been handed down uncorrupted by "our founding fathers," so that we do not lose the principle of good governing and administration of our country.

The topic of public spending control is in itself a theme that justifies a conference. But this particular conference is also important because it has been organized in collaboration with the International Monetary Fund. It is superfluous to remind everyone of the prestige of this institution, its contributions to the planning and management of economic and financial policies of industrialized and developing countries, to the compilation of statistical information, to analyses of economic trends, and, in general, to economic research.

With Italy, the International Monetary Fund has always played the important role of stimulating budget adjustments, and in this meeting, the Fund again provides this impetus.

Italy today holds an important position within the international community serviced by the Fund. This position allows us to join with the other several countries that are engaged in a coordinated effort to manage international economic policies. This conference will certainly produce useful ideas and suggestions that will be useful to us in this endeavor.

It is well known that there are controversial issues in the international debate. In recent years, these issues have related specifically to budget policies; and policymakers look to the scientific community and to conferences like the one taking place here for a clear and precise analysis that can help guide them when they are preparing agreements.

I cannot—specifically because of my constitutional role—fail to underline what an honor we consider it that an Italian location has been chosen for this worthy initiative. At the same time, as President of Università Bocconi, I express my greatest satisfaction in having our University host this conference.

Vito Tanzi

Director, Fiscal Affairs Department
International Monetary Fund

It is indeed a great honor and a pleasure for me and my colleagues from the International Monetary Fund to be here with you today. It is extremely valuable for us to join such an illustrious group of scholars, senior officials, bankers, and economic writers for an unencumbered discussion of vital international issues. We are particularly honored today by the presence of Signor Giovanni Spadolini and Signor Giuliano Amato.

This conference, organized jointly by the Centro di Economia monetaria e finanziaria of the Università Bocconi and the Fund, is part of a series of regional seminars started in 1981 by the Fund's External Relations Department as a channel for the exchange of ideas with academics, bankers, businessmen, and opinion makers in the media. The objective of these seminars is to evoke interest and debate among academics and other professionals in current economic and financial issues, to garner outside ideas in the areas of Fund competence, and to contribute to a better understanding of the role of the Fund in the international monetary system. Seventeen such seminars have been held worldwide, and the proceedings of most have been published by the Fund in several languages.

The theme of today's conference, "Fiscal Policy, Economic Adjustment, and Financial Markets," could not have been more timely. Considering the fact that planning for this seminar started about a year ago, one could say that the choice of this theme was very prophetic, and that the organizers might have been privy to some insider information! In view of the fact that Professor Monti proposed it well before the October crash, I cannot resist the temptation to paraphrase a Wall Street line and say that "when Professor Monti talks, we should all listen!"

On a more serious note, the overall theme addresses the central issue of international economic policy coordination. The relatively recent concerted efforts to foster international economic policy coordination can be traced to the Rambouillet Summit of 1975, which was followed by several meetings, the latest of which was held in Venice last year. While not enough time has elapsed to pass final judgment on these efforts, it seems clear that economic policy coordination is not an easy task and that it is complicated by almost instantaneous perceptions and reactions in world financial markets.

As stated in the conclusion of the paper I will be presenting to you shortly, those who were skeptical in the past about attempts by some countries to fine-tune their economies are likely to be even more skeptical about the proposed internationalization of these policies. In my view, this is particularly pertinent with respect to fiscal policy coordination among the industrial countries. But the complexity of the issues at hand should not prevent us from having a constructive discussion and from examining and evaluating the many issues related to economic policy coordination without the cumbersome constraints confronting the decision makers. By the end of this seminar, we hope that we shall have a sharper awareness of the issues at stake, the difficulties that lie ahead, and the perils that could befall the world economy in the absence of improved policy coordination among the industrial countries.

I would like to conclude these brief remarks by expressing my own special and personal thanks to the Director and the staff of the Centro di Economia monetaria e finanziaria, and to the Università Bocconi and its Rector, Signor Luigi Guatri, for the excellent arrangements and the warm hospitality extended to us in this beautiful city of Milan.

Thank you.

Giuliano Amato

Italian Deputy Prime Minister and Treasury Minister

The topics that will be discussed during the three days of this conference are of great interest to all persons involved in the analysis, formulation, and implementation of economic policies in all countries with close, interdependent economies. The increasingly strong ties that bind the economies of the industrialized countries force those who are responsible for economic policies in every country to be very attentive to the consequences their decisions can have on the economies of other countries. Decisions taken independently to pursue legitimate national objectives can lead to severe inequalities in economic and financial relations. In these cases, it is necessary to find effective ways of coordination.

The experience of international economic coordination has helped nations avoid taking the kind of unilateral action that could have damaged the orderly development of international commercial and financial relations. It has also contributed to various forms of cooperation between different countries in order to pursue common objectives. Many international economic institutions have contributed to this process, including the International Monetary Fund, which has played a fundamental role.

International economic cooperation becomes more effective, although more difficult, when it extends even further than mere currency relations and demand management in the short term. It is particularly effective when it extends to structural aspects of the economy and examines ways to reconcile the medium-term development of individual countries.

The internationalization of markets for goods and factors of production imposed by modern technology must be confronted. A solution must be found to those problems created by a progressive liberalization and integration of the markets themselves. At the same time, in order for liberalization to be beneficial in terms of increased efficiency, but without causing imbalances and dangerous instabilities, it is necessary to find forms of harmonizing the regulations and the institutions that preside over economic and financial activities. This will lead, in the future, to the unification of some of them and is particularly important and pressing for the financial markets.

Liberalization and integration of international markets, along with the adoption of common regulations and reliable institutions, favor fiscal adjustments required by domestic demand and the public deficit in some countries. In fact, a large deficit can be supported—or in some cases required—for some time in an economy with a marked tendency toward saving, such as the Italian economy.

But it can also become a factor of potential instability and an increasing constraint to growth possibilities, the more rapidly the economy proceeds on the path of international financial integration and currency liberalization in a context of relative exchange rate stability between countries bound by exchange agreements.

In 1987 Italy chose to accelerate the process of financial liberalization. Other steps in this direction will be taken in the near future in the form of programs for the liberalization of monetary assets and of financial services, in view of the creation of the unified European Common Market. At the same time, with the decision made in September 1987, Italy has confirmed its participation in the European Monetary System, thus contributing to the strengthening of the system.

Within this context, the adjustment process cannot be confined only to a positive differential between the growth rate of gross domestic product and the rate of interest, which is to be hoped for but is not yet a reality, or to an unwelcome and avoidable resumption of inflation. The adjustment must be based on the control of public spending and an increase in tax receipts, the latter to be obtained not by increasing tax rates but by extending the taxable base. The qualitative aspect, along with the quantitative aspect of the fiscal adjustment process is particularly important for its successful outcome, as several papers to be discussed at this conference will no doubt point out.

The results of these discussions will certainly contain new and interesting proposals, and I will be waiting to hear these proposals with great interest. In the meantime, I express my warmest appreciation to the International Monetary Fund and to Università Bocconi for organizing this conference, and my wishes to all participants for a successful and stimulating meeting.

1

International Coordination of Fiscal Policies: Current and Future Issues

Vito Tanzi

Coordination means different things to different people. Webster's *Seventh New Collegiate Dictionary* defines it as the "act of coordinating," or the "state of being coordinated," and, perhaps more interestingly, "harmonious adjustment or functioning." Thus, the word coordination conjures up in one's mind the image of an orchestra that is harmoniously led by a talented conductor. In this analogy the members of the orchestra, the players, would obviously be the countries' policymakers. It is not clear, however, who would be in the conducting role. That role could be played by the agreement reached by the policymakers at their latest summit or as a consequence of their latest consultations. Such an agreement would presumably concern only the period immediately ahead, since it is unlikely that the policymakers would or even could commit themselves for a longer period. Or, in a more permanent arrangement, the role of the conductor could be played by a set of specific rules (perhaps based on some "economic indicators") agreed upon by the policymakers. The resolution that set up the European Monetary System (EMS) provides an example of this type of arrangement. Or even, in a futuristic world, where the national authorities have devolved some of their decision-making responsibilities to an international or supranational body, that role could be played by an international organization. In the discussion that follows, only the first of these possibilities is contemplated, since the other two do not seem realistic for fiscal policy at this time.

I. The Case for Policy Coordination

The premise that there is a need to coordinate macroeconomic policies rather than letting countries independently pursue their own economic interests is a relatively radical and novel one, especially with regard to fiscal policy. However, to some extent countries have coordinated policies, especially in connection with exchange rate arrangements, for a long time (see Fischer (1987)).[1] Although this idea surfaced in the 1970s and was put to an early and not too lucky test following the Bonn summit of 1978, only very recently has it gained wide attention on the part of both policymakers and professional economists. In fact, much of the writing on this subject dates from the past few years.

The recent impetus toward policy coordination has come from at least three directions: first, the belief on the part of many observers that the economic, and specifically the fiscal, policies of the major industrial countries have been widely "misaligned" in the 1980s; second, the growing recognition that the economies of the world, and especially those of the industrial countries, have become much more interdependent than they were in the past; and third, the argument advanced by some economists that there are important externalities in policymaking; implying that when countries act independently and in their own self-interests, policy changes may not be carried to the degree necessary to maximize the collective welfare of the group of countries.

Misalignment of Fiscal Policies

The main issue regarding policy misalignment in the 1980s has been the size and sustainability of the U.S. fiscal deficit. The fiscal deficit of the central government of the United States rose by about 3 percent of gross national product (GNP) between 1980/81 and the post-1982 period. This increase occurred even though the U.S. economy was enjoying an unusually long upswing; therefore, the "structural" deficit increased even more. This increase may have contributed to the upswing that started in 1983 and accelerated in 1984, but it created several problems for both the United States and the rest of the world. When the major fiscal policy changes were introduced in 1981, the new Administration had expected that, because of the reduction of marginal tax rates and the introduction of various savings incentives (such as Individual Retirement Accounts), the household saving rate would increase by about 3 percent, and this increase would largely finance the deficit that was seen to be temporary anyway. As it turned out, the rate of saving fell and the fiscal deficit remained very high and would have been even higher if various corrective measures had not been introduced (see Palmer (1987)).

The large increase in the fiscal deficit in a large country with a very low rate of saving was at least partly responsible for the high level of real interest rates that

---

[1]For example, the proponents of the fixed exchange rate system have argued that the Bretton Woods system was successful for a long time, partly because it imposed discipline on the macroeconomic policies of the member governments. The par value system was based on, and required, a large measure of policy coordination among participants. Some have argued that the prevalence of par values provided the simplest indicator system yet devised to gauge the existence of such coordination.

have characterized the 1980s.[2] The restrictive monetary policy of 1979 and the early 1980s gave the initial upward push to real interest rates, but when monetary policy became accommodating after 1982, real interest rates were kept high by large fiscal deficits.[3] While the structural fiscal deficit of the United States rose sharply after 1981, those of the Federal Republic of Germany and Japan, two countries with much higher saving rates, became somewhat smaller. This reduction may have helped contain the rise in the world's real rate of interest (see Tanzi (1985a)).

As a consequence of these developments, the current account of the U.S. balance of payments deteriorated rapidly—from a surplus of $6.3 billion in 1981 to deficits of around $140 billion in 1986 and 1987. Japan's current account balance, which had been in deficit in 1979 and 1980, went into a small surplus in 1981 and 1982 and grew to exceed $80 billion in 1986 and 1987. Germany's current account followed a similar pattern, running a deficit as recently as 1981, which became a small surplus in 1982–84 and grew afterwards to reach $36 billion in 1986 and $35 billion in 1987.

The worsening of the U.S. current account has affected its international investment position. Table 1 shows that the net position of the United States vis-à-vis the rest of the world changed from a positive figure of $106.3 billion in 1980 to a negative figure of $263.6 billion in 1986. Up to 1981 the United States was the world's largest creditor nation. It was still a net creditor in 1984. By the end of 1986 it had become the world's largest debtor nation. By 1987 the net indebtedness of the United States exceeded 8 percent of its GNP. The figures may overstate the real net position of the United States, since the asset side includes loans to developing countries, which have much lower market values than their book values. However, the market value of other private assets may also be greater.[4]

The details in Table 1 are as important as the overall change in the net position of the United States. They show that while direct foreign investment in the United States increased by $126.3 billion, foreign investments in U.S. securities increased by $315.3 billion, and foreign investments in other U.S. bank and nonbank liabilities increased by $324.3 billion. Thus, not only did the net position of foreign investors improve sharply, but it improved in particular in

---

[2]See Bovenberg (1987), Feldstein (1986), Mortensen (1987), Muller and Price (1985), and Tanzi (1985b).

[3]The investment incentives introduced by the United States in 1981 and 1982, as well as policies aimed at deregulating financial markets, may also have played a role (see Tanzi (1985b) and Sinn (1987)).

[4]By 1987 the Federal Republic of Germany and Japan had become net creditors to the tune of 16.5 percent and 14.1 percent of their respective GNPs.

Table 1. U.S. International Investment Position
(In billions of current U.S. dollars)

Type of Investment	1980	1986	Change
U.S. net position	106.3	−263.6	369.9
Assets abroad	607.1	1,067.9	460.8
Official reserve assets	26.8	48.5	21.7
Government nonofficial reserve assets	63.8	89.4	25.6
Private assets	516.6	929.9	413.3
Direct investment abroad	215.4	259.9	44.5
Foreign securities	62.6	131.0	68.4
Other bank and nonbank claims	238.5	539.0	300.5
Foreign assets in the United States	500.8	1,331.4	830.6
Foreign official assets	176.1	240.8	64.7
Other foreign assets	324.8	1,090.6	765.8
Direct investment	83.0	209.3	126.3
U.S. securities	90.2	405.5	315.3
Other bank and nonbank liabilities	151.5	475.8	324.3

Source: Constructed by William J. Kahley from data in R.B. Scholl, "The International Investment Position of the United States in 1986," *Survey of Current Business* (Washington), Vol. 67 (June 1987), p. 40. The table is taken from William J. Kahley, "Direct Activity of Foreign Firms," *Economic Review*, Federal Reserve Bank of Atlanta (Summer 1987), p. 39.

those assets that can be disposed of quickly and for which expectations can play an important role. Table 1 also provides some indirect evidence of the relative role of high interest rates and a good investment climate in attracting foreign capital. Although direct investment increased considerably, it was not the overwhelming factor in the change in the net indebtedness position of the United States, as has sometimes been argued.[5]

The years 1980–87 have also witnessed wide swings in exchange rates. The value of the dollar first rose sharply up to 1985 and then fell equally sharply. The changes vis-à-vis the yen and the deutsche mark have been particularly significant. The rise in the value of the dollar was widely attributed to the increase in U.S. interest rates, although the differential rate of expansion of the three economies may have also played a role. The subsequent fall has often been attributed to the growing reluctance by foreigners to keep increasing the share of dollar-denominated assets in their portfolios (see Marris (1985) and (1987)).

---

[5]Some have argued that high interest rates could be a reflection of large demand for capital, owing to a good investment climate. Thus, the large inflow of portfolio capital could itself be a reflection of a good investment climate (see Sinn (1987)).

The earlier sharp increase in the value of the dollar and the continuing large U.S. current account deficit have generated protectionist pressures and other difficulties and have inevitably forced policymakers to attempt to deal with them. The Louvre Accord (1987) was generally viewed as an arrangement on exchange rates, even though it implied some commitment on economic policies by the participating countries. The "Statement of the Group of Seven," released on December 22, 1987, is more specific in listing the policy intentions and undertakings agreed upon by the finance ministers and central bank governors of the seven major industrial countries.

Growing Interdependence

There is plenty of evidence to indicate that industrial countries have become much more interdependent than they used to be. The most dramatic recent evidence of this interdependence was undoubtedly the behavior of stock markets around the world after the 508-point fall in the New York stock exchange on October 19, 1987 ("Black Monday"). Whether one considers the share of imports and exports in national incomes—shares that have increased sharply for many industrial countries in recent decades—or the size of capital movements, or the attention that policymakers now pay to the economic policies of other countries, the conclusion must be that the fiction of a closed economy—a fiction that is still kept alive in the pages of many economic textbooks—cannot provide useful insights for guiding the economic policy of the real world. The internationalization of the financial and goods markets, together with the wide and immediate availability of information, has guaranteed that what happens in one country, and especially in a large country, will be felt by other countries. What this means is that the domestic fiscal policy multipliers associated with, say, a fiscal expansion by a single country become smaller than they were in the past. Furthermore, the smaller and more open a country is, the lower these domestic multipliers are likely to be.

The Need for Cooperative Policies

Obvious benefits are associated with this interdependence and openness. International trade of products and factors among countries encourages specialization and brings about a more efficient international allocation of resources. Under normal assumptions, international trade raises the level of world income. This interdependence, however, has important implications for the conduct of fiscal and monetary policy as well. Interdependence implies that there are important externalities to some policy actions. These externalities may create inefficiencies, in the sense that policy actions may not be carried to the level that would be considered optimal from an international point of view. In a closed economy, both the costs (political and economic) and the benefits of fiscal policy actions would be fully internalized. However, in an interdependent world, some of the benefits (and some of the costs) of that action will spill over to other countries.

Assume, for example, that the policymakers of country X wish to pursue an expansionary fiscal policy to stimulate domestic economic activity and employment. Assume also that there are no offsetting actions on the part of other countries or on the part of the monetary authorities. The fiscal policy action on the part of country X is generally assumed to increase its aggregate demand in the short run and, as a consequence, its level of imports. [6] The increased exports by other countries will increase *their* level of economic activity and employment, [7] while country X will experience a deterioration in its trade account. The smaller a country is and the more open its economy, the greater will be the share of the total increase in demand that will affect other countries.

An example often mentioned to prove the above point is the expansionary fiscal policy pursued by the Mitterrand Government in the early 1980s. It has been maintained that the domestic beneficial effects of that action were largely dissipated by the openness of the French economy and the consequent low fiscal multiplier. The expansion had to be stopped soon after it started because of the deterioration in France's balance of payments. It can also be argued that a good part of the benefits *and the costs* of the U.S. fiscal expansion since 1982 accrued to other countries, either because they could maintain a higher level of economic activity because of higher exports to the United States, or because they had to bear the consequences of higher real interest rates or of fluctuating real exchange rates or terms of trade. Countries that export little to the United States but are net borrowers and are closely linked in financial markets would be particularly affected negatively. In these countries, the cost of borrowing (or servicing their stock of debt) would go up. The distribution of costs and benefits may have been unevenly distributed across countries, depending on how close in goods trade their economies were to the U.S. economy and on whether they were net lenders or borrowers.

---

[6] This generally accepted conclusion should be qualified when the fiscal expansion starts from a situation where there is either a large fiscal imbalance or a large public debt. In such cases, negative confidence effects may neutralize all or part of the expansionary effects. Furthermore, as Corden (1987) has pointed out, with flexible exchange rates it is possible that a country may expand without a deterioration in its current account.

[7] This conclusion is not true in all models. It is conceivable that an expansionary policy in country X may negatively affect other countries through effects on real interest rates and terms of trade. For example, a large fiscal expansion in the United States that increased real interest rates could conceivably have negative effects on developing countries with a large foreign debt. Ironically, if the debt is due to American banks and if it is paid, the United States could end up benefiting from this externality.

The argument presented above has implications for the coordination of fiscal policy among countries, especially when economic activity needs to be stimulated. If, acting independently, countries would be reluctant to pursue expansionary fiscal policies because of the balance of payments effects of these policies, they could all benefit—and they could neutralize the effects on the balance of payments—if they all pursued a fiscal expansion at the same time. However, given different propensities to import, different interest elasticities of investment demand, and different trade connections with countries that are not part of the coordinated group, even in this case the results are not likely to be neutral. Furthermore, the countries would have to consider the inflationary implications of their joint expansion.

The situation gets more complex when one takes into account not just the benefits but also the costs of fiscal policy actions, and when coordination calls for expansion on the part of some countries and contraction on the part of others (see Corden (1986) and (1987)). Experts on policy coordination, using game theory and other analytical tools, have described situations whereby policy coordination may reduce rather than increase the group's welfare. However, much of the literature seems to conclude that in normal circumstances coordination would be beneficial, although the benefits do not appear to be particularly large compared to situations in which countries do not coordinate.

The above example leaves unanswered, however, some important questions. First, is it as feasible to coordinate fiscal policy actions as it is to coordinate monetary policy actions? Second, is there a possibility that short-run and long-run objectives of fiscal coordination may conflict? Third, what does coordination of fiscal policy mean? These issues are briefly raised in the next section.

II. Requirements for Successful Fiscal Coordination

Coordination can have several meanings, which may range from a vague understanding that each country will do its best to keep, or to put, its own economy (and its own fiscal accounts) in good shape (under the belief that, as Fischer (1987) and others have argued, this is the best that each country can do for others), to a commitment by each country to take specific policy actions agreed jointly in coordination with other countries. For example, in a period of slow economic activity, a group of countries—say, the Group of Seven—might agree to pursue expansionary fiscal policies. Alternatively, under circumstances in which the fiscal policies of the countries are viewed as being misaligned, some country, say, the United States, might commit itself to pursuing a policy aimed at reducing its fiscal deficit on condition that other countries, say, the Federal Republic of Germany and Japan, agreed to pursue more expansionary fiscal policies, at least for the short run, than they would otherwise. The discussion that follows focuses on this kind of coordination.

In a world in which the policies of individual countries attract a lot of attention on the part of other countries and international organizations, such as the International Monetary Fund (IMF), Organization for Economic Cooperation and Development (OECD), and European Communities (EC), it is safe to assume that some implicit coordination of policies is always taking place, in the sense that countries do pay some attention to the impact that they are having on other countries or to what other countries expect them to do. For example, Article IV and World Economic Outlook (WEO) discussions by the Executive Board of the IMF, together with the preparation and distribution of the relevant documents, must inevitably have some influence on the policy behavior of countries. It would thus be unrealistic to assume that under current circumstances, and in the absence of explicit coordination agreements, the economic policies of countries would be guided by myopic behavior that totally ignores what other countries are doing or are likely to do.

Frequent interchanges among the policymakers of different countries, together with the great amount of information that is available to them, imply that rational and concerned policymakers would take into account both the impact of their policies on others and the impact of the policies of others on them. This strategic behavior is likely to produce better results than would be associated with myopic behavior and that may not, in fact, differ very much in terms of benefits from those achieved through explicit coordination (see Canzoneri and Minford (1988)).

An actively coordinated fiscal policy *that aims at demand management on a global scale rather than at correcting major fiscal imbalances in particular countries* will have to meet various requirements if it is to stand a good chance of being successful in achieving its stated objective. This section discusses some of these requirements. The discussion focuses on fiscal policy of a demand management type, although there are of course many other kinds of coordination that are not considered here.

Fiscal Coordination and Economic Forecasts

For a policy of fiscal coordination to succeed, a necessary prerequisite would be that the relevant group of countries has *jointly* recognized that there is a need for a coordinated change in policy. This need would arise from a belief among the coordinating policymakers (finance ministers and central bank governors) that, in the absence of joint policy action, the outcome, in terms of variables measuring some economic objectives, at some future time (say, one or two years ahead) would not be desirable. As already mentioned, the relevant comparison would not be with the alternative of no action but with the one of individual action based either on myopia or, more realistically, on strategic behavior—that is, a behavior that takes into account what other countries are doing and what they expect other countries to do. Thus, the first basic requirement for successful coordination seems to be a *jointly agreed and reliable forecast.* Here there are at least two issues: the reliability of the forecasts, and agreement among the countries that one of the forecasts is the right one.

It is a well-known fact that forecasts are partly applied science, partly art, and partly divination. In a recent and stimulating book dealing with the essence of science and with a major scientific revolution now taking place, James Gleick discusses the scientific basis for the forecasts made by scientists in different branches of science, including astronomers, ecologists, weather forecasters, and economists. He says that "by the seventies and eighties, economic forecasting by computer bore a real resemblance to global weather forecasting" (Gleick (1987), p. 20). His assessment of weather forecasts is sharp: ". . .beyond two or three days the world's best forecasts [are] speculative, and beyond six or seven [days] they [are] worthless" (p. 20). His assessment of economic forecasts is even sharper:

> Presumably [governments and financial institutions] knew that such variables as 'consumer optimism' were not as nicely measurable as 'humidity' and that the perfect differential equations had not yet been written for the movement of politics and fashion. But few realized how fragile was the process of modeling flows on computers, even when the data was reasonably trustworthy and the laws were purely physical, as in weather forecasting. (p. 20)

Of course, not all economic forecasts are made by computer models, and Gleick would probably agree that forecasts made for the period just ahead have a far better chance of being right than those made for longer periods. But this is precisely the difficulty with coordination of fiscal policy. As I shall argue below, it often takes quite some time before fiscal policy changes coordinated by a group of countries can be implemented and can have an effect on the world's economies. This time is likely to be somewhat longer than the period for which acceptably reliable forecasts can be made.

Forecasts are likely to be relatively reliable for the next 6 months and somewhat less so for the next 12 months. As the period is extended beyond that, they are unlikely to provide the kind of information on which policymakers would or should base their policy decisions. Of course, we are discussing fiscal policy coordination that aims at demand management, not fiscal policy actions aimed at putting the fiscal accounts of a country in order. For the latter one does not need a forecast, although the pace of adjustment must be determined on the basis of current and expected future economic conditions. The more vigorous is the current pace and the expected future pace of economic expansion, the more quickly can fiscal disequilibrium be corrected.

At this point it is perhaps important to make a distinction between coordination of monetary policy and coordination of fiscal policy. Once an agreement is reached by the policymakers of the coordinating countries, monetary policy actions can be taken immediately and well within the period for which existing forecasts provide relatively reliable results. For fiscal policy it is different. For fiscal policy, even when an agreement has been reached, it may take a long time before action can be taken. Thus, the issue being discussed at this point is not a major difficulty for monetary policy coordination, but it is for fiscal coordination.[8] In both cases, of course, there might be a long lag between the time the action is taken and the time when the results of that action are felt by the economy.

Examples of economic forecast errors for output growth and inflation for six major industrial countries are shown in Table 2 and Table 3. The tables show forecast errors made by national forecasts as well as by the WEO of the IMF. All the errors refer to forecasts made for a period just one year ahead. Such a period is often far too short for the coordination *and execution* of fiscal policy.

The tables are largely self-explanatory, but a few aspects may be highlighted. First, the errors may appear small since they are given in percentage points, but not when they are compared to the average values of the variables they are forecasting. Second, the errors would be larger if the forecasts were made for, say, two or three years ahead. Third, the errors appear to be particularly large in periods when economic conditions are changing rapidly, such as 1974 and 1982. But these are exactly the periods when one would want to have fiscal coordination of the demand-management type. Fourth, in some cases, there are significant differences between the forecasts made by the countries' national authorities (say, the Council of Economic Advisers (CEA) forecast in the United States and the official forecast in Japan) and those made by WEO (see also correlation coefficients in the tables). The differences between the forecasts made by the national authorities and those made by the Fund (or, for that matter, by OECD) tend to be particularly large in exactly those periods when the strongest case for coordination could be made.

In conclusion, one of the basic requirements for successful fiscal coordination—namely, the *availability of a jointly agreed and reliable forecast*—is unlikely to be met.[9] This has serious implications for fiscal coordination that aims at global demand management through fiscal policy changes, although it is a far less serious obstacle for monetary policy coordination or fiscal coordination that emphasizes either the correction of serious fiscal imbalances in particular countries or structural changes.

---

[8]But, of course, if there are long lags on the effectiveness of monetary policy, as Milton Friedman has often argued, then the issue is the same.

[9]Ghosh and Masson (1987) have recently argued that model uncertainty may provide a strong incentive for countries to coordinate their policies if they recognize policy uncertainty. However, they do not explicitly account for lags in implementation.

Table 2. Output Growth Forecast Errors, Year-Ahead Forecast

(In percentage points)

	United States				Japan		France		Federal Republic of Germany				Italy		United Kingdom	
	OMB[1]	CEA[2]	Consensus	WEO[3]	Official	WEO	Official	WEO	Consensus	Five Wise Men	Official	WEO	ISCO[4]	WEO	NIESR[5]	WEO
1973	…	0.8	0.2	0.4	4.3	0.5	—	—	-0.4	0.1	-0.9	-0.3	-0.9	-1.4	-0.8	-1.0
1974	…	3.2	2.9	4.9	2.7	10.8	2.5	1.4	2.6	2.1	0.6	2.6	3.1	2.6	0.4	3.6
1975	…	-1.0	1.0	0.3	0.9	1.2	4.2	4.7	6.1	5.6	5.6	5.4	3.7	4.6	3.5	4.0
1976	0.2	—	-0.1	0.2	-0.1	-0.7	-0.2	-1.8	-1.6	-1.1	-1.1	-2.2	-3.6	-4.2	-1.3	-0.7
1977	0.8	—	0.1	0.3	0.9	1.2	1.5	0.4	3.1	2.1	2.6	2.2	1.3	-2.2	-1.7	0.6
1978	1.3	0.4	-0.1	0.1	1.3	-0.8	1.2	0.1	-0.4	0.1	0.1	—	-0.6	0.4	-0.5	-0.5
1979	2.0	1.4	-0.8	1.1	0.2	-1.1	0.3	—	-0.4	-0.6	-0.4	-0.4	-1.0	-1.0	1.1	1.0
1980	1.2	-0.7	-1.1	0.2	-0.2	0.5	1.1	1.0	0.7	1.0	0.7	1.3	-2.5	-1.2	1.9	1.4
1981	-1.7	1.0	-0.7	-3.4	2.0	1.1	1.2	1.6	0.3	0.8	-0.2	2.3	-0.2	0.6	1.1	1.8
1982	5.1	4.2	2.4	2.6	1.9	2.7	1.2	0.6	2.2	1.7	2.5	3.1	1.3	2.1	0.1	-0.5
1983	1.0	-3.0	-1.3	-1.6	-0.3	0.5	1.1	1.8	-0.3	-0.3	-0.8	0.7	2.7	4.5	-0.8	-1.6
1984	-1.6	-1.1	-1.3	-2.5	-1.0	-1.8	-0.5	-0.3	-0.6	-0.1	-0.1	-0.6	…	-0.2	-0.3	-0.5
1985	1.6	1.5	0.7	1.3	0.3	-0.4	0.4	0.4	-0.5	0.5	—	-0.1	…	0.2	-0.6	-0.9
Average absolute error (1973–79)	1.075	0.971	0.743	1.043	1.486	2.329	1.414	1.200	2.086	1.671	1.614	1.871	2.029	2.343	1.329	1.629
1980–85	2.033	1.917	1.250	1.933	0.950	1.167	0.917	0.950	0.767	0.733	0.717	1.350	1.675[6]	2.100[6]	0.800	1.117
Whole Period WEO	1.650	1.408	0.977	1.454	1.239	1.792	1.185	1.085	1.477	1.239	1.200	1.631	1.900[7]	2.255[7]	1.085	1.392
Correlation coefficient, WEO	0.89	0.68	0.83	—	0.50	—	0.88	—	0.91	0.92	0.86	—	0.86	—	0.86	—

Source: Llewellyn and Arai (1984), updated and extended by Michael J. Artis, "How Accurate is the World Economic Outlook?", Part I in Staff Studies for the World Economic Outlook, (Washington: International Monetary Fund, July 1988), p. 24

Note: Forecast errors are defined as forecasts minus realization values.

[1] Office of Management and Budget.
[2] Council of Economic Advisers.
[3] World Economic Outlook.
[4] Istituto Nazionale per lo Studio della Congiuntura.
[5] National Institute of Economic and Social Research.
[6] 1980–83
[7] 1973–85

Table 3. Inflation Forecast Errors, Year-Ahead Forecast

(In percentage points)

	United States				Japan		France		Federal Republic of Germany				Italy		United Kingdom	
	OMB[1]	CEA[2]	Consensus	WEO[3]	Official	WEO	Official	WEO	Consensus	Five Wise Men	Official	WEO	ISCO[4]	WEO	NIESR[5]	WEO
1973	...	-2.3	-2.7	-2.3	-9.6	-6.3	-2.1	-2.3	-0.6	-0.1	-0.6	-0.4	-3.0	-2.3	-2.9	-0.5
1974	...	-3.2	-3.5	-4.7	-8.1	-8.6	-4.1	-4.4	0.5	1.0	0.3	0.2	-10.2	-7.6	-2.8	-4.8
1975	...	2.3	-0.2	0.5	5.1	9.0	-3.0	-2.1	-1.3	-2.3	-1.8	-1.1	1.6	-1.0	-5.6	-7.8
1976	2.0	0.9	0.7	0.6	—	-0.1	-1.9	1.1	1.4	0.9	0.9	1.2	-7.5	-2.8	-1.1	—
1977	0.1	-0.4	-0.3	-0.5	1.6	1.3	-0.4	-0.5	0.4	0.4	-0.1	0.1	-1.0	2.7	-1.0	-0.6
1978	-1.1	-2.3	-1.4	-1.3	0.9	-0.8	-2.0	-1.2	0.1	-0.4	-0.4	0.1	-1.2	-0.8	-0.3	0.4
1979	-2.2	-1.6	-1.1	-1.1	1.7	0.2	-1.5	-1.5	-0.3	-0.8	-0.3	-0.2	-3.4	-1.8	-3.2	-4.2
1980	-0.1	-1.0	-0.2	0.1	1.8	4.4	-2.4	-1.8	-0.5	-0.5	-1.0	0.1	-5.8	-6.2	-0.2	-4.6
1981	0.8	1.6	0.1	-1.3	1.5	1.6	-0.9	-3.1	0.4	-0.1	0.4	0.2	-3.5	-3.8	-0.4	1.2
1982	2.1	2.6	1.9	1.2	1.4	1.5	1.1	0.5	-0.3	-0.8	-0.8	-0.3	0.3	2.0	—	1.0
1983	2.3	1.5	1.5	1.8	1.5	2.3	-0.9	2.1	0.3	0.3	0.3	1.3	-0.1	4.1	1.7	2.2
1984	1.0	1.4	0.7	0.4	0.2	1.6	-0.5	0.3	0.6	1.1	1.1	1.1	...	...	0.5	1.8
1985	1.3	1.1	1.0	1.0	-0.1	-0.5	-0.3	-0.4	0.3	-0.2	-0.2	0.4	...	2.3	0.2	-1.1
Average absolute error (1973–79)[6]	1.350	1.857	1.414	1.571	3.857	3.757	2.143	1.871	0.657	0.843	0.629	0.471	3.986	2.714	2.414	2.614
1980–85	1.267	1.533	0.900	0.967	1.083	1.983	1.017	1.367	0.400	0.500	0.633	0.567	2.425[7]	3.500[7]	0.500	1.983
Whole Period[6]	1.300	1.708	1.177	1.292	2.577	2.938	1.623	1.638	0.538	0.685	0.631	0.515	3.418[8]	3.000[8]	1.531	2.323
Correlation coefficient, WEO	0.809	0.80	0.94	—	0.92	—	0.64	—	0.86	0.80	0.86	—	0.83	—	0.80	—

Source: Llewellyn and Arai (1984), updated and extended by Michael J. Artis, "How Accurate Is the World Economic Outlook?", Part I in *Staff Studies for the World Economic Outlook*, (Washington: International Monetary Fund, July 1988), p. 24.

Note: Forecast errors are defined as forecasts minus values for the GNP/GDP deflator (except for the United Kingdom, and NIESR where the consumer price index was used).

[1] Office of Management and Budget.
[2] Council of Economic Advisers.
[3] World Economic Outlook.
[4] Istituto Nazionale per lo Studio della Congiuntura.
[5] National Institute of Economic and Social Research.
[6] Excluding 1973–85.
[7] 1980–83.
[8] 1973–85.

Fiscal Coordination and Economic Objectives

Assuming that the coordinating policymakers have reached an agreement on the relevant forecast, the next step must be to agree on the economic objectives that should be achieved through coordination. Should the main objective be an acceleration of economic activity, a reduction in the unemployment rate, a reduction in the rate of inflation, some adjustment in the balance of payments, or a reduction in the real rates of interest? And if, as is likely, more than one objective is important, how should the various objectives be ranked in terms of priority?

There are two issues that are likely to arise: coordination *among countries*, and coordination *within countries*. Economic policy in democratic countries must, to a large extent, reflect the priorities of the citizens. If these priorities are ignored, elected policymakers are not likely to remain policymakers for long. This is, again, an area where a large difference exists between monetary and fiscal policy, especially in some countries.

Monetary policy is often made by officials who are somewhat insulated from the political process. They are appointed for a given number of years, or even for an indefinite period, and cannot be removed.[10] When Paul A. Volcker, then Chairman of the Federal Reserve Board, decided to pursue a restrictive monetary policy in 1979 to reduce the rate of inflation, he did not have to worry about the reaction of the U.S. electorate. This freedom, however, is not enjoyed by the elected officials who make fiscal policy and who have to worry about the next election and have to coordinate their actions with the legislature, which is also keeping an eye on the electorate. What this means is that it would be unrealistic to assume that in the fiscal area the policymakers of a country would, to a substantive degree, subordinate the priorities of the country's electorate to those of the policymakers of other countries. It is well known that Germans, reflecting *their* historical experiences, are more concerned with inflation than with unemployment. For Germans the worst economic experience in this century was the hyperinflation of the 1920s that wiped out the financial savings of that country's middle class. It is equally well known that Americans, also reflecting *their* historical experience, are more concerned with unemployment than with inflation. Their worst economic experience was the Depression of the 1930s. Those events still cast a long shadow on current economic policy.

---

[10]The degree of statutory independence of central banks in conducting monetary policy varies substantially among the Group of Seven countries. In some countries they are required by law to secure approval by the Treasury Minister of key monetary policy decisions. The central banks of the United States and Germany are independent.

The one important example of economic cooperation among countries, the European Monetary System (EMS), has succeeded in coordinating monetary but not fiscal policy. In fact, the evidence so far is that there has been relatively little coordination of fiscal policy among the members of the EMS (see Tanzi and Ter-Minassian (1987), and Russo and Tullio (1988)).

Fiscal Coordination Within a Country

Much of the writing on fiscal coordination has simply assumed that policymakers meet at some important summit meeting and decide on a coordinating strategy that might imply changing the money supply by a given percentage or reducing or increasing the fiscal deficit by a given amount. On the basis of this change in the fiscal deficit, some economic model can then calculate the final effect on the variables that policymakers wish to influence through coordination. In the next subsection, the relationship between changes in instruments (that is, the fiscal deficit) and changes in objectives (for example, growth, inflation) will be discussed. But first, it is worthwhile to discuss the question of what may happen between the time when a decision is made at some international meeting to change the fiscal deficit and the time when that decision becomes, if it does, the specific policy of a country. To paraphrase an old Italian saying: in fiscal policy, between the declaration of intentions and the implementation of actual policies one must deal with the role of the legislature.

Let us start with a summit agreement in which a country, say, the United States, has agreed to reduce its fiscal deficit by 1 percent of GNP. When the policymakers get back to Washington, the first decision that they will have to make is whether they will propose that the reduction be carried out through the revenue side or through the expenditure side of the budget. In either case, all they can do is propose the changes to Congress. If the proposal is on the revenue side, it will have to go to committees; these will deliberate for months and perhaps years, and could, eventually, come out with alternative proposals that may bear little relation *either quantitatively or qualitatively* to the initial proposal. In this political process, domestic priorities are likely to take precedence over international priorities. Besides, if the changes are important and they are on the revenue side, the question arises of whether the revenue-estimating models now available are good enough to be able to assess, with any degree of precision, the relationship between the changes in the statutory rates and the actual revenue changes. If the changes are on the expenditure side, the question arises of whether they are durable. In any case, the control by the executive branch over this instrument, especially in the United States, is much more tenuous than current writing on coordination implies.

If the proposal is on the expenditure side, the budgetary cycle also has to be dealt with. Table 4 provides some information on this issue for the group of seven

Table 4. Opening Stages of the Annual Budget Cycle in Seven Major Industrial Countries

Country	Decision Taken by	Nature of Decisions	Months Before Budget Presented to Legislature	Next Step
Canada	Cabinet Committee on Priorities and Planning	Total spending and broad sectoral targets (envelopes)	6	Ministers submit detailed departmental bids for approved programs, for negotiation with Treasury Board
France	Prime Minister	Broad guidelines in "lettre de cadrage"	9	Ministers prepare and negotiate requests, leading to a specific ministry target in "lettre de plafond" three months later
Germany, Federal Republic of	Minister of Finance	Total spending and broad guidelines	9	Ministers submit detailed departmental bids, for negotiation with the Minister of Finance
Italy	Treasury Minister	Changes required in total and by department	6	Ministers submit budget proposals to Treasury Minister
Japan	Cabinet	Policy guidelines on budgets	6	Ministries submit proposals to Ministry of Finance
United Kingdom	Cabinet	Planning total set for three years forward	9	Spending ministers submit bids if necessary, for amounts in excess of previously agreed baseline
United States	President	General fiscal and budget guidelines; sometimes departmental-specific	15	Spending agencies submit bids to OMB

Source: Adapted from Table 1 in OECD (1987), p. 27.

major industrial countries. The table shows that in one important case (the United States), the cycle commences some 15 months before the proposals are sent to the legislature. In three cases, it starts nine months before, and in the remaining three cases it starts six months before. The fiscal year for which the budget applies starts normally some time after the proposals are sent to the legislature. Once again, the proposals that go to the legislature are likely to be modified both quantitatively and qualitatively. Thus, even if the coordinating agreement has been made at the very beginning of the cycle, it is unlikely that it will have much of an effect on expenditure for two years, if not longer. And, of course, as has already been stated, in some countries the final result is likely to differ sharply from the original intention. Furthermore, there will be a lag between the time the fiscal action is implemented and the time its effect is felt in the economy.

Let us summarize the most likely operating scenario for pursuing a policy of fiscal coordination. Presumably, the action would start with a jointly agreed forecast for one year ahead. That forecast would send signals that some policy changes are needed. Thus, after some time, an agreement would be reached (perhaps at a summit). Such an agreement would conceivably ask different countries to reduce or increase their fiscal deficit by agreed amounts. On the basis of this agreement, proposals to change revenue or expenditure would be prepared by each country. Eventually, these proposals would go to the proper committees in the legislature where, at least in some important countries, they would be modified and sent to the full legislature. At some point they might be approved. Between the original agreement by the coordinating group and the enactment of the proposals, and between that enactment and the time when their effect is felt on the economy, a considerable amount of time is likely to have elapsed. That time is likely to be well beyond the period for which reliable forecasts can be made.

Fiscal Coordination and Policy Instruments and Objectives

Assume that (1) policy changes of the size and structure desired by the coordinating policymakers can be enacted immediately; (2) that policymakers of different countries have agreed on a forecast; (3) that they have agreed on the goals to be achieved through coordination; and (4) that they have agreed *in principle* on the policy changes to be made. Thus, what remains to be specified is the size of the change to be made to, say, the fiscal deficit or the growth of money. Since much of the literature on macroeconomic coordination has concluded that coordination improves policymaking, it should follow that there would be no reason not to coordinate. Unfortunately, even under these ideal circumstances, the important issue arises of the relationship between the policy instruments and the final objectives of policy. The issue discussed here is not limited to fiscal policy but extends to all policies.

Economics has not advanced to the point at which it can give definite and precise answers to the question of what effect a given expansion in the money supply, for example, or an increase in the fiscal deficit would have on some basic objectives such as the rate of growth, inflation, the current account in the balance of payments, and so forth. Sometimes even theoretical answers are not easy. Often, governments rely on econometric models to get some of these answers, and quite a few of these models are now serving different governments. If all of these models agreed on the answers and the answers were the correct ones, coordination would be easy. If they all agreed but the answers were the wrong ones, the gains from coordination would be reduced but policymakers might still reach an easy agreement on what to do. A more serious practical problem arises when the models give different answers to the same questions, and the policymakers of the different countries must decide whether to trust the results of their own model or those of others. Just how serious is this issue of conflicting models? An experiment at the Brookings Institution in Washington addressed this specific issue.

In this experiment the people in charge of 12 multicountry models were asked to simulate, independently, the effects of carefully specified policy changes to see how much agreement there would be in the results obtained. Two of these changes concerned fiscal policy: a permanent increase in U.S. real government expenditure of 1 percent of baseline GNP; and a permanent increase, also of 1 percent of baseline GNP in non-U.S. government expenditure. These changes were simulated, while the growth of monetary aggregates was assumed to be exogenous. The results, which are summarized in Table 5, refer to the second year after the policy changes were made and show the cumulative percentage deviation from the baseline estimates.

A remarkable feature of these results is their wide range. The U.S. fiscal expansion is seen to raise: (1) real U.S. income by anywhere between 0.4 percent and 2.1 percent by the second year, and real foreign income by anywhere between zero and 0.9 percent; (2) the U.S. consumer price index (CPI) by anywhere between –0.9 percent and 0.9 percent, and the foreign CPI by anywhere between –0.1 percent and 0.6 percent; (3) U.S. interest rates by anywhere between 0.1 percent and 2.2 percent, and the foreign rates by anywhere between zero and 1 percent; and (4) the value of the U.S. exchange rate by anywhere between –2.1 percent and 4.0 percent. The U.S. current account deteriorates by anywhere between $0.5 billion and $22.0 billion. The results of the foreign expansion on the United States can also be seen from the table. They all show equally broad ranges.

Table 5. Simulation Effect of Fiscal Expansion in Second Year After Policy Change

(In percent, except where otherwise noted)

Fiscal Expansion in the United States

Model	United States Income	CPI	Interest Rate	Currency Value	Current Account (in billions of U.S. dollars)	Non-United States Income	CPI	Interest Rate	Current Account (in billions of U.S. dollars)
MCM	+1.8	+0.4	+1.7	+2.8	−16.5	+0.7	+0.4	+0.4	+8.9
EEC[1]	+1.2	+0.6	+1.5	+0.6	−11.6	+0.3	+0.2	+0.3	+6.6
EPA	+1.7	+0.9	+2.2	+1.9	−20.5	+0.9	+0.3	+0.5	...
LINK	+1.2	+0.5	+0.2	+0.1	−6.4	+0.1	—	...	+1.9
LIVERPOOL	+0.6	+0.2	+0.4	+1.0	−7.0	—	+0.6	+0.1	+3.4
MSG	+0.9	+0.1	+0.9	+3.2	−21.6	+0.3	+0.5	+1.0	+22.7
MINIMOD	+1.0	+0.3	+1.1	+1.0	−8.5	+0.3	+0.1	+0.2	+5.5
VAR[2]	+0.4	−0.9	+0.1	+1.2	−0.5	—	—	—	−0.2
OECD	+1.1	+0.6	+1.7	+0.4	−14.2	+0.4	+0.3	+0.7	+11.4
TAYLOR[2]	+0.6	+0.5	+0.3	+4.0	...	+0.4	+0.4	+0.2	...
WHARTON	+1.4	+0.3	+1.1	−2.1	−15.4	+0.2	−0.1	+0.6	+5.3
DRI	+2.1	+0.4	+1.6	+3.2	−22.0	+0.7	+0.3	+0.4	+0.8

Fiscal Expansion in OECD Countries

Model	Non-United States Income	CPI	Interest Rate	Currency Value	Current Account (in billions of U.S. dollars)	United States Income	CPI	Interest Rate	Current Account (in billions of U.S. dollars)
MCM	+1.4	+0.3	+0.6	+0.3	−7.2	+0.5	+0.2	+0.5	+7.9
EEC[1]	+1.3	+0.8	+0.4	+0.6	−9.3	+0.2	+0.1	—	+3.0
EPA	+2.3	+0.7	+0.3	−0.7	...	+0.3	+0.3	+0.6	+4.7
LINK[3]	+1.2	+0.1	...	−0.1	−6.1	+0.2	—	—	+6.3
LIVERPOOL	+0.3	+0.8	—	+3.3	−17.2	−0.5	+3.1	+0.8	+11.9
MSG	+1.1	+0.1	+1.4	+2.9	−5.3	+0.4	+0.6	+1.3	+10.5
MINIMOD	+1.6	+0.2	+0.9	+0.6	−2.2	+0.1	+0.2	+0.3	+3.2
VAR	+0.5	−0.3	−0.2	−2.4	+1.7	+0.3	−0.1	+0.2	−2.6
OECD	+1.5	+0.7	+1.9	+0.9	−6.9	+0.1	+0.2	+0.3	+3.3
TAYLOR[2]	+1.6	+1.2	+0.6	+2.7	...	+0.6	+0.9	+0.4	...
WHARTON	+3.2	−0.8	+0.8	−2.4	+5.5	—	—	+0.1	+4.7
DRI	...	...	...	...	...	...	...	...	...

Source: Frankel (1986), p. 21.

[1] Non-U.S. short-term interest rate not available; long-term rate reported instead.

[2] U.S. CPI not available; U.S. GNP deflator reported instead.

[3] Appreciation of non-U.S. currency not available; depreciation of dollar reported instead.

Besides the wide range of what should be similar results, a few aspects merit comment. First, it should be recalled that these are largely demand-driven macroeconomic models. In some of them, expectations do not play much of a role. In those where they do, the issue is how accurately they have been modeled. For example, right now—that is, in December 1987—when the value of the U.S. currency has been falling considerably, supposedly because the financial markets do not believe that the agreement reached by the Administration and Congress to reduce the U.S. budget deficit will be complied with, it is easy to be skeptical about results that indicate that, say, an announcement by the U.S. Government to *increase* government spending by 1 percent of GNP would *raise* the value of the dollar. Second, the U.S. fiscal expansion is seen to affect non-U.S. incomes more than the non-U.S. fiscal expansion affects U.S. incomes. Third, the results shown refer to the second year after the policy changes. As one traces the effects beyond that period, some of them (for example, the positive effect on income) would vanish leaving the governments with higher public debt to service.

Finally, when the leading econometric models give results as varied as these, and when none of these models may give the true answer, it is easy to see the difficulties faced by those who negotiate agreements on policy coordination. It is difficult in this case to come up with a package of policy changes that would be accepted by all participants as the clearly optimal one. What we might have is coordination based on intuition. As Branson (1986, p. 176) has put it: "With this range of disagreement on economic analysis, how are the negotiators to reach agreement?" And if an agreement is reached, how can one be sure that it will improve the situation? Once again, one comes to the conclusion that the best form of international policy coordination, especially in the fiscal area, is the one that encourages countries to pursue policies that over the medium run put their fiscal accounts in order while paying some attention to the pace at which changes are made. In a way this conclusion argues in favor of a rule and against a policy of international fine-tuning.

Fiscal Coordination and Political Leverage

A successful policy of fiscal coordination would be facilitated if (1) all of the participating countries had the same political and economic influence; or (2) the one country that has more leverage either economically or politically was also the one with an economy that is not facing major disequilibria in some of the areas to be coordinated. One of the reasons for the success of the EMS in reducing the rate of inflation of the member countries has undoubtedly been the fact that the Federal Republic of Germany was the major economic power in the group, and Germany's inflation rate was very low. Therefore, the other EMS countries were forced to pursue monetary policies that became progressively more consistent with Germany's. Moreover, restrictive monetary policies became more credible. In some sense, the monetary authorities in other EMS countries took advantage of the stock of credibility of the German central bank. But, suppose, for example, that at the time the EMS came into existence Italy had been the major economic power in the group. Given Italy's inflation rate at that time, and its consequent monetary policy, it is conceivable that the other countries would have adjusted, at least in part, to the Italian policy. The result would probably have been a much higher rate of inflation over the longer run and the costs of anti-inflation plans would have been higher since these plans would have been less credible.

We have here what could be called the "fox-without-the-tail" syndrome. As Aesop tells us, the fox that lost its tail tried to convince the other foxes that a tail was a burden after all, and the other foxes would be better off if they cut theirs off. International coordination of fiscal policy inevitably creates pressures on those countries that have been more successful in recent years in correcting their fiscal imbalances to relax their fiscal policy to bring it more in line with that of countries where less adjustment has taken place. These pressures on the former will become stronger the less successful are the latter in putting their fiscal houses in order. If these pressures succeeded, fiscal coordination might not generate *over the medium run* the desirable results, even if it succeeded in bringing some short-run stimulation to aggregate demand.

III. Fiscal Situation of the Major Industrial Countries

The two previous sections examined various issues connected with fiscal coordination. This section takes a look at the fiscal accounts of the seven major industrial countries that have attracted the attention of experts and policymakers in connection with the coordination of macroeconomic policies. Some economists have suggested that Japan, the Federal Republic of Germany, and, perhaps, the United Kingdom should now pursue expansionary fiscal policies, since these countries have presumably already won their battle against fiscal disequilibrium. The United States, Italy, and Canada, however, should continue with their attempts to rein in their fiscal deficits. The advice to France is less clear cut.

The underlying model on which this advice is based seems to be a kind of global Keynesianism whereby the world is assumed to have and to need a given amount of aggregate demand; therefore, to prevent a recession, if demand is reduced by fiscal restraints in some important countries, the reduction must be compensated by fiscal expansion in others. Of course, monetary policy could be used as a substitute for fiscal policy, but this aspect is ignored in this discussion, although it plays a large role in the current discussions on coordination of macroeconomic policies.

The case for fiscal expansion by some countries has, perhaps, been made most forcefully by Willem Buiter in several articles. In a recent article he writes:

> There should be a 'supply-side friendly' fiscal expansion in the fiscally strong industrial countries, such as Japan, Germany, and the United Kingdom. The behaviour of their debt/GDP ratios, their primary deficit and, in the case of Japan and Germany, their current account deficits suggest that these countries have ample fiscal elbow room. In addition there is considerable real slack in all three economies. . . . (Buiter, 1987, p. iii).

He considers the recently announced fiscal stimulus in Japan (equal to about $35 billion) ". . . a step in the right direction but. . . very small in relation to both the macroeconomic and the structural needs of both Japan and the world economy." He also considers "the German decision to bring forward some already scheduled tax cuts (0.9% of GDP in 1988) . . . inadequate" (p. iv). Furthermore, "The 'unsustainability' of the current U.S. fiscal position has been much exaggerated" (p. v).

Since at least 1982, the International Monetary Fund has been advising industrial countries with large fiscal deficits to reduce them (see de Larosière (1982 and 1984)). This strategy was recently outlined in some detail in the April 1987 *World Economic Outlook (WEO)*, the Fund's yearly assessment of the international economic situation. In that study the Fund reaffirmed its belief in the need for medium-term correction in the fiscal accounts of industrial countries. At the same time, *WEO* warned that a too-sudden reduction in the U.S. fiscal deficit could reduce government demand faster than the private sectors in the United States and abroad could pick up the slack, thus possibly leading to a worldwide slowdown of economic activity. Nonetheless, "[i]n the case of the United States, the danger in not proceeding promptly and vigorously with fiscal restraint is that financial markets may eventually react unfavorably to continued large borrowing needs on the part of the government" (International Monetary Fund, 1987, p. 20). A reduction in the U.S. fiscal deficit, by reducing interest rates, would stimulate investment in the United States and abroad. Furthermore, the removal of a major worry from the economic scene would contribute to a climate more favorable to an expansion of private sector activity.

The suggestion was made in *WEO* that Italy and Canada should give consideration to policies "that would achieve cuts in the fiscal deficit more quickly," whereas for the Federal Republic of Germany, "relatively greater concern attaches to sustaining the pace of demand and output" (p. 20). There is thus no doubt about the medium-run direction of the policy advocated by the Fund vis-à-vis fiscal consolidation.

Given these contrasting positions between those who advocate a fiscal activism that minimizes the need for fiscal adjustment (or the potential dangers of fiscal expansion) and those who emphasize the objective of medium-run fiscal consolidation, it may be worthwhile to comment briefly on the current fiscal situation in the major industrial countries.

Table 6 gives the fiscal balances of the general governments of the Group of Seven countries as percentages of GDPs or GNPs. The improvement in recent years in the fiscal accounts of the Federal Republic of Germany and Japan is obvious. However, the table shows also that in 1987 the fiscal accounts of all the countries, except Japan, were still running deficits and some (Italy, Canada, the United States, and France) were running relatively large deficits. Furthermore, various fiscal maneuvers (temporary taxes, sales of assets, amnesties, windfall revenues) had temporarily reduced these deficits in some of the countries, so that the "core" deficits were somewhat higher. For example, the U.S. Congressional Budget Office (1988) has estimated that these temporary factors had reduced the U.S. fiscal deficit by $37 billion in 1987. In the United Kingdom the sale of assets generated revenue close to 1 percent of GDP in 1986–87. In the United States the fiscal deficit of the central government was expected to go up again in the absence of significant policy changes.

Table 6. General Government Fiscal Balances

(In percent of GDP or GNP)

Country	1980	1981	1982	1983	1984	1985	1986	1987
United States[1]	−1.3	−1.0	−3.5	−3.8	−2.8	−3.3	−3.4	−2.3
United Kingdom[2]	−3.4	−2.5	−2.4	−3.4	−3.9	−2.9	−2.4	−1.4
France[2]	—	−1.9	−2.8	−3.2	−2.8	−2.8	−2.9	−2.4
Germany, Federal Republic of[1]	−2.9	−3.7	−3.3	−2.5	−1.9	−1.1	−1.3	−1.8
Italy[2]	−8.5	−11.3	−11.3	−10.6	−11.5	−12.5	−11.4	−10.5
Canada[2]	−2.8	−1.5	−5.9	−6.9	−6.4	−7.0	−5.5	−4.6
Japan[1]	−4.4	−3.8	−3.6	−3.7	−2.1	−0.8	−0.9	0.6

Source: International Monetary Fund (1987).
Note: A minus sign indicates a deficit.
[1]Percent of GNP.
[2]Percent of GDP.

The fall in the rate of inflation has also reduced the nominally measured deficits. Furthermore, large surpluses of the social security systems are, in some countries (such as the United States), hiding large deficits of the rest of the public sector. For example, the U.S. Congressional Budget Office has projected that the federal funds deficit (that is, the deficit net of social security and other trust funds) would be close to $300 billion between 1989 and 1993 (U.S. Congressional Budget Office (1988), pp. 76–77). Of course, the surpluses of these trust funds are accumulated to build reserves to meet future needs and not to finance the rest of the government.

Aggregated data for the Group of Seven countries indicate that their fiscal deficits for the general government, as shares of combined GDPs, reached a peak of 4.1 percent in 1983, fell to 3.3 percent in 1984 and 1985, and declined to 3.1 percent in 1986 and 2.7 percent in 1987. As percentages of aggregate net private savings, the deficits reached a peak of 70 percent in 1983 and fell to 48 percent in 1986, and 42 percent in 1987.

The change in the fiscal situation in the three major countries since the early 1980s implies that the fiscal deficits have fallen in economies with large domestic savings (Japan and Germany), where they could more easily be financed through domestic sources, and have increased in the United States, which has a low and falling saving rate. This has meant that a large share of the U.S. indebtedness had to be financed from foreign sources, which has sharply increased the share of dollar assets in the hands of foreigners. [11]

The demand for dollar assets on the part of foreigners is likely to depend on the relative rates of return to dollar assets as compared to other assets, and on the perception of risk on the part of the foreign lenders. One type of risk is associated with the depreciation of the dollar. Another closely related risk is inflation in the United States. In fact, the U.S. Government is in the enviable position of being able to inflate itself out of some of its foreign debt, since this debt is held in dollars. However, since much of the U.S. debt is short term, expected inflation would quickly lead to increases in interest rates, thus sharply limiting this possibility. Over the past two years, Japanese and German investors have suffered large losses on their holdings in U.S. securities because of the depreciation of the dollar. A continuation of large (even if falling) deficits in the United States would require that foreigners keep increasing their stock of dollar-denominated assets unless the U.S. savings rate goes up or the U.S. investment rate falls. It does not seem reasonable to assume that foreigners would be willing to accommodate progressively larger dollar balances in their portfolios without demanding higher rates of return. An increase in the fiscal deficit of Japan and Germany, by creating an additional demand for funds, would not make the financing of the U.S. fiscal deficit any easier and would hurt other net borrowers such as indebted countries.

Table 7 gives the total debt of the general government as a share of GDP or GNP. Since the early 1980s the shares are either growing (United States, France, Italy, and Canada) or relatively stable (United Kingdom, Germany, and

---

[11]Between 1982 and 1985 the general government fiscal deficit of the United States was absorbing around 20 percent of the total net private savings of the Group of Seven countries. The depreciation of the dollar after 1985 implied that a smaller share of the total savings of the Group of Seven countries was necessary to finance the U.S. deficit. This might help explain some of the decline in real interest rates in the past few years.

Table 7. General Government Total Gross Debt
(In percent of GDP or GNP)

Country	1980	1981	1982	1983	1984	1985	1986	1987
United States[1]	37.9	37.2	41.3	44.1	45.2	48.4	51.2	51.6
United Kingdom[2]	54.6	54.7	53.4	53.6	54.9	53.6	52.9	50.4
France[2,3]	37.3	36.4	40.1	41.4	43.9	45.5	46.0	47.3
Germany, Federal Republic of[1]	32.5	36.3	39.5	40.9	41.5	42.2	42.4	43.2
Italy[2]	58.5	60.5	66.3	71.9	77.0	83.6	87.9	91.3
Canada[2]	44.7	45.1	50.5	54.5	58.0	63.4	67.2	69.0
Japan[1]	52.0	57.0	61.1	66.9	68.4	69.4	69.3	68.6

Source: Organization for Economic Cooperation and Development, *Economic Outlook*, 44, (Paris: OECD, December 1988).
[1]Percent of GNP.
[2]Percent of GDP.
[3]Does not exclude public sector mutual indebtedness.

Japan). Whether increasing or stable, large public debts bring about large public spending (because of interest payments), which in turn, when other expenditures cannot be reduced, brings about high taxes with disincentive effects.[12] Both Tables 6 and 7 and the related comments in the text indicate that the fight against fiscal disequilibrium is far from over. There are other reasons as well why it might be imprudent to push Japan and Germany to pursue expansionary fiscal policies.

The experience of many countries, both industrial and developing, indicates that fiscal policy is not like a faucet that can be turned on and off. This is another area where the difference between fiscal and monetary policy is considerable. It is relatively easy to create a large deficit, as the United States proved in 1981. It is very difficult to reduce a large deficit, as the United States has been proving since 1982. There is a clear asymmetry in fiscal policy. Most spending programs once in place cannot be easily removed. Taxes are easier to reduce than to increase. These facts should bias the attitude of policymakers toward caution.

Another important factor—the aging of the population—is also highly relevant in this context, especially in connection with Japan and Germany. This factor will, in time, have two major consequences. First, it will bring about substantial

---

[12]In the OECD countries, larger expenditure for interest payments has been accompanied by smaller capital expenditure by the government. For the Group of Seven countries combined, the public debt ratio to GDP increased from around 40 percent in the 1976-81 period to 58.3 percent in 1987. For the 1984-87 period, the ratios were, respectively, 51.7 percent in 1984, 54.5 percent in 1985, 56.8 percent in 1986, and 58.3 percent in 1987. Because of the depreciation of the dollar, the share of the U.S. public debt in the total Group of Seven countries' public debt fell from 46 percent in 1985 to 37 percent in 1987.

increases in social expenditure. Second, it will reduce the private saving rate of the countries, as the proportion of the population with high propensities to consume rises. Take Japan as an example. In a recent study on the reasons for that country's high saving rate, Horioka (1986, pp. 25–26) has concluded:

> With respect of future trends in Japan's private saving rate, the dominant influence will be the dramatic changes in the age structure of the population: a decline in the ratio of the young will cause the savings rate to increase slightly until 1995 while a rapid increase in the ratio of the aged will lead to a precipitous decline in the rate thereafter.

It is only six years until 1995. A Fund study on aging and social expenditure observes that the "impact of demographic change on the Japanese economy is likely to be the most extreme among the Group of Seven" (Heller and others (1986), p. 8). The study forecasts a rise in the elderly dependency rate of 65 percent in the 15 years from 1986 and a rise in the social expenditure ratio of almost 40 percent by the year 2000, which "would imply the need for considerable fiscal adjustment" (p. 8).

Given these factors, and the inertia of fiscal changes, it would seem prudent not to create a fiscal situation that in a few years might generate problems that would be difficult to solve.

In policymaking there is another bias to worry about: the one that leads policymakers to apply much higher rates of discount to benefits that come further in the future than to benefits that come immediately. In other words, there is a tendency to alleviate current problems at the cost of more serious future problems. Larger fiscal deficits might bring immediate benefits in terms of higher economic activities but at costs that may be considerable over the longer term.

Table 8, based on the Federal Reserve Board Multicountry Model, helps make this point. The results in the table were part of the Brookings experiment reported earlier. The table traces the effects of fiscal expansion, both by the United States and by other OECD countries, through a period of six years. It indicates that an increase in U.S. real government expenditure equal to 1 percent of U.S. GNP would increase U.S. GNP by 1.6 percent in the first year and 1.8 percent in the second year over the baseline. After that, the benefits from the fiscal expansion begin to fall. By the sixth year the fiscal expansion would leave the United States (1) with GNP no higher than it would have been without the fiscal expansion; (2) with a price level that is 2.3 percent higher; and (3) with a government expenditure (and presumably a fiscal deficit and a public debt) higher than it would have been. Presumably, though this result was not reported, the impact of the fiscal expansion on the GNP for periods beyond the sixth year would be negative. Thus, if one believes the results of this exercise, short-term benefits have been bought at long-term costs. The table shows also that a foreign

Table 8. The Impact of Fiscal Expansion Over Time

(Cumulative percentage deviations from baseline)

Fiscal Expansion	Year					
	1	2	3	4	5	6
United States[1]						
U.S. GNP	1.6	1.8	1.4	0.9	0.5	0.1
U.S. prices	0.1	0.4	0.9	1.4	1.9	2.3
Foreign GNP	0.3	0.7	0.9	0.9	1.0	1.0
Foreign prices	0.2	0.4	0.6	0.7	1.0	1.2
Foreign[2]						
U.S. GNP	0.3	0.5	0.4	0.2	0.1	—
U.S. prices	—	0.2	0.3	0.4	0.6	0.7
Foreign GNP	1.1	1.4	1.3	1.2	1.1	1.1
Foreign prices	—	0.3	0.6	0.9	1.2	1.6

Source: Adopted from Table 1 in Edison and Tryon (July 1986), p. 6.
[1]A permanent increase of U.S. real government expenditures of 1 percent of baseline GNP.
[2]A permanent increase in foreign real government expenditures of 1 percent of baseline GNP.

fiscal expansion would have a relatively small impact in the short run on the United States and none over the medium run.

IV. Concluding Remarks

In this paper some major issues related to international macroeconomic policy coordination have been surveyed. The focus has been on the coordination of fiscal policy. Issues that arise specifically in the context of the coordination of monetary policies or exchange rate policies have been largely ignored, even though they are obviously important. The relatively negative conclusions reached here about the coordination of fiscal policies may not be equally relevant to these other forms of coordination.

Two aspects have been highlighted. First, many practical difficulties would arise in any attempt to coordinate fiscal policy among industrial countries. Some of these difficulties have been ignored by proponents of fiscal coordination. Second, the paper has taken issue with those who maintain that countries such as Japan, the Federal Republic of Germany, and the United Kingdom have fully overcome their fiscal difficulties and are now in a situation where they could, and should, pursue more expansionary fiscal policies. Such a policy, these advocates of expansionary policy claim, would help pull the world economy from its low-growth path and bring the current account balances of the major industrial countries closer to a sustainable path. What is being proposed is, in fact, some sort of fine-tuning on a global scale.

Those who were skeptical in the past about attempts by some countries to fine-tune their economies are likely to be even more skeptical at this proposed internationalization of policies. The connection between expansionary fiscal policies and faster growth rates is tenuous at best. There is simply no convincing evidence that the countries that have pursued more restrictive fiscal policies have grown any less fast than those that have pursued expansionary fiscal policies. The United Kingdom, for example, has done relatively well in recent years in spite of a conservative fiscal policy. In the United States the rate of growth of the economy accelerated in 1987 in spite of a sharp reduction in the fiscal deficit. In Denmark the general government fiscal balance changed from a deficit of 9 percent of GDP in 1982 to a surplus of 3 percent in 1986. This remarkable change was accompanied by a very fast *increase* in demand. In Belgium the fiscal deficit was reduced by 2.7 percent of GDP in 1987 without any negative effects on the economy. All these reductions in fiscal deficits were the result of explicit government policies and not the natural outcome of fast-growing economies. Yet, the fiscal expansion of the second half of the 1970s in many industrial countries did not make them grow any faster than the others. Often the opposite was true.

Where coordination of fiscal policy may be highly relevant is with respect to some structural aspects, particularly tax reform. Well-designed major reforms of the tax system, even when they are revenue-neutral, are likely to have an important impact on growth as well as on the movements of financial capital and factors of production. This is an area where coordination would yield large dividends, since tax reforms can be used by countries to gain a competitive advantage over other countries. However, in this area there are also serious practical difficulties in coordination. If "supply-side-friendly" tax reforms could be coordinated, they would help promote faster world growth and more efficient economies (see Tanzi (1987)). In this respect, the recently proposed reduction in tax rates by Germany is highly welcome, even though it may not have gone far enough in reducing marginal rates and removing tax-induced disincentives. That reduction, however, is welcome for its efficiency aspects more than for its demand-promoting effects.

The same can be said for the recent commitment by the Japanese Government to increase its spending for public works. The final consumption expenditure of government as a percentage of GDP is much lower in Japan than in other OECD countries—9.7 percent, as compared to 17.2 percent for total OECD in 1985. An increase in this expenditure, if directed toward bottlenecks in infrastructures, could give important returns, regardless of whether or not it increased Japan's fiscal deficit. A full discussion of these structural aspects must be left for another opportunity.

References

Blanchard, Olivier J., and Lawrence H. Summers, "Perspectives on High World Interest Rates," *Brookings Papers on Economic Activity: 2* (1984), The Brookings Institution (Washington), pp. 273–324.

————, Rudiger Dornbusch, and Richard Layard, eds., *Restoring Europe's Prosperity* (Cambridge, Massachusetts: MIT Press, 1986).

Bovenberg, A. Lans, "Long-Term and Short-Term Interest Rates in the United States: An Empirical Analysis," IMF Working Paper 87/84 (mimeographed, International Monetary Fund, December 10, 1987).

Branson, William, "The Limits of Monetary Coordination as Exchange Rate Policy," *Brookings Papers on Economic Activity: 1* (1986), The Brookings Institution (Washington), pp. 175–94.

Bryant, Ralph C., and others, eds., *Empirical Macroeconomics for Interdependent Economies* (Washington: The Brookings Institution, 1988).

Buiter, Willem, "The Current Economic Situation, Outlook and Policy Options, with Special Emphasis on Fiscal Policy Issues," Discussion Paper Series No. 210 (London: Centre for Economic Policy Research, November 1987).

————, and Richard C. Marston, eds., *International Economic Policy Coordination* (Cambridge: Cambridge University Press, 1985).

Calvo, Guillermo, A., "Servicing the Public Debt: The Role of Expectations" (mimeographed, July 1987).

Canzoneri, Matthew B., and Patrick Minford, "When International Policy Coordination Matters: An Empirical Analysis," *Applied Economics* (London), Vol. 20 (September 1988), pp. 1137–54.

Commission of the European Communities, *Annual Economic Report* (Brussels: Commission of the European Communities, 1987/88).

Cooper, Richard N., "International Economic Cooperation: Is It Desirable? Is It Likely?" International Monetary Fund Seminar Series No. 1987–10, presented at IMF Seminar, October 29, 1987 (mimeographed, Washington: International Monetary Fund, 1987).

————, "Economic Interdependence and Coordination of Economic Policies," Chap. 23 in *Handbook of International Economics*, Vol. II, ed. by Ronald W. Jones and Peter B. Kenen (New York: North Holland, 1985).

Corden, W. Max, "Fiscal Polices, Current Accounts and Real Exchange Rates: In Search of a Logic of International Policy Coordination," *Weltwirtschaftliches Archiv* (Tübingen), Vol. 122, No. 3 (1986), pp. 423–38.

_____, "How Valid Is International Keynesianism?" IMF Working Paper 87/56 (mimeographed, Washington: International Monetary Fund, August 28, 1987).

de Larosière, J., "Restoring Fiscal Discipline: A Vital Element of a Policy for Economic Recovery," *IMF Survey* (Washington), Vol. 11 (March 22, 1982), p. 81.

_____, "The Growth of Public Debt and the Need for Fiscal Discipline," *IMF Survey* (Washington), Vol. 13 (September 3, 1984), p. 261.

Dornbusch, Rudiger, *Dollars, Debts, and Deficits* (Cambridge: MIT Press, 1986).

Edison, Hali J., and Ralph Tryon, "An Empirical Analysis of Policy Coordination in the United States, Japan and Europe," International Finance Discussion Papers No. 286 (Washington: Board of Governors of the Federal Reserve System, July 1986).

Feldstein, Martin, "Budget Deficits, Tax Rules, and Real Interest Rates," NBER Working Paper 1970 (Cambridge, Massachusetts: National Bureau of Economic Research, July 1986).

_____, "U.S. Budget Deficits and the European Economies: Resolving the Political Economy Puzzle," *American Economic Review* (Nashville, Tennessee), Vol. 76 (May 1986), pp. 342–46.

Fischer, Stanley, "International Macroeconomic Policy Coordination," NBER Working Paper 1925 (Cambridge, Massachusetts: National Bureau of Economic Research, October 1987).

Frankel, Jeffrey A., "The Sources of Disagreement Among the International Macro Models and Implications for Policy Coordination," NBER Working Paper 1925 (Cambridge, Massachusetts: National Bureau of Economic Research, May 1986).

_____, and Katharine Rocket, "International Macroeconomic Policy Coordination When Policy-Makers Disagree on the Model," NBER Working Paper 2059 (Cambridge, Massachusetts: National Bureau of Economic Research, October 1986).

Frenkel, Jacob A., and Assaf Razin, *Fiscal Policies and the World Economy: An Intertemporal Approach* (Cambridge, Massachusetts: MIT Press, 1987).

Ghosh, Atish R., "The Growth of Public Debt and the Need for Fiscal Discipline," *IMF Survey* (Washington), Vol. 13 (September 3, 1984), p. 261.

_____, and Paul R. Masson, "International Policy Coordination in a World with Model Uncertainty," *Staff Papers* (International Monetary Fund), Vol. 35 (June 1988).

Gleick, James, *Chaos: Making a New Science* (New York: Viking, 1987).

Guitián, Manuel, "The European Monetary System: A Balance Between Rules and Discretion," Part I in *Policy Coordination in the European Monetary System,* Occasional Paper No. 61 (Washington: International Monetary Fund, 1988).

Heller, Peter, and others, *Aging and Social Expenditure in the Major Industrial Countries, 1980–2025,* Occasional Paper No. 47 (Washington: International Monetary Fund, 1986).

Holtham, Gerald, and Andrew Hughes Hallett, "International Policy Cooperation and Model Uncertainty," Chap. 5 in *Global Macroeconomics: Policy Conflict and Cooperation,* ed. by Ralph C. Bryant and Richard Portes (New York: St. Martin's Press, in association with the International Economic Association and the Centre for Economic Policy Research, 1987).

Hooper, Peter, "International Repercussions of the U.S. Budget Deficit," Brookings Discussion Papers in International Economics, No. 27 (February 1985), The Brookings Institution (Washington), pp. 1–31.

————, and Catherine L. Mann, "The U.S. Fiscal Deficit: Its Causes and Persistence," International Finance Discussion Papers No. 316 (Washington: Board of Governors of the Federal Reserve System, November 1987).

Horioka, Charles Yuji, "Why is Japan's Private Savings Rate so High?" (unpublished, International Monetary Fund, June 26, 1986).

International Monetary Fund, *World Economic Outlook* (Washington: International Monetary Fund, April 1987).

Kehoe, Patrick J., "Coordination of Fiscal Policies in a World Economy," *Journal of Monetary Economics* (Amsterdam), Vol. 19 (May 1987), pp. 349–76; originally appeared, under the same title, in Staff Report No. 98 (Minneapolis, Minnesota: Federal Reserve Bank of Minneapolis, Research Department, February 1986).

Llewellyn, John, and Haruhito Arai, "International Aspects of Forecasting Accuracy," *OECD Economic Studies* (Autumn 1984), Organization for Economic Cooperation and Development (Paris), pp. 73–117.

————, Stephen Potter, and Lee Samuelson, *Economic Forecasting and Policy—The International Dimension* (London; Boston: Routledge and Kegan Paul, 1985).

Mansur, Ahsan, "Fiscal-Monetary Mix and Exchange Rate Movements in the Major Economic Countries, 1980–84," IMF Working Paper 88/3 (mimeographed, International Monetary Fund, January 20, 1988).

Marris, Stephen, *Deficits and the Dollar: The World Economy at Risk* (Washington: Institute for International Economics, 1985).

————, *Deficits and the Dollar Revisited: The World Economy at Risk* (Washington: Institute for International Economics, rev. ed., 1987).

Masson, Paul, and Adrian Blundell-Wignall, "Fiscal Policy and the Exchange Rate in the Big Seven: Transmission of U.S. Government Spending Shocks," *European Economic Review* (Amsterdam), Vol. 28 (June/July 1985), pp. 43–52.

McKibbin, Warwick J., and Jeffrey D. Sachs, "Coordination of Monetary and Fiscal Policies in the OECD," NBER Working Paper 1800 (Cambridge, Massachusetts: National Bureau of Economic Research, January 1986).

Meade, James, "Inernational Co-operation in Macro-economic Policies," *Economic Papers* No. 28 (Brussels: Commission of the European Communities, February 1984).

Mortensen, Jorgen, "Profitability, Real Interest Rates, and Fiscal Crowding-Out Hypothesis in the OECD Area, 1960–1985: An Examination of the Crowding-Out Hypothesis Within a Portfolio Model," *Economic Papers* No. 59 (Brussels: Commission of the European Communities, October 1987).

Muller, Patrice, and Robert Price, "Public Sector Indebtedness and Long-Term Interest Rates" (unpublished, World Bank Staff Working Paper, 1985).

Organization for Economic Cooperation and Development, *The Control and Management of Government Expenditure* (Paris: OECD, 1987).

Oudiz, Gilles, and Jeffrey Sachs, "Macroeconomic Policy Coordination Among the Industrial Economies," *Brookings Papers on Economic Activity: 1* (1984), The Brookings Institution (Washington), pp. 1–75.

Palmer, John L., "The Changing Structure of the Deficit," *National Tax Journal* (Columbus, Ohio), Vol. 3 (September 1987), pp. 285–97.

Poehl, Karl Otto, "You Can't Robotize Policymaking," *The International Economy* (Washington), Vol. 1 (October/November 1987), pp. 20–26.

Russo, Massimo, and Giuseppe Tullio, "Monetary Coordination Within the European Monetary Sysem: Is There a Rule?" Part II in *Policy Coordination in the European Monetary System*, Occasional Paper No. 61 (Washington: International Monetary Fund, 1988).

Sinn, Hans-Werner, "The Policy of Tax-Cum-Base Broadening: Implications for International Capital Movements," paper presented to the 43rd Congress of the IIPF, August 24–28, 1987 (unpublished, Paris: IIPF, 1987).

Tabellini, Guido, "Domestic Politics and the International Coordination of Fiscal Policies," Discussion Paper No. 226 (London: Centre for Economic Policy Research, January 1988).

Tanzi, Vito (1985a), "The Deficit Experience in Industrial Countries," Chap. 4 in *The Economy in Deficit*, ed. by Phillip Cagan (Washington: American Enterprise Institute, 1985).

————— (1985b), "Fiscal Deficits and Interest Rates in the United States," *Staff Papers*, International Monetary Fund (Washington), Vol. 33 (December 1985), pp. 551–76.

—————, "Tax Reform in Industrial Countries and the Impact of the U.S. Tax Reform Act of 1986," IMF Working Paper 87/61 (mimeographed, Internatonal Monetary Fund, September 21, 1987).

—————, and Teresa Ter-Minassian, "The European Monetary System and Fiscal Policies," Chap. 13 in *Tax Coordination in the European Community*, Series on International Taxation No. 7, ed. by Sijbren Cnossen (Boston: Kluwer Law and Taxation Publishers, 1987).

U.S. Congressional Budget Office, "The Economic and Budget Outlook: Fiscal Years 1988–1992," *Annual Report*, Part 1 (Washington: U.S. Congressional Budget Office, February 1988).

Williamson, John, and M.H. Miller, *Targets and Indicators: A Blueprint for the International Coordination of Economic Policy* (Washington: Institute for International Economics, 1987).

Comment

Rudiger Dornbusch

The occasion of discussing Vito Tanzi's stimulating and provocative paper provides a welcome opportunity to express professional acknowledgment and appreciation for the important research effort on fiscal policy over which he has presided at the International Monetary Fund. The work is welcome not only in the area of data development, but also on the side of analysis. Tanzi's own contribution and his openness to discussion are an excellent example in an otherwise overly closed institution.

I will first take issue with some detailed points. In some instances, I wish to highlight a particular point Tanzi makes; in other there is a need to comment and disagree. Then, I shall take up the central point of my discussion—the world economy after U.S. budget cuts.

One point needs to be raised before the details come. Tanzi's paper is wide-ranging, and it is a vehicle for letting off steam on a number of issues, principally the U.S. budget deficit. Tanzi's beliefs are very catholic. In fiscal matters there is only one precept: get your house in order—the sooner the better. Budgets should be balanced! There is at best a reluctant recognition of a cyclical role for fiscal policy. If hard-pressed, I suspect Tanzi would confess that he thinks that, too, is an exaggerated concern.

This view leads him to argue that the U.S. fiscal expansion of 1982 and beyond was misguided, not only on domestic grounds, but also because of adverse effects on the world economy. This view is controversial. Surely it must be recognized that the monetary tightening of 1981–82, *together* with the fiscal expansion, brought about the high interest rate-strong dollar configuration that hurt, for example, commodity exporting debtor countries. But imagine that there had only been tight money. Interest rates would still have been high (though perhaps not quite as much), but there also would have been a deep recession. That, too, would have hurt countries abroad. Indeed, this was the case in 1982, before the tax cuts pushed the United States on a growth path. The simple fact is that the world economy was going to be hurt by the unanimous demand for an end to inflation. You cannot make an omelette without breaking some eggs.

I shall return to this point, but I want to register here my disbelief in the proposition that a U.S. recession is a good thing for the world economy. The direct effects are undesirable, and the inevitable protectionist consequences would be even more so. The problem is to find a world monetary-fiscal mix that is sustainable and consistent. I shall argue below that a world real interest rate reduction is the most likely step to reconcile the need for more balanced budgets and the overriding concern for growth.

I. Technical Issues

Tanzi argues that coordination is difficult if not infeasible because of coordination issues. These issues are already hard enough at the national level. They are even harder when considered at a multilateral level. He highlights in particular two aspects; both, I believe, are vastly exaggerated.

The first concern is with lags. Fiscal policy, he argues, unlike monetary policy, cannot be part of coordination, because the decision and implementation lags are far too long. Two responses are appropriate. Although it may be true that the decision lags for monetary policy are short, it takes far longer for monetary policy to exert any effects. The mean lag is more than three quarters, whereas fiscal policy becomes effective within the quarter of policy change. At best, there is a trade-off between implementation and reaction lags.

But, in fact, decision lags for fiscal policy can be dramatically short, as in the U.S. experience in 1975 when tax cuts were implemented retroactively within a single quarter. Furthermore, the special pressure of international coordination provides far more clout in persuading legislatures to take difficult fiscal measures. The reason is that coordination is a positive sum game—there is something to be gained! I would also add that if fiscal lags are believed to be as long as Tanzi makes them out to be, then there is even more of a need to coordinate. This is so in order to avoid catastrophic mismatches in policy that cannot, because of the alleged lags, be corrected in time. I do not wish to minimize either lags or difficulties in coordination. I simply find Tanzi's argument unpersuasive on this point.

I note in passing that Tanzi's argument about forecasting problems is at least as unpersuasive. Often, as for example, in the Great Depression, it is enough to know the level of the current aggregrates in order to determine the direction in which the policy thrust should move. The risk of overshooting is remote. It may be true, and I would agree, that the room for fine-tuning is very small. But, today, the question is what European offset there will be to a massive U.S. fiscal contraction. That is not fine-tuning. Either the other major industrial countries respond or they will experience a deep recession.

Rather than being a question of forecasting, I would have thought the chief problem in coordination was a quasi-religious one: differences in the perception of how the world works and what the state of the respective economies is. U.S.

policymakers think of Europe as a land of devastating unemployment and pervasive rigidity of mind and institution. Europeans believe the U.S. economy is recklessly overheated by deeply unsound fiscal management. Coordination in such circumstances is genuinely difficult because there is no place for the dialogue to start. That highlights above all a deficiency in leadership. The Federal Republic of Germany, through hyperinflation histrionics and under the guise of disinflation, has failed by turning Europe into a stagnation area. The United States has failed by not offering a serious assessment of its fiscal and saving problem.

Tanzi takes issue with the persistent effects of fiscal expansion. Econometric models predict that any effects of a sustained fiscal expansion (near full employment, without monetary accommodation) are soon dampened and in fact undone by crowding-out due to increased interest rates. But that is a red herring. In all cases I can think of, fiscal policy should, quite explicitly, give only transitory stimulus. A case in point might be helping economies recover from a slump or lifting them out of a depression. Combined with the right monetary policy, there is simply no issue. Of course, one might argue that fiscal discipline cannot be endangered by such yo-yo use. But the counterargument is that recessions, even though they ultimately may be self-liquidating, do leave important hysteresis effects. This point is altogether clear in comparing the United States and Europe today.

Tanzi also argues that there is pervasive uncertainty about the exact effects of a fiscal expansion program. Fiscal policy has uncertain effects; hence, do not use it. The literature has long rejected this argument. The correct view is that policymakers must take into account the nature of the uncertainty—lags, multipliers, reactions—in structuring the policy. There are two further arguments against this exaggerated skepticism. One is that much of the uncertainty about fiscal policy in an individual country may stem from uncertainty about foreign responses. Hence, coordination cuts down on uncertainty. The other argument, forcefully developed by Diamond (1985), is that there is no such thing as "no policy." What is the counterfactual? Even a policy rule of a full employment-balanced budget may have to react to current developments to stay on course. It is interesting that Tanzi is not reluctant to recommend putting one's house in order, even though, by his own arguments, the consequences of such a policy are unpredictable.

In concluding the discussion on these more detailed points, I would like to take issue with Tanzi's sweeping assertion:

> The connection between expansionary fiscal policies and faster growth rates is tenuous at best. There is simply no convincing evidence that the countries that have pursued more restrictive fiscal policies have grown any less fast than those that have pursued expansionary fiscal policies. The United Kingdom, for example, has done relatively well in recent years in spite of a conservative fiscal policy (p. 33).

In the case of the United Kingdom, as is well known, oil revenue and significant asset sales were used to finance a shortfall of taxes relative to current outlays. The *European Economy* (November 1987, p. 108) comments as follows:

> The buoyancy of non-oil revenues and the acceleration of the privatization programme enabled the long-term objective of bringing the public sector borrowing requirement down to 1% of GDP to be achieved ahead of schedule. . . .

In fact, the decline in the central government's financial balance using Organization for Economic Cooperation and Development (OECD) measures was smaller than the revenues from privatization, which were close to 1 percent of gross domestic product (GDP). A macroeconomic specification of the thrust of fiscal policy would look for the aggregate demand side effects of balancing the budget. Asset sales do not have a restrictive demand effect and, hence, are a clever way of keeping books balanced while exerting an expansionary fiscal policy stance. The U.K. example thus serves poorly to make the point that fiscal restraint is a source of growth. I hasten to add that I favor U.S. budget balancing and am not suggesting that budgets should be in deficit. I simply point out that there is no shred of evidence to support Tanzi's assertion that budget balancing is easily achieved with growth. On the contrary, the European experience contradicts it squarely. Budget balancing may be necessary, but let nobody try to persuade us that it does not make a difference in short-run growth. For the individual country it is possible to export unemployment; at the world level there is a serious adding-up problem when a major country starts cutting the budgets.

II. U.S. Adjustment and Real Interest Rates

Aesop's fox leaves footprints all over Tanzi's paper. The tailless fox of the fable, making the best of a bad situation, is trying to persuade all other foxes that not having a tail is true chic. Tanzi's fox is the United States, seeking to spread worldwide fiscal laxity. But all the foxes know better: The United States needs a good recession, a "Reinigungskrise" as it is called at the Bundesbank.[1] I do not concur in this view. The "crying wolf" strategy of Europe over all and any policy-induced growth will backfire when the imbalances created by U.S. adjustment put Europe into a bind.

The U.S. fiscal problem has been by and large resolved through the tax reform of the past years. The broadening of the tax base and the reduction in the deficit

[1]The same view was expressed in *The Economist* (January 26, 1988), in an article entitled "How to Crack Japan."

to around 3.5 percent of gross national product (GNP) assures that the path of
the debt-income ratio is not explosive. Table 1 reports OECD data for the United
States.

Table 1. U.S. General Government Fiscal Deficit and Debt

(In percent of GDP)

Component	1982–84	1985	1986	1987	1988
Budget deficit	3.3	3.3	3.5	2.5	2.4
Noninterest deficit	1.4	1.0	1.2	0.1	—
Net debt	23.4	26.5	26.3	26.6	—
Gross debt	65.4	69.4	69.2	69.5	—

Source: Organization for Economic Cooperation and Development, *Economic Outlook*
(Paris: OECD, various issues).

There is considerable year-to-year fluctuation in the U.S. budget deficit due to
summitry masquerading of deficit cuts. But the basic message is that of a
gradually (if too slowly) declining *nominal* deficit and hence a falling deficit GDP
ration. The latest forecast of the U.S. Congressional Budget Office (CBO) shows
a federal deficit averaging 3.13 percent of GDP in 1988–90. What does this imply
for debt dynamics? The growth of the debt/GDP ratio is given by the familiar
equation:

$$x = (r - y) x - v, \tag{1}$$

where x is the debt/GDP ratio, r and y are the real interest rate and the growth
rate of output, respectively, and v is the noninterest budget. The noninterest
budget is nearly balanced and on a path to surplus. But the real interest rate
exceeds the growth rate of trend output, which is about 2.5 percent. But the
excess applies to only a moderate debt ratio. Thus, even with a 5 percent real
interest rate and a balanced noninterest budget, the debt ratio would only rise by
1.5 percent a year. With reasonable real interest rates (say, 2 percent) the debt
ratio would be more than stabilized. In this sense, there is no longer a fiscal crisis
in the United States. There is simply no explosive debt situation. Figure 1 shows
the CBO's forecast of the stabilization of the federal government's debt ration
toward 1990.

Now consider the question of U.S. budget balancing. Why should the budget
be balanced and what is the monetary policy that should accompany the budget
correction? The first point has a clear answer. U.S. saving is very low, for any
number of reasons; my own explanation is that financial liberalization has removed credit constraints even from the last worker. The interaction of full
employment and financial liberalization shows up in powerful spending effects
and, as a result, in low personal saving. This interpretation is borne out by a
glance at the behavior of the saving rate and consumer credit.

Figure 1. U.S. Debt Ratio, 1955–94

(In percent of GDP)

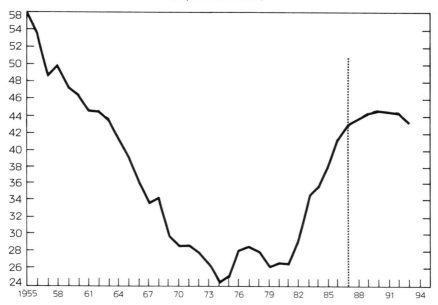

Source: U.S. Congressional Budget Office.

The low saving rate in the United States implies that high investment is possible only at the cost of sustained external imbalance. But sustained budget deficits might well carry a price in terms of a loss of control over the dollar, interest rates, and inflation much further down the road. Thus, I see budget correction as the essential step for raising national saving, making up for the far too low private saving. In raising national saving, budget correction frees resources for investment.

The next question is how to sustain growth in the face of a major budget cut— say, 3 percent of GDP over three years. A critical ingredient here is a major reduction in interest rates. The interest rate will have to be reduced, not cyclically as a result of recession, but actively to accommodate growth. Crowding-in of investment to offset the impact of budget cuts is a delicate task in respect to timing. Ideally, interest rate cuts should run ahead, since their lags are quite long. But, unfortunately, poor leadership in the United States has precluded superplay, allowing the country to get to full employment without initiating the appropriate policy corrections. More attention must be paid at this stage to international coordination.

A full-employment policy in the United States does require much lower interest rates and/or a much lower value of the dollar. Since lower interest rates are compatible with a stable dollar only if they fall significantly abroad, there is a clear interdependence problem. If the rest of the world does not catch on, it is bound to end up in a deep recession.

It is clear that correction of the two deficits requires major adjustment abroad. A U.S. recession would be the worst possible outcome. Europe and Japan would lose exports, just as they would with dollar depreciation. But with a recession, an ambitious program of fiscal correction in the United States would become impossible.

A sharp deterioration in economic conditions would, of course, lead to a deterioration in the fiscal climate. Recession and high real interest rates (as Europe has been experiencing) do more havoc to budgets and debt than do a few years of reckless tax cuts. The numbers provided by a recent CBO analysis are revealing. Table 2 shows the impact of different economic scenarios for the U.S. federal budget.

Table 2. Rules of Thumb: Effect on Budget Deficit

(In billions of U.S. dollars)

Change	1988	1992
1 percent lower growth	7	48
1 percent higher unemployment	29	57
1 percent higher interest rates	3	20
1 percent higher inflation	−2	−1

Source: U.S. Congressional Budget Office,*The Economic and Budget Options. Fiscal Years 1990–1994* (Washington: CBO, January 1989), p. 51.

The table highlights the central role of growth and interest rates in shaping the U.S. budget. The wide tax base assures that growth has a powerful effect on revenues. Higher interest rates, because of the relatively high federal debt ratio, have an adverse effect. The data in Table 2 make clear that a policy of budget balancing that sustains growth by reducing interest rates carries extra payoffs in terms of the budget: direct budget balancing effects and an important bonus in terms of reduced interest payments.

My conclusion is that a major reduction in real interest rates worldwide is an essential ingredient for a soft landing of the world economy. The United States could have a soft landing without cutting interest rates and allowing the dollar to fall so as to stimulate net exports. Clearly such a beggar-thy-neighbor policy can do the job, but it does so at the expense of recession abroad. Strangely, the problem posed by the U.S. deficit will be almost entirely that of adjustments in the rest of the world.

Tanzi's paper does not pay much attention to real interest rates, except to note that they are high because of deficits. Insufficient liquefaction in the aftermath of world disinflation does not appear as a hypothesis. But even Friedman (1983) has argued that liquefaction is essential in the transition to a low-inflation regime.

> If a reduction in monetary growth leads to a decline in inflation, and that decline is embedded in anticipated inflation, the resulting lower cost of holding money will produce an increase in the quantity of real balances demanded. Velocity, which rises because of the reverse effect when inflation accelerates, and stabilizes when inflation stabilizes, will tend to decline when inflation declines. An ideal policy would therefore involve an initial decline in monetary growth, a subsequent rise when declining inflation reduces velocity, and a final decline to the desired long-run level when velocity stabilizes (pp. 5–6).

In these terms the world economy has not experienced sufficient monetization to reduce real interest rates to the habitual levels (see Figure 1). Further monetization becomes essential to achieve a soft landing when fiscal correction is undertaken. Failure to heed Friedman's advice on monetization (prudently, moderately, but certainly) is now the chief danger for the world economy. Long-run fiscal frugality is essential for growth in the standard of living, but getting there on a course of full employment is as essential, and easy monetary policy is the critical complement.

References

Brainard, William C., "Uncertainty and the Effectiveness of Policy," *American Economic Review, Papers and Proceedings of the Seventy-Ninth Annual Meeting of the American Economic Association* (Nashville, Tennessee), Vol. 57 (May 1967), pp. 411–25.

Commission of the European Communities, *European Economy* (Brussels), No. 34 (November 1987), p. 108.

Diamond, P., "Ignorance and Monetary Policy" (mimeographed, Cambridge, Massachusetts: Massachusetts Institute of Technology, January 1985).

Friedman, Milton, "Monetarism in Rhetoric and in Practice," *Monetary and Economic Studies*, Bank of Japan (Tokyo), Vol. 1 (October 1983), pp. 1–14.

Comment

Patrick Minford

I very much agree with Vito Tanzi's general attack on activist fiscal policy coordination. I will comment first on some details of his analysis and then develop a case—implicitly supported by Tanzi's paper—for nonactivist fiscal coordination, in support of monetary rules for price stability.

First, the details. Forecast inaccuracy may undermine ambitious attempts at fine-tuning, but it does not destroy the general case for rough-tuning, since, plainly, forecasts are able to track the direction of output relative to capacity with some success—even with all the errors shown in Tanzi's tables. Nor is model disagreement fatal. Policy instruments, or some aspects of them, directed at specific targets, can generate improvement, according to a large spread of models, including those used by the coordinators. Holtham and Hallett (1987) recently explored this possibility and found a few hypothetical examples.

Of course, we have not as yet worked out measures of how large the gains could have been in practical cases. In our recent study (Canzoneri and Minford (1988)), Canzoneri and I concluded that even with a single model with large spillovers, coordination yielded gains that were small relative to the accuracy with which policy could be implemented—a form of forecast error. In practice, the objections Tanzi raises may be impossible to overcome.

Tanzi mentions the absence from many models of rational expectations, which he feels—and I agree—are the best available modeling tool for expectations. Although this situation is changing—a number of the models presented at the Brookings conference Tanzi mentions embodied rational expectations—it remains true that the models in widespread use by forecasters and policymakers do not. Again, this is a relevant problem for practical coordination.

Of the four remaining problems Tanzi lists, I rate two of them as serious. The other two—disagreement on objectives, and asymmetry of power—are not strictly problems. Coordination brings gains to participating parties, whatever their objectives, because of spillovers; the spillovers are the opportunity of trade, as it were, and the objectives define the offers to trade. Asymmetry of power will affect the noncooperative equilibrium, making it, for example, a Stackelberg equilibrium, rather than a Nash one, but cooperation will still yield gains if there are spillovers.

The inside lag of domestic policy seems to pose an insuperable problem for fiscal policy as a stabilization tool. True, it may be easy to get quick agreement from the U.S. Congress or the Italian Parliament for tax cuts and expenditure rises, but not for measures in the opposite direction.

And finally, the possibility of negative fiscal multipliers should be taken very seriously. This problem is linked to the point made earlier about expectations, in that adverse confidence effects (or their opposite, which Walters (1986) contends occurred in Britain in 1981 when the budget contraction took place in the recession trough) may well offset the usual direct effects. Of course, if the multipliers were reliably negative, we could simply change the sign of the fiscal response. But the multipliers can move around, depending on the precise future policy pattern expected, and this expectation will generally be independent of policy intentions and announcements. Our models cannot yet deal with this dimension.

I would add two arguments against coordinated fine-tuning. First, it might provide vested interests with greater opportunities to expand the size of public programs in the name of action to stimulate the economy; yet once started for this purpose, such expansions are hard to reverse, imparting an upward bias to public spending and fine-tuning.

Second, time-inconsistency is likely to be worsened by such coordination. Whereas a domestic rule can be monitored by the public, an international agreement introduces the loophole of a foreign party's views. As for monitoring by the foreign power, what sanctions could the foreign power apply? We have seen recently how difficult it was for the rest of the Organization for Economic Cooperation and Development (OECD) to persuade the United States to reverse its budget deficit, following the expansionary spirit of the early 1980s. Essentially, coordinated fine-tuning is just discretion exercised jointly by two or more parties; and is as much prey to time-inconsistency as discretion by one government. I fear that such fine-tuning would produce stagflation, as people began to anticipate the mutual exploitation of Phillips curves (see Rogoff (1985)).

I. Non-Activist Fiscal Coordination

The case for fiscal rules at the international level is the same as that underlying the Medium-Term Financial Strategy in the United Kingdom. To build credibility for monetary control, deficits must also be limited; otherwise, monetization comes to be seen as the politically irresistible option for holding down the ratio of debt to gross domestic product (GDP). So, if major countries all wish to achieve price stability and, as a by-product, can stabilize their exchange rates, fiscal rules are the corollary, and they might as well be coordinated—that is, mutually policed—to reinforce the commitment to stability. The benefits of this regime would be the reduction of monetary uncertainty and transaction costs in international trade.

The rules would impose ranges for deficit/GDP ratios, outside which corrective action would be required for monetary reasons. The ranges would not interfere with the normal fluctuations associated with the business cycle or with unpredictable public finance needs (such as those arising from strikes or wars). For countries far from fiscal equilibrium, such as—dare I say it—Italy, there would be a transitional range, as there has been in the United Kingdom from 1979 to date.

This type of coordination is better able to confront the above-mentioned difficulties associated with fine-tuning. Forecasts and models are needed, but in an appropriate role—that of determining ranges large enough to permit appropriate flexibility, their midpoints set to reflect the savings propensities of each country. Public choice pressures and time-inconsistency should be reduced by the policing of agreed international rules. The inside lag becomes an advantage, because once agreed on, fiscal policies are less easy to tamper with.

The key obstacle is the residual political desire for freedom to inflate. I say "residual," because most major countries played with that freedom in the 1970s and early 1980s, and have learned that it only buys trouble. Recently, we heard from some U.S. politicians that they wanted this freedom in 1988—an election year. What an irony that a supposedly conservative government should demand such a freedom! But following the dollar's plunge in the free-fall reaction to such wants, wiser counsels have prevailed. Could it be that the United States is at last genuinely interested in playing by a set of world rules for price and exchange rate stability? If so, the last major obstacle to a proper Louvre Accord has probably been eliminated, since other OECD governments have learned—often the hard way—to prize stability. But I wonder: since John Connally tore up the Bretton Woods Agreement, the United States has always resisted allied attempts to impose half-agreed new rules whenever domestic political pressures called for such resistance. Clearly, any new framework would have to be set up and led by non-U.S. governments, and U.S. participation would have to be accepted as a bonus.

II. Conclusions

Tanzi rightly criticizes those who demand coordinated fiscal activism at the present time; notable demands for fiscal expansion have come from the Centre for European Policy Studies group originally associated with Rudiger Dornbusch (see Blanchard, Dornbusch, and Layard (1986)). Even the inclusion of "supply-side-friendly," "right-handed" measures does not make the package seductive, since deficits today will have to be paid for later, presumably by supply-side-unfriendly fiscal contraction or by higher inflation.

I would merely add that if surpluses are likely to result from public sector reforms, for example, then tax cuts and fiscal loosening are the right actions to take. This is the situation now in the United Kingdom where privatization revenues have been used to pay for tax cuts, but only against a strongly improving trend in public finances (itself partly the result of privatization).

Tanzi favors the coordination of supply-side policy. I am not so sure; cutting top tax rates has been greatly stimulated by the United States leading the way on tax reform. But certainly there are areas, such as protectionism, where cooperation is good for consumer interests.

To conclude, coordinated fiscal discretion falls into essentially the same traps as independent fiscal discretion. Just as the latter has given way in most of the OECD countries to limits on fiscal deficits, so should discretion at the international level give way to rules, so as to extend the greater national price stability across frontiers. The Louvre Accord may be the first sign of such a tendency. Vito Tanzi's paper points us in that direction too, and is an encouraging index of where International Monetary Fund thinking may be going.

References

Blanchard, Olivier, Rudiger Dornbusch, and Richard Layard, eds., *Restoring Europe's Prosperity: Macroeconomic Papers from the Centre for European Policy Studies* (Cambridge, Massachusetts: MIT Press, 1986).

Canzoneri, Matthew B., and Patrick Minford, "When International Policy Coordination Matters: An Empirical Analysis," *Applied Economics* (London), Vol. 20 (September 1988), pp. 1137–54.

Holtham, Gerald, and Andrew Hughes Hallett, "International Policy Cooperation and Model Uncertainty," Chap. 5 in *Global Macroeconomics: Policy Conflict and Cooperation*, ed. by Ralph C. Bryant and Richard Portes (New York: St. Martin's Press, in association with the International Economic Association and the Centre for Economic Policy Research, 1987).

Rogoff, Kenneth, "Can International Policy Cooperation Be Counter-Productive?" *Journal of International Economics* (Amsterdam), Vol. 18 (May 1985), pp. 199–217.

Walters, A.A., *Britain's Economic Renaissance: Margaret Thatcher's Reforms, 1979–1984* (New York: Oxford University Press, 1986).

Comment

Antonio Pedone

Inherent in both fiscal policy and international cooperation are many limitations having to do with design, implementation, and effects. It is thus no surprise that the international coordination of fiscal policy will embody many more limitations than fiscal policy within a country or the international coordination of monetary policy.

Tanzi's paper contains a complete list of the issues facing any attempt at coordinating fiscal policy that aims at demand management on a global scale, rather than at correcting major fiscal imbalances in particular countries. Tanzi thinks that "where coordination of fiscal policy may be highly relevant is with respect to some structural aspects, particularly tax reform" (p. 33). I agree that structural fiscal policy should play an important role in international economic coordination, but I think that we must also confront the difficulties and find solutions to the problems of short-term fiscal policy coordination.

This last point becomes more evident if we look at fiscal policy coordination in the context of the coordination of monetary policies and exchange rate policies, and if we recall, as Tanzi does, the impetus toward policy coordination coming from the need to reduce the large external imbalances of the three leading industrial countries. Econometric studies have shown that any substantial reduction of the external imbalances undertaken by major industrial countries, while maintaining a stable and high growth rate and a sufficient volume of world trade so as not to aggravate the situation of the most indebted developing countries, could not be the result of a single economic policy measure, however effective or timely, nor of the domestic policy of a single country, however important and influential.

The distribution of the adjustment process over a broad range of measures in different countries would reduce the costs involved in drastic and uncertain changes in economic policies and would make it possible to reverse them should the results differ widely from those expected. This pragmatic approach assumes that wide fluctuations in exchange rates are costly, because they increase the uncertainty of trade and investment operations, and because they may make it worthwhile to shift from foreign markets to the domestic market and from free sectors exposed to international competition toward more protected sectors;

and because the coverage of risks connected with exchange rate fluctuations is expensive, unequal, and incomplete.

If it is assumed desirable to avoid "excessive" variability in exchange rates, while at the same time keeping the objectives of growth and reduction of external imbalances, then the economic policies of the major industrial countries require some coordination. Of course, the inconsistency of national economic policies is not automatically reduced by international economic cooperation. But international cooperation may be necessary to avoid unilateral actions, which could be disruptive of world trade and financial markets.

The role of international economic cooperation cannot be defined—nor dismissed—independently of the role assigned to monetary policy and to exchange rate and trade policies. Viewed in this way, international economic cooperation could make a positive contribution to the reduction of inconsistencies in national economic policies. But we must all be aware of its practical difficulties, which are rightly emphasized in Tanzi's paper.

We all know how weak the statistical foundations of many international comparisons and financial variables are; but here, the International Monetary Fund and other international institutions could help to improve the standards used. Tanzi also emphasizes the difficulty of agreeing on a reliable forecast, and argues that "this has serious implications for fiscal coordination that aims at global demand management through fiscal policy changes, although it is a far less serious obstacle for monetary policy coordination or fiscal coordination that emphasizes . . . the correction of serious fiscal imbalances in particular countries . . ." (p. 16). The problem arises because the implementation lag of financial policy is longer than the period for which acceptably reliable forecasts can be made. But the long-term fiscal adjustment process also requires (long-term) economic forecasts. And what if the errors become larger when the forecasts extend across longer periods?

I think that an agreement on forecasts could be made easier if they met three commonsense requirements: agreement of evidence should come from a host of indicators rather than a single forecast; less attention should be given to exceptional values and more to well-defined trends that are potentially cumulative and destabilizing; and only quantitatively significant deviations from the target values should be selected.

The difficulty of reaching an agreement on the economic objectives that should be achieved through international economic cooperation can be overcome by the choice of an appropriate set of indicators. Tanzi argues that even clear signals from different indicators may be conflicting and subject to different, if not contrasting, interpretations. I think that this real danger can be mitigated in many ways: by separating the different indicators into homogeneous groups; by setting a range of target values for each of them; by varying the list of the indicators according to their use and to the frequency with which target values are updated; and by adapting the procedures on the use of indicators to the extent of the deviations from the various agreed-upon target values.

It must be said that disagreement on economic objectives and economic analysis would also affect discussion on the desirability and timing of changes in medium-term fiscal policy, and on economic policy in general. Is the "zero-economic policy" advocated in the end by Tanzi preferable to the inclusion of "commonsense international economic cooperation" with structural and medium-term fiscal policy?

It is true that the problems of shortening fiscal policy lags (particularly the decision lag) and improving the budgetary process remain crucial to the success of international economic cooperation. They become more crucial if one of the objectives of international economic cooperation is to reduce exchange rate variability. In fact, independence in monetary policy is somewhat reduced if target values for exchange rates are fixed; so it becomes more important that public budget instruments regain full flexibility and efficacy. As the experience of the European Monetary System has shown, any kind of managed exchange rate system implies that monetary policy is no longer completely free for domestic objectives. When monetary policy is mainly assigned to an exchange rate objective, some other instrument is needed to influence domestic demand and to offset the effects at the micro level of external shocks and large swings and relative prices. The effective use of fiscal policy toward these ends becomes crucial. But here, some fundamental problems arise that, in practice, may hinder the whole process of international economic cooperation.

Fiscal policy decisions usually require a long time to be taken, since, unlike decisions about monetary policy, they must have parliamentary approval. In addition, fiscal policy decisions are often asymmetrical and not reversible; it is much easier to cut taxes or increase public expenditure than to increase taxes or reduce public expenditure. Thus, as Tanzi suggests, when an expansionary fiscal policy is called for, the risk of compromising the medium-term sustainability makes some governments overcautious about adopting all the expansionary measures required. Conversely, when a contractionary fiscal policy is called for, most governments find it difficult, if not impossible, to get parliamentary approval for all the proposed tax and public expenditure changes.

These are the practical difficulties that could prevent any progress toward fiscal policy coordination, as underlined in Tanzi's paper, but these same difficulties could also hinder the implementation of a medium-term financial adjustment. Some appropriate institutional changes must be adopted to increase the flexibility of fiscal policy. These changes could include the use of tax regulators tied to the values of some economic international and/or domestic variables; the indexation of public expenditures to macreconomic variables; and some changes in the budgetary process, so as to take into account the short-run adjustment needs and medium-term sustainability of fiscal policy. Without some improvement in these institutional areas, governments cannot effectively control the policy mix and are unable to commit themselves fully to the adoption of the domestic policies required by international economic cooperation—be it aimed at demand management or medium-term fiscal adjustment.

The Impact of Fiscal Policy on the Balance of Payments: Recent Experience in the United States

John H. Makin

The connection between fiscal policy and the balance of payments has received much attention in the mid-1980s. The simultaneous appearance of the United States' "twin deficits"—the federal budget deficit and the trade deficit—has been much discussed and debated among economists and policymakers (see Figure 1). Much of the disagreement has been about whether a causal relationship exists between the twin deficits and, in particular, whether a sharp reduction in the U.S. budget deficit is a necessary condition for a reduction in its trade deficit.

This paper will explore the connection between fiscal policy and measures of external balance. Fiscal policy will be largely construed to mean budget policy, but some discussion of tax policy will be included, since it is relevant to the U.S. experience during the 1980s. The phrase "measures of external balance" is used on occasion in the text in place of the "balance of payments" used in the paper's title, because the balance of payments in a formal sense always balances, and it is necessary to specify whether one wishes to examine the much touted and maligned merchandise trade balance or alternatives, such as the current account balance or its mirror image, net capital inflows.

It is also important to specify whether one is operating under a regime of freely flexible, partly flexible, or fixed exchange rates. The transition from flexible to partly flexible exchange rates, particularly since the February 1987 Louvre Accord, is important to recognize, since it affects the observed adjustment mechanism that operates in response to a fiscal disturbance like a larger budget deficit.

I shall begin with a general discussion of fiscal policy and the balance of payments and then examine some familiar ground within the context of a simple full-employment model for a small country. Next, the discussion is modified to

Figure 1. Overall U.S. Deficit and Foreign Investment, 1979–87

(In billions of U.S. dollars, from first quarter to first quarter)

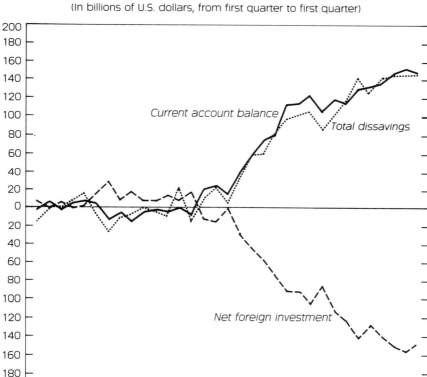

Source : U.S. Department of Commerce, *Survey of Current Business,* various issues.

more readily accommodate the case of the United States in the 1980s. Assumptions of a small country and full employment are relaxed. These discussions are next employed in conjunction with the behavior of other Group of Seven countries to focus explicitly on the recent U.S. experience with fiscal policy and external imbalances. Where appropriate, the role of attendant monetary policies is discussed in conjunction with fiscal policy.

The discussion throughout is heuristic, eschewing specific modeling with equations or diagrams. Those who prefer more specificity or who wish to read "between the lines" are referred to Makin (1986).[1]

---

[1]Chapter 2 contains a specific model that underlies much of the general discussion presented here.

I. A General Discussion of Fiscal Policy and the Balance of Payments

The proximate impact of fiscal policy on the balance of payments is simple enough to explain. If by "fiscal policy," one means the relationship between government spending and tax revenues, and by "balance of payments," one means the current account balance (merchandise trade plus net services and investment income), the following is true: more government spending, while holding constant revenues and net private saving (private saving minus private investment), will enlarge the current account deficit largely by raising the merchandise trade deficit. The corollary proposition is that the current account deficit (capital inflows) cannot fall without a corresponding (not causal) fall in the budget deficit unless net private saving rises. The rise in net private saving may coincide with a collapse of private investment and a recession, particularly if accommodating capital inflows are only available at a higher interest rate.

A relationship between fiscal (tax and spending) policy and the balance of payments would normally be discussed within the context of a regime of fixed exchange rates. More expansionary fiscal policy would put incipient upward pressure on domestic interest rates. In a Mundellian, small-country world with infinite mobility of capital, capital inflows accommodate the fiscal expansion at a given world interest rate. The positive impact upon aggregate demand is not mitigated by the "crowding-out" that results in a closed-economy setting in the absence of monetary accommodation by the central bank or an infinitely elastic (with respect to interest rates) money demand schedule.

The net impact of fiscal expansion on the balance of payments in the fixed-exchange-rate case is zero, but that masks a change in its components. The increased capital inflow will, barring a change in private net saving or official intervention in foreign exchange markets, be reflected by an equal rise in the current account deficit. In short, a rise in national dissaving is accommodated by a capital inflow from abroad, which, in turn, is reflected in a larger current account deficit.

If private capital is not infinitely mobile, part of the capital inflow may come from official intervention in the foreign exchange market aimed at pegging the exchange rate, provided that the higher interest rate does not raise net private saving by an amount exactly equal to the rise in government dissaving. If the increase in net private saving is below that critical level and private capital inflows are inadequate to match the rise in national dissaving, then there will be an excess demand for foreign exchange. If the exchange rate is fully flexible, the currency depreciates until a combination of higher interest rates and currency depreciation increases net private saving by an amount equal to the increase in government dissaving.

If, alternatively, the exchange rate is pegged, official intervention in support of the home currency will, if not sterilized (not allowed to affect the money supply), reduce the domestic money supply and/or raise the money supply abroad. All of the adjustment pressure is thereby thrust upon the interest rate, which must rise by enough at home to elevate private net saving and capital inflows by an amount equal to the increase in government dissaving. A drop in the foreign interest rate enhances capital inflows. Higher prices at home and lower prices abroad help the adjustment by increasing imports and cutting exports, thereby raising required capital inflows. Higher prices at home may also elevate private net saving at home, and lower prices abroad may cut net private saving abroad through the real balance effect on saving. If the intervention employed to peg the exchange rate is sterilized, the adjustment mechanism is prevented from operating. The excess demand for foreign exchange by the home country becomes chronic, and intervention continues until the prospect of sharp adjustment (usually a devaluation by the deficit country) is realized, at which time a combination of currency devaluation and higher interest rates brings about either the needed reduction or net private dissaving.

II. U.S. Fiscal Policy and External Adjustment: A Large Open Economy With Flexible Exchange Rates

A discussion of the impact of U.S. fiscal policy in the 1980s on the external balance might better be focused on exchange rates than on the balance of payments. A careful study of the external effects of countercyclical fiscal policy in a large open economy with flexible exchange rates and a significant non-traded-goods sector reveals that, contrary to the conclusions reached with small-country models developed by Robert A. Mundell, J. Marcus Fleming, and others in the 1960s, fiscal policy is a potent countercyclical tool.

A corollary, seemingly obvious, conclusion is that exchange rate stability requires active coordination of fiscal and monetary policies among large open economies. Notwithstanding a stated desire for exchange rate stability by most Group of Seven finance ministers and central bankers, no such coordination has emerged during the 1980s.

An appropriate engine of analysis for consideration of the external effects of fiscal and other policy measures in a large open economy requires some modification of the simpler models developed for small open economies that were discussed in the preceding section. The minimum serviceable model includes, in addition to the usual equilibrium conditions in the traded-goods sector and the monetary sector, a market-clearing condition in the non-traded-goods sector, specification of equilibrium conditions in labor markets, and equations satisfying interest parity, Fisher conditions, and purchasing power parity. Such a model, developed in Makin (1986), can be solved to endogenize the home country's terms of trade, which in turn determines the impact of changes in fiscal and/or monetary policy on exchange rates, output, and employment.

Such a model, augmented with ad hoc expectations-generating mechanisms, captures well the U.S. experience of the 1980s. Expansionary fiscal policy results in sharp currency appreciation, which in turn puts deflationary pressure on prices. The deflationary pressure from currency appreciation moderates money-wage demand, which, along with an improvement in the terms of trade, causes output and employment to rise. Such a combination of events characterized the U.S. economy in 1984. During 1987/88, in Japan, following the introduction of a fiscal expansion package, coupled with currency appreciation, the Japanese situation resembled the 1984 U.S. experience.

If the exchange rate is relatively ineffective at eliminating an excess demand or supply condition in the market for traded goods, as it is in the United States, the model under consideration suggests that wide swings in exchange rates may also accompany shifts in monetary policy undertaken to offset the negative impact on the supply side of the traded-goods sector arising from a sharp currency appreciation.

With this framework in mind, it is possible to review some broad, stylized facts concerning U.S. fiscal policy during the 1980s and accompanying policies elsewhere. Viewed broadly, the 1980s was a period of fiscal retrenchment for most large industrial countries outside the United States. In the seven largest Organization for Economic Cooperation and Development (OECD) economies, public expenditure had risen from 33 percent of gross domestic product (GDP) in 1972 to 41 percent of GDP in 1982. But by 1982, the OECD's measure of government financial balances indicated a sharply expansionary posture in the United States, a neutral posture in Japan, and a strongly contractionary posture in the Federal Republic of Germany (see Figure 2). In the following two years, the U.S. posture remained sharply expansionary, Japan's posture turned contractionary, and the German posture remained contractionary, though slightly less so than in 1982.

The broad pattern of fiscal retrenchment outside the United States exacerbated the pressure on dollar appreciation created by the highly expansionary posture of U.S. fiscal policy. The effect outside the United States was to cushion the domestic impact of fiscal retrenchment. The strong dollar and the rapid pace of U.S. economic growth, especially in 1984, permitted a sharp increase in exports to the United States or other dollar areas.

After the Plaza Accord (1985), and especially during 1986, the U.S. monetary policy eased sharply, and the dollar began to depreciate against most currencies, but most drastically against the yen and the deutsche mark. During 1987, the pressure for a weaker dollar was intensified by a move in U.S. fiscal policy to a

Figure 2.   Change in Structural Budget Balance, Inflation-Adjusted, 1980–88

(In percent of nominal GNP/GDP)

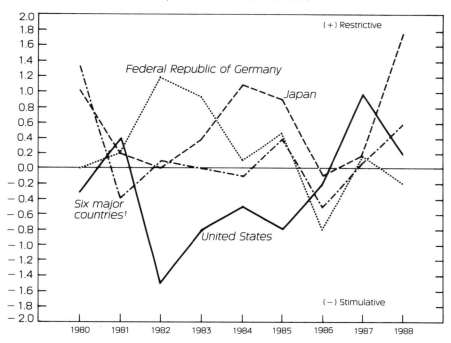

Source: *OECD Economic Outlook* (Paris: Organization for Economic Cooperation and Development, various issues).
[1]Average of six major countries, excluding the United States.

more restrictive stance and an easing of Japanese fiscal policy, coupled with some sterilization of the Bank of Japan's dollar support during the middle of 1987.

By 1987, especially after the February Louvre Accord, a macroeconomic dilemma had become evident in the United States. Five years later than most industrial countries, the United States was beginning to move to control its fiscal deficits. The result was that fiscal policy was stuck in neutral, or slightly in reverse, and was therefore not available as a countercyclical tool.

A decision to peg the dollar exchange rate in a narrow range against the deutsche mark and the yen at a time when accommodating capital flows to the private sector from abroad were beginning to slow created a dangerous situation. Strictly speaking, a country with an exchange rate target loses control over monetary policy. In the case of the United States during 1987, the central banks of Germany, Japan, and elsewhere provided $100 billion-plus of accommodating inflows in an attempt to peg the dollar exchange rate at a time when U.S. absorption was not dropping rapidly enough to allow a falloff in capital inflows.

Contrary to the stated objectives of many Group of Seven policymakers outside the United States to bring about more U.S. adjustment, the extra liquidity provided by official intervention in support of the dollar only delayed U.S. adjustment by accommodating U.S. absorption on easier terms. Of course, the objective of the dollar support was to cushion the loss of exports to dollar markets. It revealed a powerful ambivalence that has always characterized the attitude in more open economies to a U.S. adjustment: "the United States should spend less, but not on imports from my country; the (great, big) United States should not expect to eliminate a merchandise trade or current account deficit by selling more to my (poor, little) country."

The exchange rate-pegging exercise ran into difficulty in May–June 1987 when Japan embarked on an expansionary fiscal policy, coupled with some sterilization of its intervention in support of the dollar. The expansionary fiscal policy placed strong upward pressure on Japanese interest rates, which was accentuated by a housing construction boom during the summer of 1987.

As a result of exchange rate pegging, the higher interest rates in Japan were transmitted to the United States. By September, the United States was forced to tighten monetary policy in view of its agreement to peg the exchange rate within a narrow range. This move highlighted the dilemma facing the Federal Reserve. Maintaining expansion called for easier money, whereas defending the dollar called for tighter money. Unable to do both, the Federal Reserve opted for slightly tighter money and raised the discount rate by ½ of 1 percent early in September. In effect, the Fed was making an adjustment that ought to have been made in April after the initial sharp run-up in interest rates.

The upward pressure on U.S. interest rates intensified in October, especially after the October 14 release of the August trade deficit. By October 19—"Black Monday"—interest rates had risen so high that the temptation to sell stocks and then to buy bonds became unbearable. The result was a collapse of equity prices, as investors rushed to the relative safety of bonds.

The pervasive view was that if a cycle of weak trade numbers and higher interest rates were to continue until the U.S. recovery was choked off, the outlook for corporate earnings was bleak. The reaction was therefore to sell shares. Once the sale of shares accelerated on Black Monday, the combination of 10 percent-plus interest rates on government bonds and a prospective recession caused the rush into bonds. The only check on further bond buying since has been the fear of a possible rise in inflation due either to a dollar collapse, faster money growth, or both.

The stock market collapse was in part the result of an accumulated need for a correction of U.S. fiscal policy. Viewed in the simplest terms, it reflected a stark fact: foreign capital would accommodate U.S. consumption in excess of production only with interest rates at a level high enough to undercut equity prices, particularly when those equity prices had reached price/earnings multiples above their historical norms.

More broadly, the market crash signaled a vision of the future. The United States would have to reduce consumption either by means of ever higher interest rates or by means of a negative wealth effect created by a collapse of equity values, which would, in turn, reduce U.S. consumption and investment and, thereby, U.S. absorption, to a point at which accommodative capital inflows would occur at an interest rate consistent with equity prices.

The interconnections between commodity and financial markets were made unusually clear during the last quarter of 1987. Excess U.S. outlays on commodities—the current account deficit—caused bond prices to fall until interest rates threatened to cut expenditure sharply. Then, share prices fell and bond prices rose to less than half their March 1987 highs. The markets are now groping for a new configuration of equity and bond prices that will clear markets at levels consistent with a level of U.S. net absorption that external lenders will accommodate. That level of accommodation depends on the rate at which non-U.S. markets increase absorption of U.S. exports and the rate at which the United States cuts absorption of non-U.S. exports.

III. U.S. Fiscal Policy and Structural Adjustment

Discussion so far has focused on the macroeconomic effects of the unusual configuration of U.S. fiscal policy during the 1980s. The unusual nature of that policy, coupled with some major changes in tax structure enacted in 1981 that tended to exacerbate the effects of the budgetary impact of lower tax revenues and higher spending, resulted in significant structural microeconomic effects that must be analyzed to understand the overall impact of U.S. fiscal policy in an international setting.

A thorough understanding of the profound structural effects on the U.S. economy that resulted from tax and budget measures enacted in 1981 and 1982 provides a broader basis for an understanding of the origins of the U.S. trade legislation that emerged during 1986 and 1987. An understanding of these structural factors is also helpful for predicting the likely course of U.S. trade legislation in the immediate future. The microeconomic tax changes effected by the 1981/82 tax reform acts, when coupled with the budgetary and exchange rate impact of changes in aggregate spending and taxation, created a dangerous combination for U.S. manufacturers in the traded-goods sector.

The aggregate tax cuts enacted in 1981 were part of a normal correction for the upward creep in U.S. tax burdens that routinely occurs as a result of a largely unindexed tax system. The rapid inflation of the 1970s had sharply increased marginal effective tax rates on income from capital as well as tax rates faced by individuals. Total revenues of the federal government as a share of gross national product (GNP) had risen above 19 percent, somewhat above the 1962–85 average of 18.5 percent.

As a result of the tax cuts and incentives put into place in 1981–82, revenues as a share of GNP fell briefly to 18 percent in 1983–84 and then began to rise back to above-normal, post-World War II levels, reaching over 19 percent by 1987. The major budgetary impact came from a sharp increase in spending. In effect, spending on entitlements programs, nearly half of total federal outlays, continued to rise rapidly, accompanied by a brief but even more rapid acceleration of military spending. As the deficits accumulated, spending on interest on the debt also rose.

The major structural or microeconomic feature of the 1981/82 tax acts was a sharp reduction in the marginal effective tax rate on new investment. This was accompanied by a liberalization of accelerated depreciation allowances, along with investment tax credits that amounted to partial expensing allowances for qualified investments. Such measures sharply reduced marginal effective tax rates on income from new investments, and in some cases—equipment investments in particular—marginal effective tax rates were negative. The federal government was actually paying private firms to purchase certain forms of qualified equipment.

The effect of measures to stimulate investment is temporary. A reduction in the tax burden on new investment creates an increase in the desired capital stock for firms eligible for the investment incentives. As a result, other things being equal, these firms increase their purchases of capital. The observable counterpart is a rise in investment flows that continues until the capital stock reaches its desired level. At that time, the only net, ongoing impact on investment is a small increase in gross investment, provided that firms continue to replace the depreciated portion of a larger capital stock.

The positive impact on new investment of the 1981/82 tax incentives was delayed by the recession of 1982. By late 1983, private investment in the United States was accelerating rapidly, just as the federal budget deficit was beginning to rise as well. The result was a sharp increase in overall U.S. expenditure that was not matched by an increase either in government tax revenues or private saving.

The sharp increase in U.S. absorption was accommodated on unusually easy terms by a large increase in lending from abroad. This was due partly to a continuous relaxation of controls on capital outflows in Japan and elsewhere and partly to the attraction of a rapidly growing U.S. economy in which it appeared that inflation was being brought under control.

The problem for U.S. traded-goods industries lay with the sharp appreciation of the dollar that accompanied the surge in private investment and government spending during 1983/84. Many of the U.S. companies that responded to the investment incentives in the 1981/82 tax acts found that they were unable to sell the goods produced with new stocks of capital when faced with competition (both in domestic and foreign markets) from goods produced abroad. In effect, the failure to anticipate the sharp appreciation of the dollar implicit in the unusual configuration of U.S. fiscal and monetary policies and the accompanying retrenchment of fiscal policies abroad caused U.S. investors to set hurdle rates too low for investment projects in traded-goods industries. As a result, by 1985 much of the new addition to the capital stock in the United States had been rendered economically redundant by virtue of a sharp appreciation of the dollar.

The U.S. economy in 1985 was really two economies. The nontraded sector was prospering, thanks to the stimulative effects of a surge in government and private spending; and the traded- or manufactured-goods sector was saddled with heavy excess capacity and an inability to compete in U.S. and world markets.

This uncomfortable dual economy set two forces in motion. The first was legislative, which took the form of heavy lobbying by U.S. industry for a trade bill with heavy emphasis on the opening up of foreign markets and the removal of nontariff barriers impeding sales abroad. Second, at the Plaza meeting in September 1985, the Reagan Administration reversed its stance on the dollar and indicated a willingness, and indeed a perceived need, for dollar depreciation. A rapid growth in the U.S. money stock, accompanied temporarily by monetary tightening in Japan, gave additional momentum to a dollar depreciation that had begun earlier in 1985.

The extreme pressure on the international competitiveness of U.S. manufacturing during the 1981–85 period resulted in structural adjustments that meant that the U.S. current account balance would likely be less responsive to exchange rate adjustment than has historically been the case. As a result of a long-sustained real appreciation of the dollar, many U.S. companies accelerated or initiated plans to locate manufacturing facilities abroad. This relocation trend is not likely to be reversed, but rather to be maintained as a hedge against the problems related to exchange rate volatility that come from competing in world markets. It is important to remember that the volatility, in turn, flows from a failure to coordinate economic policies among industrial countries.

The internationalization of U.S. business has of course been matched by the internationalization of businesses whose managements are based in other countries. A typical pattern shows managerial expertise in financial and research areas headquartered in a home or base country, with manufacturing facilities located around the world. This is partly due to the above-mentioned need to hedge against sharp changes in exchange rates. It is also likely due to the large economies of scale that can be realized by virtue of centralized financial and managerial capital. A multinational firm that operates worldwide, sourcing and manufacturing in markets dictated by financial and real market conditions, is very likely to be an increasingly prevalent phenomenon. The rapidly increasing presence of "American" firms in Europe and Japan and "Japanese" and "European" firms manufacturing and operating in the United States only serves to underscore this point.

The consequences for policymakers of this internationalization of business will be many. First, standard measures of merchandise trade balances may have to be discarded, or at least read with additional qualifications in mind. The more a country's firms tend to locate their manufacturing facilities abroad, the smaller will be that country's recorded commodity exports. Yet, such a weak showing on traditional merchandise trade figures may mask a sharp increase in dominance in world markets by the country's manufacturers.

The results of U.S. budgetary and tax policy in the 1980s will also require a rethinking of policies developed largely in a closed-economy setting. No thought was given by U.S. policymakers in 1981, when investment incentive measures were enacted into the tax code, to the possibility that the budgetary implications of revenues lost through investment incentives, coupled with deficit increases resulting from other deficit-increasing measures, would result in an exchange rate appreciation that frustrated the original purpose of the tax incentives. The crowding-out of investment occurred ex post due to currency appreciation, instead of ex ante due to higher interest rates. Unfortunately, the new investment could not be undone in the face of ex post crowding-out. The new investments, given the depreciation of the dollar, have since become more viable, but the wait for the delayed positive returns was costly.

More broadly, the advisability of tax measures designed to enhance competitiveness where exports are capital-intensive is called into question by traditional trade theory. If a country like the United States enacts measures that lead to a large increase in the capital stock, then, as we know from the Rybczynski theorem, the relative price of capital-intensive exports will fall, or, equivalently, the United States' terms of trade will deteriorate. The result is that many of the supposed benefits of investment incentives spill out of the United States to the rest of the world.

There has been much talk of loss of U.S. competitiveness and the ability of tax policy to restore that competitiveness. Based on comparisons with Japan, U.S. competitiveness in the early 1980s had largely been restored to the level of 1970, prior to adjustment for exchange rate changes. Figure 3 shows the path of U.S. competitiveness versus Japanese competitiveness in the manufacturing sector,

Figure 3. Measures of U.S.-Japanese Competitiveness, 1970–86

(Competitiveness index)[1]

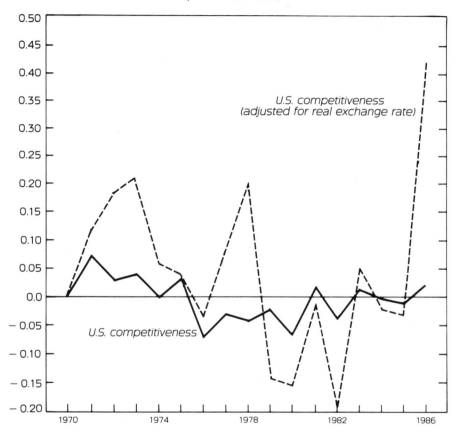

Source: U.S. Department of Labor, Bureau of Labor Statistics, various releases.
[1]For additional details, see Makin (1987).

with 1970 set at zero, based on the path of labor productivity and labor compensation.[2] The second line shows the real appreciation of the dollar and the subsequent impact on competitiveness that resulted from sharp dollar appreciation. The effect on competitiveness of exchange rate volatility dominated the effect of traditional measures based on movements in the productivity and real cost of factors of production.

―――――――
[2]For additional details, see Makin (1987).

Figure 3 also shows that the rapid depreciation of the dollar that began after 1985 ought to have more than compensated for the level of real competitiveness based on relative factor productivity and relative factor cost. The failure of the U.S. merchandise trade balance measured in dollars to fall even in 1987, two years after the depreciation of the U.S. dollar began, is a reflection of two factors: first, the large volume of U.S. imports relative to exports, which means that price effects dominate quantity effects, particularly in view of relative elasticities that favor foreign suppliers to the U.S. market; and second, strategies of non-U.S. exporters to maintain their U.S. market share even in the face of a much weaker dollar.

IV. Looking Ahead: The Process of Adjustment to U.S. Fiscal Policy in the 1980s

The persistence, although at considerably reduced levels, of the U.S. trade and current account deficits three years after the depreciation of the dollar began is a symptom of the fact that the broad adjustment to the U.S. fiscal experiment of the 1980s continues. The required adjustments are made more extreme by the fact that the post-1981 fiscal expansion coincided with a widespread fiscal retrenchment in other Group of Seven countries, especially Japan, the Federal Republic of Germany, and the United Kingdom.

The basic question facing the United States and the world economy is whether the adjustment can be achieved without a U.S. recession. In theory as well as in practice, such an adjustment without a U.S. recession requires that the United States spend less while the rest of the world spends more. Specifically, in terms of the theory outlined in this paper, the United States needs to continue its fiscal retrenchment in exchange for an easing of monetary policy in other Group of Seven countries, especially Japan and Germany.

Both adjustments have so far been only partially completed. A structural, downward adjustment in the U.S. budget deficit will require fundamental changes on the expenditure side. The entitlements programs, which constitute half of total federal spending and remain the largest and most rapidly growing budget category, will have to be modified with new legislation. The growth of entitlements benefits, including social security and government and military retirement programs, will have to be slowed by an adjustment of the formula that indexes the outlays on these programs to inflation. A widely discussed approach would be to subtract 2 percent from the inflation rate when cost of living adjustments are calculated for these programs. Such a change, given currently foreseen rates of inflation, would reduce outlays on these programs by nearly $80 billion over the next five years.

The savings would continue to grow over time, owing to a lowering of the growth path of outlays on entitlements. Such spending reductions would not be subject to alterations by congressional appropriations committees as would discretionary spending programs. As such, they would provide stable, prospective deficit reductions needed for a long-run, successful structural realignment of U.S. fiscal policy.

The recipients under entitlements programs are typically retired middle-class citizens, well organized by special interest groups such as the American Association of Retired Persons. Voter participation among these groups is unusually high. For these and other reasons, politicians are reluctant to adjust these programs.

The other major category of U.S. spending—defense—has already been curbed. Defense spending in nominal dollar terms has been virtually flat for two years and falling in real terms.

Many have argued that in view of the political difficulty hampering the adjustment of U.S. federal government spending, new sources of revenue ought to be sought. It is to be hoped that revenue proposals will be guided by sound basic principles of taxation. Any new taxes should be levied at low rates on a broad base.

For a country with the world's lowest saving rate, a broad-based consumption tax comes to mind. The rough rule of thumb is that each percentage point of a consumption tax, with protection for low-income taxpayers built in, yields about $15 billion in revenue. A national value-added or sales tax in the 3 percent to 5 percent range would yield $45 billion to $75 billion annually.

An administratively simpler and perhaps preferable alternative to a national sales tax, which requires an elaborate machinery to implement, might be a broadly based devaluation of the United States' $400 billion worth of tax preferences. Currently, tax preferences that allow deduction from taxable income of interest, tax, and other expenses associated with owner-occupied housing, health insurance premiums, and many other measures constitute a regressive revenue loss for the federal government. If all tax preferences were devalued by about 20 percent, roughly $60–70 billion in revenues would be available.

The approach featuring devaluation of deductions and tax preferences has the great benefit of administrative simplicity. Taxpayers could simply calculate their deductions under the existing code and then be allowed to take only 80 percent of the value of the calculated deductions as a reduction in taxable income. The revenue yield would be sufficient to bring the U.S. structural budget deficit back into line with pre-1981 levels.

When considering the stubbornness of the U.S. budget deficit, it is useful to remember that if the total outstanding debt of the federal government stood now at its 1981 level, the U.S. budget deficit would be in the $40–50 billion range.

That level is typical in absolute terms of the past 25 years and, at about 1 percent, unusually low as a share of GNP.

The addition of $1.3 trillion of national debt has meant that the interest burden on debt has risen by about 2 percent of GNP, or a steady-state total of $90–100 billion. The useful guidelines, therefore, for revenue measures would be to design measures that are aimed at servicing the new larger stock of debt while ensuring that other large programs like entitlements are not allowed to increase outlays too rapidly. A value-added tax in the 3–5 percent range or a 20 percent devaluation of tax preferences would accomplish this. As already noted, the tax preference devaluation measure has in its favor administrative simplicity. It could also be put into effect more quickly and with far less administrative cost than a value-added tax.

Viewed broadly, the U.S. current account and budget deficits of the late 1980s are manifestations of the late stages of a major economic shock rolling through the industrial world. Long-run studies of growth, like that conducted by Maddison (1987), suggest that secular growth rates in industrial countries tilted downward after 1973. For the 1950–73 portion of the postwar period, the real growth rate for five countries outside the United States (France, Germany, Japan, Netherlands, and United Kingdom) was 5.6 percent. For the United States, the average 1950–73 growth rate was 3.7 percent. For the 1973–84 period, the five-country rate decelerated to 2.1 percent, and the U.S. rate decelerated to 2.3 percent. There was a recognition delay in most industrial countries during the latter 1970s. As a result, budgetary stringency was not applied, deficits mounted, and pressure for monetary accommodation grew until inflation surged worldwide in 1979/80.

It has been widely noted that most major industrial countries, excluding the United States, began fiscal retrenchment in the early 1980s. It has also been widely noted that the adjustment was made far more easy for countries like Germany, Japan, and the United Kingdom by the fiscal monetary configuration in the United States after 1981. By 1983, this configuration had resulted in a rapidly growing U.S. economy and an appreciating dollar, both of which combined to allow a surge in export sales to the United States; these exports, in turn, acted as a cushion for the fiscal retrenchment in the countries sending the exports.

Another factor contributing to earlier adjustment by the five countries outside the United States may have been the sharper post-1973 growth slowdown: 5.6 percent down to 2.1 percent for the five countries, versus 3.7 percent down to 2.3 percent for the United States. The 1950–73 period saw a more rapid resurgence of growth outside the United States due to replacement of production facilities destroyed during World War II, whereas the growth surge in the United States was less sharp, and the post-1973 slowdown, less dramatic.

Whatever the reasons for the unsynchronized fiscal retrenchment in industrial countries, there have been disquieting signs that an inability to coordinate fiscal policy among the Group of Seven countries has created extreme tension in financial markets. The collapse of the U.S. equity market in October 1987 signaled that the level of interest rates required to provide capital inflows to the United States sufficient to finance its current account deficits is inconsistent with attractive prospects for growth of the U.S. economy.

What is clear in the aftermath of the collapse of equity markets is that, barring any significant expansionary policies abroad, the reduction of U.S. absorption will be accomplished either by a high level of interest rates or, as now seems more likely, by a negative wealth effect achieved by means of a further collapse in equity markets.

The U.S. trade and current account deficits cannot be reduced arithmetically without a reduction in the U.S. budget deficit unless there is either a collapse of investment or a surge of private saving. The discouraging spectacle of desultory budget negotiations in the United States after the 1987 crash suggested that public sector dissaving would not be reduced by much. The modest reduction in government dissaving during fiscal 1987/88 was in fact accompanied by some reduction in private sector absorption. A combination of high real interest rates and a sharp drop in equity values and, thereby, in the wealth of U.S. equity owners, helped to reduce private absorption.

The role of official intervention in currency markets in this process has been largely to postpone adjustment. The largely sterilized $100 billion intervention to support the dollar after the February 1987 Louvre Accord suggests an ambivalence on the part of other countries about U.S. adjustment. As noted earlier, most countries act as if they would like the United States to reduce its absorption while continuing to buy exports from that country and not successfully selling to that country. Rather, there is a preference for the United States to reduce its absorption through higher taxes and lower government spending. Significant adjustment of this sort seems unlikely. Meanwhile, world financial markets are left to struggle with a prolonged delay in structural fiscal adjustment termed "muddling through" in the United States.

V. Summary and Concluding Comments

During the 1980s the impact of U.S. fiscal policy has been more unusual by virtue of its size and persistence than by its inconsistency with standard macroeconomic theory.

A combination of very expansionary fiscal and nonaccommodative monetary policy in the United States from 1981 to 1984, with some intervals of monetary relaxation, produced rapid economic growth by 1983 and the onset of sharp dollar appreciation. Mirroring these events was a sharp deterioration of the U.S. trade and current account balances and an attendant improvement in comparable balances elsewhere.

Exacerbating the responses to the policy mix just described were micro-incentives enacted in the U.S. tax code in 1981/82, which encouraged investment and thereby increased U.S. net dissaving. At the same time, Japan's progressive relaxation of controls on capital outflows from December of 1980 acted, along with other capital flows, to encourage the transition to a large deficit in the U.S. current account. The requisite capital inflows were provided at lower than expected interest rates, owing partly to the release of a large pool of Japanese and European savings into U.S. financial markets and partly to the relative attractiveness of investments in U.S. financial and real assets.

The major adjustment undertaken thus far to the imbalances engendered by the U.S. program of fiscal expansion, coupled with fiscal retrenchment programs in other major industrial countries, has been to allow the dollar to depreciate rapidly against other major currencies, especially the yen and the deutsche mark. In view of the high level of U.S. imports relative to exports, elasticities generally unfavorable to rapid U.S. adjustment to external imbalances, and market strategies of exporters to the United States designed to maintain market share, the expenditure-switching engendered by the sharp depreciation of the dollar has been insufficient to reduce the dollar level of the U.S. merchandise trade deficit below $160 billion. The current account deficit has persisted in the $140–150 billion range.

Completion of the adjustment process still requires expenditure-reducing measures in the United States, such as lower government spending, higher taxes, or both. Failing these, reduction of private sector dissaving will be accomplished by market forces either in the form of collapse in equity values, high real interest rates, or both.

Since the U.S. economy accounts for over one third of economic activity in the industrial world and absorbs nearly one quarter of all world exports, it seems desirable from a worldwide economic viewpoint to cushion the required adjustment in the United States by means of modest demand-expansion measures undertaken in other industrial countries. These measures should take the form of easier monetary policies in the Federal Republic of Germany and Japan, coupled with maximum reduction of trade barriers.

Although growth of monetary aggregates in those countries is high by historical standards, the evidence of consistent appreciation of their currencies and the absence of any pressure on commodity prices measured in their currencies suggests that the demand for money is growing more rapidly than the supply of money. This is a situation reminiscent of the United States' situation in 1982. The deflationary atmosphere brought on by a strongly appreciating dollar caused sharp growth of money demand, evidenced by sharp drops in velocity. Stable prices were consistent with high rates of growth of the money supply. The corollary: monetary policy was tighter than the central banks imagined it to be.

The broad lesson of the 1980s is that a regime of flexible exchange rates is no more congenial to poorly coordinated fiscal policies than it was to poorly coordinated monetary policies in the 1970s. Exchange rate volatility or, more specifically, the sharp rise and fall of the dollar from 1983 to 1988 is only a symptom of a low level of fiscal policy coordination, largely among the Group of Seven countries.

If past experience is any guide, industrial countries will continue to have difficulty undertaking coordination of policies. This in itself is a bearable though difficult fact of life for an increasingly integrated world economy. The major danger inherent in the large trade imbalances and exchange rate volatility that accompany poor coordination of monetary and fiscal policies is ill-advised attempts to treat symptoms rather than underlying causes. Attempts, such as the Louvre Accord, to peg exchange rates when poor policy coordination ultimately requires adjustment elevate rather than lower the negative by-products of uncertainty about future exchange rates. Attempts to reduce trade imbalances by restrictive trade legislation, tariff and nontariff barriers, or beggar-thy-neighbor efforts to undervalue currencies raise the risk of curtailing world trade, thereby sharply lowering living standards worldwide.

References

Maddison, Angus, "Growth and Slowdown in Advanced Capitalist Economies," *Journal of Economic Literature* (Nashville, Tennessee), Vol. 25 (June 1987), pp. 649–98.

Makin, John H., *U.S. Fiscal Policy: Its Effects At Home and Abroad* (Washington, D.C.: American Enterprise Institute for Public Policy Research, 1986).

————, "American Competitiveness," Working Paper No. 13 (Washington: American Enterprise Institute for Public Policy Research, October 1987).

Comment

Gert Haller

John Makin's paper gives a clear and comprehensive description of U.S. fiscal policy and its international repercussions. I have little to add to the overall analysis. But since I come from the Federal Republic of Germany, a country on which the impact of economic policies in the United States is strong and far-reaching, I would like to focus a little more on the German economic situation and the stance of German fiscal and financial policies. If I may, I would like to look at the picture from a German point of view.

For me, it was interesting to learn that the U.S. budget deficit is not so much the outcome of the tax cuts in the early 1980s, but more the result of an inability to limit the increase in public spending, especially the growth of entitlements and transfer payments. I recall very well the famous bipartisan decision of the U.S. Congress in the summer of 1981. At that time, one could have gained the impression—at least I had the impression—that the U.S. Administration and Congress had succeeded in permanently cutting government outlays by some $30 billion or $40 billion, and had thus paved the way for the intended tax cuts. It was some time before I learned that only a few of these spending cuts actually passed the related congressional appropriations committees. This inability to reduce public spending contrasts sharply with the political announcements before and after the presidential election of 1980.

Three aspects of the U.S. fiscal and current account deficits and their international consequences deserve special attention: the significance of public deficits for business activity; the policy mix in the United States; and the stance of fiscal and financial policies in the main trading partners of the United States. It is common theory that in the traditional Mundell-Fleming world with flexible exchange rates, fiscal policy is a rather blunt tool for stimulating economic activity. In the U.S. case, however, the Mundell-Fleming model does not work. As Makin very clearly describes, for the U.S. economy, which has a large non-traded-goods sector, an expansionary fiscal policy proved to be a powerful tool for strengthening economic activity, even with flexible exchange rates. However, it seems doubtful to me whether this example can simply be transferred to other countries. In contrast to the United States, the export sector of the Federal Republic of Germany accounts for more than 30 percent of the whole economy.

Empirical studies show, moreover, that Germany's foreign sector is closely interlinked with the rest of the German economy. Therefore, the strong appreciation of the deutsche mark since 1985 harmed not only export business but also most other parts of the economy. Current slow growth in business investments is not least an outcome of the fast rise of the exchange rate between the deutsche mark and the U.S. dollar.

This brings me to my second point. A comprehensive description of economic policies in the United States in the early 1980s must focus especially on monetary policy. At a time of increasing fiscal relaxation, the stance of U.S. monetary policy was still highly restrictive. I think it is not unfair to say that at that time the policy mix of the United States was to some extent extreme. Thus, the combination of an expansionary fiscal policy and a restrictive monetary policy resulted in extremely high interest rates, both in nominal and in real terms.

It is certainly true that the strong economic expansion in the United States and the appreciation of the dollar have helped to cushion the negative impact of fiscal retrenchment outside the United States. But it is also true that a different policy mix in the United States would have permitted different monetary policies in other countries and, thus, a different pattern of economic events. High interest rates in the United States prompted the capital inflows from abroad (in particular from Japan, but also from Germany). Of course, this is the mirror image of the U.S. current account deficit. These high capital flows to the United States had a threefold effect: high interest rates outside the United States; a loss of funds that could have been invested at home; and the accompanying rise in current account surpluses. Of course, all these effects are interrelated; they reflect the same thing from a different point of view.

From a German perspective it is noteworthy that the German central bank, the Bundesbank, found itself in a difficult situation. By trying to stop, or at least to slow, the depreciation of the deutsche mark—a policy the Bundesbank called "leaning against the wind"—it made monetary policy in Germany rather restrictive, both in terms of the development of monetary aggregates and in terms of real interest rates.

I will not deny, of course, that the increasing imports of the United States had an expansionary effect on other countries, not least on Germany. But one could certainly ask whether this is only a short-run argument. In the longer run, high capital outflows and strong exports contributed—other things being equal—to a smaller capital base in Germany and to an overexpansion of the export sector. When the dollar reached its peak of US\$1 = DM 3.50, even shoelaces were shipped to the United States. I am not convinced that these kinds of exports from Germany to another highly developed country like the United States are a contribution to an efficient international division of labor.

To come to the current situation in the Federal Republic of Germany, I would first like to say a few words on the general stance of German fiscal and financial policies. To evaluate these policies correctly, one has to go back again to the early 1980s when the German Government decided to reduce the ratio of public spending to gross national product (GNP), which had risen over the 1970s by more than 10 percentage points. In contrast to the intentions of the United States to bring down public spending, in Germany, this policy has succeeded. By a strict limitation on expenditure growth, the ratio of public spending to GNP was brought down between 1982 and 1986 from some 50 percent to about 46½ percent. Up to 1985, the scope thus created was used primarily to reduce the high deficit of public budgets.

Starting in 1986, a program of tax cuts and tax reform was undertaken. Net tax relief was set to be as follows.

1986 DM 10.9 billion, or roughly 0.6 percent of GNP
1988 DM 13.7 billion, or 0.7 percent of GNP (including DM 5.2 billion brought forward as agreed in the Louvre Accord)
1990 DM 20 billion, or roughly 1 percent of GNP

This program will provide total net tax relief of about DM 50 billion, or 2½ percent of GNP. By 1990, taxes will take a share of some 22 percent of GNP—the lowest this ratio has been since 1958.

These tax reform measures have led and will further lead to a renewed increase in public sector deficits (central government figures are in parentheses).

	Billions of DM	Percent of GNP
1985	39.3 (22.7)	2.1 (1.2)
1986	41.0 (23.3)	2.2 (1.2)
1987	54.0 (28.5)	2.5 (1.4)
1988	68.0 (40.0)	3–3.5* (2.0)*

Since 1985, when the appreciation of the deutsche mark started, monetary policy in the Federal Republic of Germany has clearly been on an expansionary path. Money market rates have been lowered successively, and in 1986 and 1987 monetary growth was above money supply targets. Germany had the lowest discount rate in the 112-year history of German central banks and, second to Switzerland, the lowest money market rate of all major industrial countries.

I think it is well known that there had been some discussion within the board of the Bundesbank on the question of whether monetary policy was too expansionary. However one answers this question, monetary policy has in the present

*Approximately.

situation clearly reached its limits. The present monetary situation could be described as a kind of "liquidity trap." Money demand is highly elastic. In the present situation, it seems that long-term interest rates cannot be brought down appreciably below 6 percent. In view of low money market rates, the interest curve is steep, which clearly indicates an expansionary stance of monetary policy.

In accordance with the shift in economic demand components required to eliminate current account imbalances, domestic demand in Germany has been appreciably higher than aggregate growth since 1986. Growth is thus being fueled exclusively by domestic demand. In contrast, the external surplus has been declining since 1986, both in nominal and, with even greater effect, in real terms as well. Its influence on economic growth is thus inevitably negative.

The following figures show the year-on-year changes in domestic demand and GNP (at 1980 prices).

	Domestic Demand	GNP
1985	1.0	2.0
1986	3.7	2.5
1987	3.0	1.5–2.0
1988	2.5–3.0	1.5–2.0

The foreign balance in billions of deutsche mark developed as follows (the figures in parentheses show percent of GNP).

	Nominal Terms	Real Terms
1985	77.2 (4.2)	82.5 (5.2)
1986	110.6 (5.7)	65.5 (4.0)
1987	109.3 (5.4)	47.6 (2.9)
1988	102.0 (4.9)	36.5 (2.2)

Economic trends in the Federal Republic of Germany are thus exerting a positive influence on the world economy.

Needless to say, asking Germany to increase its contributions to the international adjustment process by faster growth is asking for a rise in internal demand, which has to increase the more the foreign surplus is to be reduced. A reduction in the German current account surplus to a range from 1 percent to $1/2$ percent of GNP by 1990/91 would require a rise in internal demand of about $3^{1}/_{2}$ percent a year. I am quite certain that this figure could only be reached if Germany decided to revert to inflationary policies.

Thus, it will certainly take time to reach a more stable and balanced international economic situation. This conference is not the place to decide the question of whether economics is a moral science, as Kenneth Boulding once put it. There is no use in asking who has to take the blame for the present disequilibria. The problem confronting us is simply due to the inability of the major industrialized countries to coordinate their policies.

What conclusions do we have to draw? First, I fully agree with Makin that there must be some burden-sharing between deficit and surplus countries. A lower rate of government spending in the United States would certainly help. In the Federal Republic of Germany, the increase in public deficits in the years to come will probably be more marked than it presently seems. I am not sure whether there is scope for a more expansionary monetary policy in Germany. To avoid a collapse of world trade, everybody is well-advised to abstain from protectionist measures. The situation requires patience and self-control.

Second, I also fully agree with the conclusion that flexible exchange rates do not allow one country to depart very much from the policies of other countries. The experiment of past years—that is, putting the burden of adjustment almost exclusively on the shoulders of the exchange rate—has proved to be very expensive. This is especially valid for countries with a large foreign sector. Wide exchange rate fluctuations in both directions tend to depress private investment over the whole cycle. When the dollar/deustsche mark exchange climbed to US$1 = DM 3.50, German shoelace producers were well aware that this situation would not last forever.

Third, if policy coordination in a highly interlinked world turns out to be insufficient, then the question arises of whether we need improvements in the exchange rate system, which will increase the obligation to coordinate policies.

Comment

*Carlo Santini**

I found Professor Makin's paper both analytically interesting and highly relevant to the policy issues currently facing the United States and other economies in the world.

I shall not present a full-fledged discussion of his arguments, but will address a selected set of points that I regard as being of special interest for the conference. In discussing these points, I shall roughly follow the order that Makin follows in his reasoning.

One can broadly accept his account of the U.S. experience of the early 1980s, when the dollar appreciation, induced by a policy mix of fiscal expansion and monetary restraint, helped to slow down price inflation and wage dynamics. In this context, the terms of trade improved and output and employment expanded.

I have greater difficulty in accepting the strongly worded proposition that "the exchange rate is relatively ineffective at eliminating an excess demand or supply condition in the market for traded goods, as it is in the United States . . . " (page 58). There is, of course, an element of truth in this rather general statement, but it needs to be qualified, either by reference to the conditions specified in theoretical models or in the light of the abundant evidence collected in empirical studies of the U.S. trade performance.

More specifically, the argument developed in the paper regarding the increasingly dualistic nature of the U.S. economy and the resulting slowness of the adjustment of trade flows to exchange rate movements certainly deserves great attention. Makin's contention that the decline in U.S. competitiveness caused by the appreciation of the dollar forced companies to relocate manufacturing facilities abroad on a large scale and that this development is not likely to be reversed as the dollar depreciates is of great intellectual appeal but is somewhat lacking in empirical support. Needless to say, it would be interesting to see the relevant statistical evidence. Has the shift really been so large, when account is taken of the lead times involved in investing in new operating facilities overseas? In

---

*The views expressed here are the author's and not necessarily those of the Bank of Italy.

addition, I find it hard to believe that U.S. companies responded to the appreciating dollar primarily by internationalizing production instead of by reorganizing
their domestic activities. This would be an interesting contrast to the experience
in Italy, where companies reacted to the strong exchange rate policy by reducing
inefficiencies, cutting costs, and enhancing innovation.

If U.S. corporations followed the same course—and it is plausible to presume
that they did, at least to some extent—the return of the real rate of the dollar to
its 1980 level should have put them in a favorable competitive position. Surely,
the recent strong export performance of the U.S. economy indicates that this
might actually be the case.

I am in broad agreement with the paper's analysis of the impact on the dollar of
the expansionary fiscal posture in the United States and of budgetary retrenchment elsewhere. One could actually buttress this argument with some empirical
evidence about the relationships between saving and investment in the three
major economies and the interplay between their current account balances.
According to the Organization for Economic Cooperation and Development
(OECD), between 1981 and 1986 the ratio of the budget deficit to gross national
product (GNP) in the United States increased by 2.5 percentage points, whereas
in Japan and the Federal Republic of Germany, it declined by 3.0 and 2.5 percentage points, respectively. The results are similar if the changes are computed
on a structural budget basis. Comparable changes in the opposite direction
occurred in the current account balances of the three countries: in terms of gross
domestic product (GDP), the U.S. current balance moved into deficit by 3.5 percentage points; the Japanese surplus increased by 3.9 percentage points; and the
German balance recorded a swing into surplus of almost 5 percentage points. My
view is that the shifts in budgetary policies in the three countries, together with
the relative stability of the financial balances desired by the private sector
(households, corporations, financial institutions), played a significant role in
determining the movements in external payments through their influence on the
pattern of domestic savings and investment.

I agree with Professor Makin's suggestion that Europe greatly benefited from
the strong U.S. expansion and rapidly appreciating dollar in 1983 and 1984.
These developments propagated economic growth in Europe and other areas of
the world economy by way of the foreign trade multiplier and, as the paper
correctly argues, provided a cushion for the fiscal retrenchment in the countries
exporting to the United States.

A good deal of empirical work has been conducted by the Bank of Italy's
Research Department on this subject, with the aim of investigating the trade and
output effects on the three major European Monetary System (EMS) countries
of the large real appreciation of the dollar and the strong recovery of the U.S.

economy. [1] The model used is a partial equilibrium one, with a structure similar to that of the International Monetary Fund's world trade model, except that it encompasses two separate areas rather than the whole world. This permits distinct parameter estimates according to the area considered—that is, the EMS or the non-EMS-OECD area. Several shocks have been simulated, of which the most interesting for the purposes of this discussion is a devaluation of the EMS currencies with respect to the dollar and an increase of domestic demand in the United States.

The exercise shows that the trade balances of the three countries respond significantly to changes occurring outside the EMS area, especially in aggregate demand. Exchange rate changes have a smaller impact because the domestic price reaction dampens their effect on price competitiveness.

In sum, the appreciation of the dollar and the faster growth of U.S. domestic demand facilitated external adjustment in the three EMS countries. The benefits were especially important for France and Italy, since they came in a period when both nations were pursuing anti-inflationary policies that caused their real exchange rates to appreciate. Since no support was provided during that period by the sluggish demand growth in the low-inflation countries of the EMS, it is doubtful whether France and Italy would have been able to follow the same policies in the absence of the external stimulus provided by the United States.

On the issue raised in the paper of the ambivalent attitudes of most of the United States' major trading partners to the prospect of a substantial external adjustment in the United States, my view would be the following. The counterpart of the necessary correction in the U.S. external deficit will, of course, be shrinking surpluses. These will obviously have to occur mostly in the rest of the OECD area, since we cannot count on the indebted developing countries in view of the fragility of their financial situation. Yet the reduction of the U.S. deficit should not be absorbed randomly by its partners in proportion to their present payments position, which is what would happen with unchanged policies abroad, in the event of a sharp contraction in the United States. Rather, the adjustment should be managed smoothly and targeted to the major surplus countries. This process would require differentiated demand policies in the OECD area outside the United States, so as to generate sufficient growth in domestic absorption and offset the negative impact of declining net exports to the United States while simultaneously reducing the existing payments imbalances.

---

[1]See Stefano Vona and Lorenzo Bini Smaghi, "Economic Growth and Exchange Rates in the EMS: Their Trade Effects in a Changing External Environment," Chap. 6 in *The European Monetary System: Proceedings of a Conference Organised by the Banca d'Italia, STEP and CEPR*, ed. by Franco Giavazzi, Stefano Micossi, and Marcus Miller (Cambridge: Cambridge University Press, 1988).

As far as the European Economic Community is concerned, although a lower overall surplus is certainly warranted, the distribution of the related adjustment, chiefly between Germany and the other member countries, is a matter of concern and continuing debate, centered on policies designed to produce changes in relative demand growth and on the appropriateness of today's EMS central rates. The importance of relative demand growth is also being boosted by the increasing priority the EMS countries are giving to stability in exchange rate relations.

Lastly, in his discussion of the policy prescriptions for the near future, I was interested in Professor Makin's advocacy of a concerted or cooperative package in which the United States should be prepared to offer a "fiscal retrenchment in exchange for an easing of monetary policy in other Group of Seven countries, especially Japan and Germany" (p. 66), with a view to preventing a recession in the United States and other world economies. On this score I have two remarks to make, which perhaps complicate rather than answer Professor Makin's queries. The first concerns the issue of worldwide fiscal discord and its implications for the observed instability in currency and equity markets. It is, I think, more clearly recognized today, at least by some of the Group of Seven nations, that fiscal policy decisions should be better attuned to the needs of international adjustment; the stimulative action announced in 1987 by Japan is exemplary in this respect. I am of the view that if the leading countries were able to negotiate a fiscal compromise involving less U.S. spending and more spending elsewhere, it would have a considerable stabilizing effect on financial markets (in the short run) and contribute to a reduction in the external imbalances (over the longer term). Yet, I see no mention of the possibility of such international policy coordination in the paper.

My second related point is concerned with the paper's "optimum policy scenario." The paper is rather pessimistic about the prospects of fiscal correction in the United States, claiming that "public sector dissaving would not be reduced by much" (p. 69), and that there will be a "prolonged delay in structural fiscal adjustment" (p. 69). The political complexities of the budgetary process in the United States mean that Professor Makin is probably right on this score. He then suggests that we may be facing a catastrophe: a sharp market reaction to the failure or inadequacy of policy decisions in the form of a further collapse of equity prices or a sudden rise in interest rates, resulting in a recession. I find it hard to believe that such a negative scenario can be prevented by coupling fiscal restraint in the United States with easier money in Japan and Germany alone. I still believe that action is needed on the fiscal front as well, and that there is scope for such action in both countries.

Comment

Charles Wyplosz

So much has been written about the U.S. twin deficits that it is becoming hard these days to write a paper that floats new ideas that are not outrageous. John Makin has wisely chosen to present a balanced account of the events since the beginning of this decade. That leaves the discussant with few bones to chew on. I shall therefore concentrate on some theoretical points first, and then bring up the European receiving end of the U.S. deficits.

This paper, as I see it, confirms the strong and growing recognition that the Mundell-Fleming model is after all the most efficient framework for interpreting the world macroeconomy. This is amazing for three reasons. First, the Mundell-Fleming model is the open economy version of the *IS-LM* model that is hardly mentioned in some recent influential macroeconomics textbooks. Second, this model, which is now more than 25 years old, has none of the components that have so changed what graduate students learn and do nowadays, ranging from rational expectations to intertemporal maximization, including time-inconsistency and equilibrium business cycles.

The last reason is that the model is surprisingly robust to a large number of restrictive assumptions, probably setting a record in the application of the parsimony principle, which sometimes escapes modern users. For example, Makin notes that, contrary to a literal reading of the model, the recent experience has shown that fiscal policy is able to affect output under flexible exchange rates. (Remember that according to the Mundell-Fleming model, a fiscal expansion leads to an exchange rate appreciation, and the resulting trade deficit eliminates the impact of fiscal policy.) In describing the effects of the investment tax advantage, Makin points out, quite interestingly, that U.S. firms were prompted to speed up their investment plans, only to discover that the dollar had risen while new equipment was being put in place, so that their overseas markets had shrunk to the point of making the newly installed capital useless. This is, of course, exactly the current account crowding-out effect predicted by the Mundell-Fleming model, with the "simple" distinction that in the model time is collapsed to comparative statics. One could push the advantage further and note that this is a perfect example of a successful case of time-inconsistency. Indeed, once the additional capital is in place, it may well be optimal to tax it (in the U.S.

case, to repeal the tax concessions and achieve a terms of trade advantage via an exchange rate appreciation). Forward-looking agents are not supposed to fall into such a trap, and yet they did! Or did they?

This really brings me to one aspect that is overlooked by Makin— namely, the dynamic aspects of fiscal policy. Because any deficit (budgetary or external) leads to debt accumulation, stability conditions require that it be eventually compensated by a primary surplus that is at least sufficient to stabilize the ratio of debt to gross national product (GNP), if not to bring the debt back down in initial level (see Sachs and Wyplosz (1984)). Thus, the eventual reversal of the U.S. twin deficits and the dollar depreciation were predetermined all along from the first day of Reaganomics. Whereas U.S. firms in early 1985 might have felt that they were trapped with excess capital, the same firms in 1988 must be happy to have invested in time to take advantage of the low dollar at a time of near full employment. This is why it makes sense for the United States to hope for a demand expansion abroad when it can finally deal with its budget deficit. The question is whether it made any sense to shift investment spending intertemporally.

In order to answer this question, we must ask ourselves what would have happened in the absence of the investment tax incentives. Belaboring the identity that forms the backbone of Makin's argument:

$$(S - I) - CA = (G - T),$$

it is clear that the budget deficit increase $(G - T)$ could have led to a crowding-out either via net private savings $(S - I)$ or via the current account (CA). With the savings rate notoriously unresponsive to policy actions (notwithstanding the Ricardian equivalence principle), the investment tax concessions pushed all the adjustment onto the current account, thus financing the budget deficit through foreign borrowing, instead of crowding out investment. The question raised above can now be answered as follows. With no investment tax advantage and 100 percent crowding-out of private investment, the policy move would have been smart if the net social return of the budget deficit had exceeded the net social return of displaced investment. With the tax advantage and 100 percent leakage to the current account, the criterion is now whether the net social return of the (larger) deficit exceeds the real cost of foreign borrowing. A case can be made that the latter criterion is less stringent than the former (although not necessarily that it is satisfied; this may depend, among other things, on future foreign demand for U.S. goods). Yet, a superior alternative would have been to limit the sharp interest rate increase and the equally sharp dollar appreciation with a more accommodating monetary policy.

Turning now to the European side, I find Makin's explanation of "Black Monday" (October 1987) a bit parochial. He notes that the reduction of the U.S. current deficit requires a fall in U.S. absorption (which is correct only because the United States operates at close to full employment). With a serious cut in the budget deficit slow in coming and hard to come by, the absorption can only be reduced through tight monetary policy or a negative wealth effect, or both. Hence, according to Makin, the financial markets simply anticipated the unavoidable. But then, why did stock prices plunge worldwide? Is it not true that absorption should rise outside the United States to help with the adjustment? Are not the world financial markets providing the cure and the poison at the same time? For, if absorption falls overseas and reduces U.S. exports, we are not getting any closer to the solution.

Following Makin's insight that the stock market crash of 1987 "signaled a vision of the future" (p. 61), then Europe's future is bleak despite years of financial retrenchment and record high unemployment. The same logic would interpret the simultaneity of crashes as an indication that the United States, where it all started, is pulling Europe into trouble. The truth is probably the opposite. Stock prices fall because of lower expected profits, in present value terms.[1] For U.S. prices to fall then, what must happen is either an (expected) increase in real interest rates or an (expected) reduction of future profits. The latter comes as the consequence of a fall in output, not in absorption. If foreign demand for U.S. goods grows sufficiently, a reduction in U.S. absorption need not lead to lower U.S. output and profits. Thus, the crash cannot be explained only by reference to the U.S. situation. The complete story must include the absence of faster growth overseas.

The important issue, then, is why Europe has not taken the expansionary measures that could have prevented stock crashes worldwide. [2] There are two broad answers. The first one is that the United States was an outlier once in 1982–85 when it embarked on a strong fiscal expansion. It now has to face the second stage of that policy, stabilizing its public debt and, hence, being an outlier again. Although cooperation is, in theory, superior to noncooperation, it does not follow that the rest of the world should always play seesaw with the United States. Indeed, some writers have suggested that Europe should have expanded along with the United States after 1982. Do they suggest a contraction now? Or, if one argues for an expansion now, based on cooperative arguments, was it wise for Europe to contract in the early 1980s? We cannot have it both ways.[3]

---

[1] Some writers have interpreted Black Monday as the happy bursting of a bubble. With hindsight, that explanation is not quite convincing.

[2] In Japan, where some expansionary moves have been accomplished, the fall in stock prices was relatively mild.

[3] Contrary to Makin's assertions, Europe did not view the U.S. expansion as a help at the time when budget deficits were being reduced in 1982–85. Inflation was then a main target, and the dollar appreciation was perceived as exported inflation with a strong beggar-thy-neighbor flavor. As a result, the European monetary-fiscal mix was probably tightened up further (some econometric evidence is presented in Wyplosz (1989)).

There seem to be two main views. The expansionary-prone view wanted a matching expansion then and wants a compensating expansion now. The tough-minded view wanted restraint then and still wants it now. In both cases, the argument is ultimately predicated upon a particular view of internal conditions in Europe—pretty much as internal conditions exert the dominant influence on U.S. policymaking. Thus, revealed preferences confirm the growing evidence that the gains from transatlantic coordination are too small to be at the forefront of the agenda, notwithstanding summitry rhetoric. The point is simply that the European Communities (EC) and the United States are both fairly closed economies, so that an expansion in the EC would have to be very strong to have significant effects on the United States. For example, simulations conducted with the Organization for Economic Cooperation and Development's (OECD) Inter-link model show that an increase of public investment in all EC countries of 1 percent of gross domestic product (GDP) only worsens the current account of the EC by 0.1 percent of GDP.[4] It would take a boost of 10 percent of GDP to bring the current account down by 1 percent, and only a fraction of this would go to the United States (which has a GDP of about the same level as the EC, so that percentages are comparable). Makin's call for "modest demand-expansion measures" (p. 70) misses that point.

The second broad explanation for Europe's inaction emphasizes its own economic conditions. European governments appear to be obsessed with the need to continue to apply fiscal and monetary restraint (the United Kingdom being a notable exception, on which more below). This is all the more surprising, given that inflation is now safely locked at low levels; employment, although declining, remained at record high levels outside the United Kingdom; and growth remains slow in comparison with the EC average of 4.8 percent a year over the 1960s. One argument for continuing restraint is that budget deficits in Europe are at least as high as in the United States (4.4 percent of GDP for the 12 EC countries; 2.4 percent for the United States). A second argument is that its economy suffers from "structural problems," so that the currently high levels of unemployment conceal almost full use of existing capacities. In this view, any expansion would be inflationary. These arguments cannot be dismissed lightly. Until they are, calls for European action based on international cooperation are unlikely to be heeded.

Evidence, however, has begun to accumulate that extreme conclusions are unwarranted. Various studies seem to indicate that most European countries suffer from a mixture of supply-side constraints and somewhat subdued final

---

[4]See Commission of the European Communities, *European Economy* (Brussels), No. 34 (November 1987), Table 29.

demand. A reasonable position, given what we know, is that some demand expansion is possible, would reduce unemployment without seriously re-igniting inflation, and would help with the U.S. current deficit.

Of course, what is true for Europe as a whole is not true for each country. Either of the two arguments for no European action may be of more relevance to some countries than to others. In particular, the need for budgetary austerity is overriding in such highly indebted countries as Belgium, Italy, and Ireland. It is hard to take it seriously, however, for the largest European countries (on this point and what follows, see Dreze and others (1987)).

The conclusion is that we ought to differentiate among European countries. Given the relatively high degree of economic integration within Europe, coordination becomes a crucial issue, should any serious change in the policy mix be considered. This contrasts with the low degree of interdependence between Europe and the United States.

The problem, then, is not coordination between the United States and Europe: both sides could benefit from an expansion of demand in Europe. The real problem is a lack of coordination in Europe, at least among the European Monetary System (EMS) countries. The Federal Republic of Germany could alleviate the U.S. deficit just by dealing with its own considerable surplus. As the center country of a de facto asymmetric EMS,[5] it would then allow other European countries to adopt a less restrictive stance as well. Indeed, experience has shown that even the larger EMS countries, like France, cannot act on their own, and Italy is quite constrained by its budgetary situation. But Germany shows no sign of moving away from its near-zero inflation target and from a rather strict budgetary orthodoxy. Meanwhile, other countries are certainly not willing to threaten the smooth functioning of the EMS for the sake of contributing to better worldwide balances, unless, of course, another stock market disaster demonstrates that economic independence may be a serious threat.

References

Commission of the European Communities, *European Economy* (Brussels), No. 34 (November 1987), Table 29.

Dreze, Jacques, and others, "The Two-Handed Growth Strategy for Europe: Autonomy Through Flexible Cooperation," CEPS Paper No. 34 (Brussels: Centre for Economic Policy Studies, December 1987).

Giavazzi, Francesco, and Alberto Giovannini, *Limiting Exchange Rate Flexibility: the European Monetary System* (Cambridge, Massachusetts: MIT Press, 1989).

---

[5]The asymmetry argument is developed in Giavazzi and Giovannini (1989).

Sachs Jeffrey D., and Charles Wyplosz, "Real Exchange Rate Effects of Fiscal Policy,"
NBER Working Paper 1255 (Cambridge, Massachusetts: National Bureau of Economic
Research, January 1984).

Wyplosz, Charles, "The Swinging Dollar: Is Europe Out of Step?" in *The Economics of the
Dollar Cycle*, ed. by Stefan Gerlach and Peter A. Petri (Cambridge, Massachusetts:
MIT Press, 1989).

3

Economic Policy and Adjustment in Denmark

Claus Vastrup

Within the last decade, Denmark has experienced important changes in both its external economic situation and its economic policy. Since these changes might provide some lessons for other small open economies, this paper will discuss the recent Danish experience with stabilization policy in general and financial markets and monetary policy in particular.

The business cycle and changes in overall economic policy since 1979/80 will be discussed, followed by a consideration of the conduct and the efficiency of financial markets. The paper concludes with a discussion of the reduction in the nominal rate of interest that occurred between 1983 and 1985 and the question of autonomy in monetary policy.

I. Internal Balance, External Balance, and Economic Policy

The turn of the decade 1979/80 is a good starting point for an evaluation of the recent Danish experience with general macroeconomic policy. At that time, the worldwide increase in oil prices had worsened the international economic situation and turned the terms of trade against Denmark and other oil importing countries. Also in 1979, Denmark joined the system of fixed but adjustable exchange rates within the European Monetary System (EMS).

The period 1979/80 to the present can be divided into two periods (1979–82 and 1983–87). The two general instruments of economic policy—expenditure-switching policy and demand management—were both used in these two periods, but the way in which they were used differed. Thus, from 1979 until October 1982, the competitiveness of the Danish economy was increased through successive devaluations, and fiscal policy was relatively expansionary; nevertheless, the Danish economy went into a recession. In the period from October 1982, the exchange rate was stable within the EMS, and fiscal policy was tight in most years; nevertheless, the Danish economy grew rapidly until 1987.

The international economic scene also changed in 1982/83, from a situation of high inflation, increasing rates of interest, and slow or almost no economic growth, to one of rapidly declining inflation and interest rates and somewhat higher rates of growth.

The Recession, 1979–82

The international recession that followed the second oil shock led to a reduction in the growth rate of Danish export markets from 3–3½ percent a year in real terms to around zero in 1981–82. Also in this period, the competitive position of the Danish economy improved by somewhat more than 20 percent as a result of a few devaluations within the EMS (Figure 1). Exports, in real terms, increased by almost the same amount.

Figure 1. Danish Competitiveness, 1978–86

(Index, 1985 = 100)

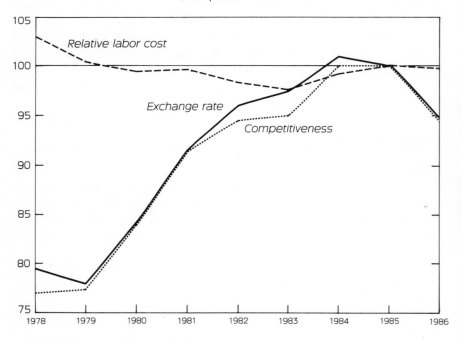

Sources: Economic Council (1987); and *Danish Economy* (December 1987).

The stated objective of fiscal policy in this period was to increase employment and at the same time to reduce, or at least not to increase, imports. To that end, public consumption was allowed to grow at rates between 2¼ percent and 4 percent a year, but public investment was constrained. Taxes were increased to restrict both private consumption and imports (Tables 1 and 2).

The purposes to which demand management were put during this period appear to suggest that fiscal policy was expansionary. According to measures used by the Organization for Economic Cooperation and Development (OECD), the total change in the cyclically adjusted balance of the general government was −4.1 percent of gross domestic product (GDP) for all three years (OECD (1986)). Since taxes were increased mostly at the beginning of the period and expenditure was increased mostly at the end of the period, fiscal policy would appear to have become increasingly expansionary in the three years (Table 3).

Despite the expansionary stance of fiscal policy, gross fixed capital formation, both residential and nonresidential, fell by over 25 percent during 1979–82 (nearly 30 percent during 1979–81), and private consumption declined by 6 percent in 1980–81 and recovered only slightly in 1982. However, since Denmark's competitive position and its exports increased, the decline in gross capital formation and private consumption can most likely be ascribed either to the supply shock caused by the oil price increase or adverse expectations generated by fiscal policy.

Only a small part of the reduction in private demand can be accounted for by the long-term rate of interest, which rose from around 16 percent in 1979 to 21 percent in 1982, since quantitative restrictions on lending by banks and mortgage institutions were relaxed and inflation increased over the same period. A more likely explanation for most of the reduction in private demand is the deterioration in real disposable income of the private sector, which, after increasing by 3½ percent on average in the three years before 1979, grew by only ½ of 1 percent a year in the period 1979–82. Since the change in the terms of trade amounted to only about two thirds of the increase in direct taxes in 1980–81, it is reasonable to assume that in addition to the effects of the oil shock, the fall in the growth rate of private sector disposable income also had a significant negative effect not only on private consumption, but also on capital formation and, in particular, private residential investment.

Since private capital formation and real consumption in absolute terms fell by much more than the increase in public consumption, fiscal policy can be said to have had a negative effect on total domestic demand. This assertion is borne out by the soaring deficit on the government accounts, which might also explain some of the rise in the interest rate during the period.

During each of the first two years of the first period (1979/80 and 1980/81), total domestic demand fell by 4 percent, but recovered to some extent in 1982. With imports of goods and services following the same pattern, net exports in real terms increased by more than 7 percent of GDP between 1979 and 1981, and then fell somewhat in 1982. The offsetting effect of net exports kept production

Table 1. Denmark: Changes in Selected Economic Indicators, 1980–86

(Absolute changes in billions of Danish kroner, in constant 1980 prices)

Indicator	1980	1981	1982	1983	1984	1985	1986
Private consumption	-8.0	-4.8	3.0	5.3	6.0	11.7	9.2
Public consumption	4.1	2.6	3.1	0.0	-1.0	2.4	0.5
Gross fixed capital formation	-10.1	-13.6	4.0	1.3	6.6	7.7	13.1
Private residential investment	-4.0	-5.1	-1.2	1.5	2.4	-0.2	4.0
Business fixed investment	-3.9	-6.3	6.2	1.2	4.2	6.9	9.3
Public investment	-2.2	-2.2	-1.0	-1.5	0.0	1.0	-0.2
Stockbuilding	-2.8	0.4	2.5	-1.3	4.1	0.6	0.8
Total domestic demand	-16.8	-15.4	12.6	5.3	15.8	22.4	23.7
Exports of goods and services	6.0	10.0	3.3	6.6	4.8	6.2	0.3
Imports of goods and services	-9.2	-2.1	4.7	2.3	6.7	11.9	9.5
Gross domestic product	-1.6	-3.3	11.2	9.6	13.9	16.7	14.4

Source: Economic Council (1987).

Table 2. Denmark: Changes in Selected Economic Indicators, 1980–86

(In percent, based on constant 1980 prices, unless otherwise noted)

Indicator	1980	1981	1982	1983	1984	1985	1986
Private consumption	-3.7	-2.3	1.4	2.6	2.8	5.3	4.0
Public consumption	4.3	2.6	3.1	0.0	-0.9	2.3	0.5
Gross fixed capital formation	-12.5	-19.3	7.0	2.1	10.7	11.2	17.2
Private residential investment	-16.8	-25.7	-8.5	11.5	15.7	-1.3	23.6
Business fixed investment	-9.4	-16.7	19.7	3.1	10.8	16.1	18.6
Public investment	-14.4	-17.1	-9.3	-15.1	0.7	12.0	-2.4
Stockbuilding (in percent of GDP)	-0.4	-0.3	0.4	0.0	1.1	1.2	1.4
Total domestic demand	-4.3	-4.1	3.5	1.4	4.2	5.7	5.7
Exports of goods and services	5.2	8.2	2.5	4.9	3.5	4.1	0.2
Imports of goods and services	-6.8	-1.7	3.8	1.8	5.1	8.6	6.4
Gross domestic product	-0.3	-0.9	3.0	2.5	3.5	4.1	3.4
Memorandum items:							
Consumer prices (implicit private consumption deflator)	10.7	12.0	10.2	6.8	6.5	4.9	3.6
Unemployment (percent of total labor force)	7.0	9.2	9.8	10.4	10.1	9.0	7.8
Current account (in billions of kroner, current prices)	-13.4	-12.3	-19.2	-12.8	-17.8	-29.1	-34.6
Current account (in percent of GDP)	-3.6	-3.0	-4.1	-2.5	-3.1	-4.7	-5.1
Hourly wage earnings	9.7	8.8	9.9	6.7	4.7	4.6	5.4
Terms of trade	-7.0	-5.1	0.3	1.7	0.0	0.8	5.8

Source: Economic Council (1987).

Table 3. Denmark: Discretionary Fiscal Policy, 1980–86

(In percent of GDP)

Change	1980	1981	1982	1983	1984	1985	1986
Change in cyclically adjusted balance	+0.3	−1.3	−3.1	+1.6	+1.6	+1.5	+4.6
Automatic budget reaction	−1.9	−2.3	+0.9	+0.2	+1.4	+0.4	+0.8
Total change in general government's actual balance	−1.6	−3.6	−2.2	+1.8	+3.0	+1.9	+5.5
of which due to:							
Direct effects of changes in interest rates	−0.3	−0.6	−0.6	—	+1.0	+0.6	+1.3
Tax on interest income of pension funds	—	—	—	+0.6	—	+0.3	+0.2

Sources: Organization for Economic Cooperation and Development (1986 and 1987); *Finansredegrelsen* (Copenhagen: Government of Denmark, December 1985); and Economic Ministry, various publications.

Note: A positive sign (+) indicates a move toward restriction (surplus), and a negative sign (−) indicates a move toward expansion (deficit).

from following domestic demand, and GDP declined by only a little more than 1 percent between 1979 and 1981, and then increased by 3 percent in 1982.

Over the period 1979–82, employment fell in line with declining production and rising labor productivity. With a growing labor supply, unemployment rose from 7 percent of the total labor force in 1979 to 10 percent in 1982 (Table 2 and Figure 2). Finally, despite the considerable increase in net exports in real terms, the terms of trade deteriorated, and the current account showed a deficit of 3–4 percent of GDP in each of the years 1980–82.

The Recovery, 1983–86

The second period was characterized by an international recovery and an even stronger recovery in Denmark, owing to circumstances specific to Denmark. Beginning in 1983, with the improvement in the international economic situation, Danish export markets grew by 2–3 percent a year in the next three years. The competitive position improved somewhat in 1984 and deteriorated in 1986, but was almost unchanged compared to 1982 (Figure 2). Exports in real terms grew by more than 4 percent a year in 1983–85, and leveled off in 1986.

With the formation of a new government in the autumn of 1982, economic policy was almost completely reversed. Fiscal policy was tightened as overall public expenditure was frozen and taxes slightly but successively increased. Exchange rate policy, which had been characterized by small, successive de-

Figure 2. Unemployment, 1978–86

(In percent)

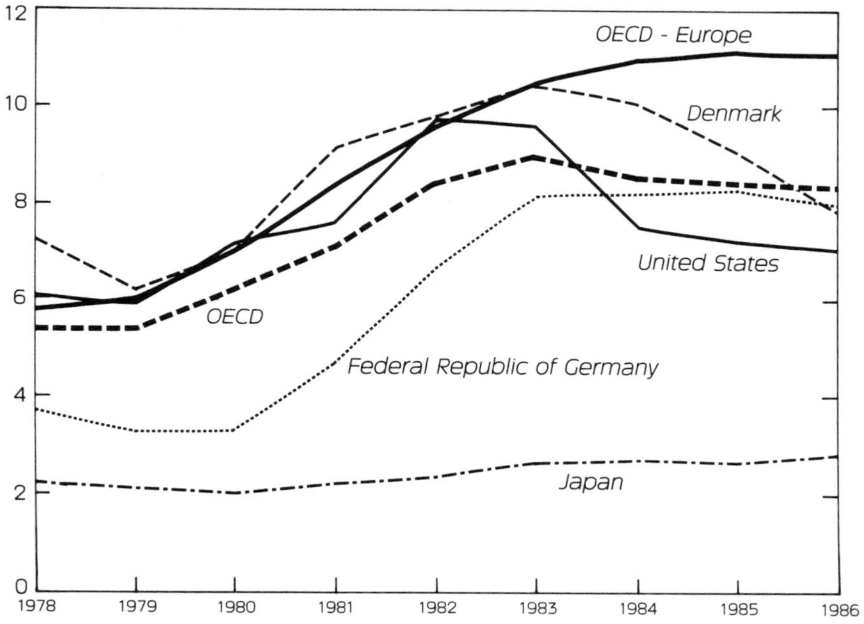

Sources: Economic Council (1987); and *Danish Economy* (December 1987).

valuations, was also changed, and the Danish krone was kept stable against other currencies within the EMS. Incomes policy was tightened, and inflation was reduced through the abolition of price indexation of wages and other provisions. However, since inflation abroad also fell, the competitive position of the Danish economy improved only in the early part of the second period.

The restrictive effects of the fiscal policy could have been offset somewhat by a steep fall in the nominal rate of interest and the associated capital gains in 1982/83 and again in 1985. But since inflation was also being brought down, the real rate of interest, measured as the difference between simultaneous values of nominal interest rates and inflation, did not fall nearly as much as the nominal rate.

Domestic demand increased by only 1½ percent in 1983, but picked up to 4–6 percent in 1984–86. Import growth kept pace with domestic demand in the first years of the period, but shot upward in 1985–86. The balance of goods and services, after showing some improvement, later deteriorated sharply in real terms, as production grew more steadily than domestic demand and imports. GDP grew by 2½ percent in 1983 and 3½–4 percent˙a year during 1984–86.

Although fiscal policy was considerably tighter in 1983–86 than in 1979–82, employment, which might have been expected to fall, actually increased by more than 7 percent from 1982 to 1986. The increase was almost exclusively in the private sector. Likewise, the international recovery and the improvement in the competitive position of the Danish economy during the first period might also have been expected to improve the current account balance. However, although the deficit in the current account moved from 4 percent of GDP in 1982 to 2½ percent in 1983, it later doubled to about 5 percent of GDP in 1985 and remained at that level in 1986, even after falling oil and other import prices had improved the terms of trade.

The 1983–86 period saw a remarkable improvement in the government budget. From a deficit of 9 percent of GDP in 1982, the balance turned to a surplus of 3 percent of GDP in 1986, although it fell somewhat in 1987. The improvement was due to discretionary as well as to automatic changes. According to OECD calculations, 75 percent of the improvement of 12 percent of GDP in the balance of the general government budget between 1983 and 1986 was due to discretionary fiscal policy (including fiscal drag; see Table 3). However, half of this improvement took place in 1986, and some of the remaining fiscal changes in 1983–85 reflected the effects on the government budget of lower interest rates and a new tax on the interest income of pension funds. Thus, part of the improvement in the government's budget in 1983–85 was due to special circumstances that were unrelated to the tightening of fiscal policy, and part of the improvement took place in 1986 following discretionary measures that reduced economic activity primarily in 1987–88.

Business fixed investment almost doubled from 1981 to 1986. In each year, capital formation was more or less evenly spread over the open sectors as well as the sheltered sectors of the economy, with a slightly decreasing proportion in domestic services (Economic Council (1987)). There thus appears to have been little evidence of capacity constraints in the open sectors.

The two main reasons for the upturn in business investment were probably the international recovery and the more favorable competitive position of the Danish economy following the devaluations in 1979–82. As noted previously, domestic demand surged, after some delay, in the second period. A possible reason for the delay is that due to adjustments, irreversibility, and the slow return of credibility, investment took some time to respond positively to the perceived increased profitability of capital. A similar, but less delayed, reaction by the general public with respect to private consumption and the financial markets provides additional evidence in support of this explanation.

The stabilization of public expenditure might also have contributed to rising expectations about a stabilization of the future tax burden. Thus, even as current taxes were increased, the improvement in the government budget might have prompted the rise in consumption and residential investment. The effects of rising expectations can be seen in the private consumption income ratio, which increased by 8–10 percent between 1982 and 1986.

Two extreme explanations might be advanced for the increase in production and employment. The increases were either due to a pickup in total demand in a Keynesian demand-constraint regime or to a profit-determined but lagged reaction in a classical regime.

A less radical explanation might be the gradual change from a Keynesian regime in 1982–84 to a classical regime in 1985–86. This explanation better accounts for the parallel increase in domestic demand and production from the bottom and in the first part of the upturn, on the one hand, and the subsequent strong increase in net imports, on the other hand. The increase in domestic demand might then be viewed as taking place in a demand-constraint regime; and the increase in net imports might be viewed as a consequence of the trade balance being determined as the difference between the high domestic demand and production constrained by real wages in response to profitability conditions.

The even distribution of investments over sectors is not at odds with this point of view. The lagged reaction by investment to changing conditions owing to adjustment costs and irreversibility is more obvious than it is for production and employment. Therefore, the changing regimes appear to be a reasonable explanation.

Some Policy Lessons Learned

Both the reduction of domestic demand in the first period and its revival along with production in the second period demonstrate the importance of expectations and credibility in the determination of private investment and consumption. Therefore, the impact of exchange rate policy and fiscal policy has to be evaluated with due regard to their intertemporal or expectational effects on private demand. The Danish experience during 1982–84, compared to that of 1985–86 (and perhaps 1979–81), provides some evidence of how an economy, even a small one with unemployment, may operate under different regimes (that is, demand-restraint as opposed to profit- or real-wage-constraint).

The change in regimes does not exclude the possibility that the increasing credibility of the policy pursued in 1983–86 may have influenced the demand for investment and consumption goods and, in particular, the response in the financial markets (see below). But this credibility might not have been established had not the real exchange rate of the Danish krone remained at the same level following the devaluations in 1979–82. The reason is that long-term credibility in an open economy requires a real exchange rate near or gradually approaching the rate compatible with equilibrium on both the labor and the foreign exchange markets.

The two periods provide some evidence of the comparative advantage of employing the two general economic policy instruments in a small open economy like Denmark. In particular, under the classical regime in 1985–86 (and possibly in 1979–81), domestic demand management tended to have the greatest impact on net exports of goods and services, and much less on employment. But employment was much more strongly influenced, compared to net exports, by switching policies. The conclusion seems to be that in a small open economy like Denmark, demand management should be employed to deal with the current account, and switching policies should deal with employment.

II. Financial Markets and Monetary Policy

The working of the financial markets and institutions in Denmark changed considerably in the 1980s. These changes should be seen in connection with changes in the exchange rate regime and in monetary policy.

Liberalization of Internal and External Restrictions

Compared with other Nordic countries, Denmark has a relatively liberal tradition with respect to internal restrictions and regulation of financial markets (OECD (1987)). However, in the period 1969/70 to 1980/81 various restrictions on financial institutions were successively imposed and tightened. The overall purpose was to keep interest rates lower than they would have been in a free market.

Reserve requirements for both commercial and savings banks were introduced in 1965 along with restrictions on lending by mortgage institutions. In 1970 the reserve requirements for banks were converted to ceilings in absolute terms based on total lending of the individual banks. This action potentially tightened the restrictions on the market for bank loans, but in such a way that in case of a binding restriction, the normal competitive connection between the deposit or money market rate and the lending rate was cut off. When the demand for loans picked up a few years later, the banks tended to substitute price rationing for the original quantity restriction. The margin between the lending and the deposit rates thus increased considerably (Figure 3). In 1975, as a consequence, a law was enacted introducing a maximum margin between the average lending and deposit rate for each bank.

Figure 3. Denmark: Average Margin Between Bank Lending and Deposit Rates, 1965–87

(In percent)

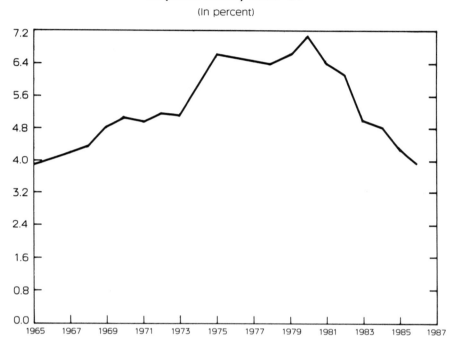

Sources: Economic Council (1987); and *Danish Economy* (November 1986).

The two restrictions made portfolio choice and rate setting much more complicated for the banks than would have been the case in a free market. Since it was possible for banks to charge the lending rates for the higher cost of deposits without losing business, the interest rate policy of the central bank was out of order. In addition, a maximum average deposit rate was introduced for each bank (later replaced by a maximum average lending rate).

In 1980/81, following the onset of the recession brought about by the second oil shock, all of the restrictions on banks were abolished. The lending activities of mortgage institutions were also liberalized in an attempt to stem the recession that had hit residential construction, which was also beset by externally induced rising interest rates.

A large part of the changes in the margin between the average lending and average deposit rates can be explained by the monetary policy instruments used in the 1970s. The Danish experience indicates that quantitative restrictions work against the efficiency of the financial markets and are inappropriate as monetary policy tools.

The change in the 1980s from a system of quantity constraints to a market-oriented monetary policy was followed by the introduction in 1985 of a system of direct management of the money market rate in place of the former system of fixed allocations of central bank credit to the banks. The interest rate had already become, by the late 1970s, the major instrument in the markets for medium- and long-term bonds, because from 1975 the Government had been financing its current account deficit by the sale of medium- and long-term bonds (this form of financing continued into 1985). As a result of the liberalizations in the 1980s, the interest rate finally became the main instrument both on the customer market and on the money market.

Restrictions on external capital flows were tightened just before Denmark joined the EMS in 1979. The restrictions were prompted by the occurrence of an inflow of capital, mainly in the form of exports of medium-term government bonds. The restrictions were meant to preserve the high domestic interest rates that prevailed at a time when the country was entering an exchange rate system with more or less fixed exchange rates, and, thereby, to maintain some autonomy over domestic monetary policy. In the years following entry into the EMS, the Danish krone was devalued a few times, and some bonds were sold back to Denmark, although the interest rates on these bonds were higher in Denmark than abroad (Jensen and Hald (1986)).

From May 1983, the restrictions on the purchase of Danish bonds by for-eigners were lifted. Exchange restrictions on capital flows were further relaxed in January 1984 and in June 1985. Danish foreign exchange restrictions, which apply mainly to bank deposits and short-term money market papers, are now among the most liberal within Europe (OECD (1987)).

Some market participants might have taken the progressive liberalization of capital flows as a signal of permanently fixed exchange rates. But since it is still possible to change the exchange rate within the EMS overnight or over the weekend, the external liberalization has not had much effect on expectations or uncertainty about the exchange rate. Therefore, although the liberalization might have reduced the autonomy of domestic monetary policy, the new exchange rate policy in operation since 1982 has probably had a much greater impact.[1] The external liberalization did intensify the competition among banks in the financial markets that had already begun with the internal liberalization in 1980/81.

Several lessons can be drawn from the Danish experience with internal restrictions and the subsequent liberalization on the financial markets. Quantity

---

[1]See the 1985 report of the Economic Council (1985), which emphasizes the importance of the external liberalization.

restrictions tend to increase the margins and decrease the efficiency of financial institutions and markets. Ceilings (or floors) on lending and deposit rates are in many respects preferable to quantity constraints, but financial flows tend to circumvent all kinds of artificial constraints. Similar problems arise with respect to foreign exchange restrictions, which is why these restrictions are no longer used as an instrument of monetary policy in Denmark.

The liberalizations have increased competition on the financial markets, and the instruments of monetary policy have changed accordingly. Since 1985 the interest rate on the money market has been the central bank's main instrument. To some extent, but less visibly, price-fixing on long- and medium-term government bonds has also been used.

The Exchange Rate and the Interest Rate

In September 1982, faced with increasing unemployment and deficits on both the current account and government finances and saddled with an economic policy that had resulted in a number of devaluations and increasing interest rates, the government resigned. In contrast to the other Nordic countries, which were devaluing their currencies, the new government announced that the exchange rate would be kept fixed within the EMS. The government also announced that incomes and fiscal policy would be tightened.

In mid-October 1982, the Danish Parliament passed legislation that imposed a temporary standstill on wage and profit margins and suspended (later abolished) all price indexation of wages. This signal of a switch to a nonaccommodating policy was immediately followed by a reduction in bond yields, which in September had been around 21–23 percent. Later in the same year, fiscal policy was tightened, and early in March 1983 an agreement to limit wage increases to about 4 percent, or half the previous increases, was concluded between the trade union federation and the central employers' association.

Later in March, the financial markets were sent another signal of the nonaccommodative policy and exchange rate regime, when, following a realignment of exchange rates within the EMS, the government kept the Danish krone stable against other currencies. Following these events, bond yields dropped to about 15 percent. In mid-April the government announced the liberalization of foreign capital controls, effective May 1, and short bond rates dropped again, but only by $1\frac{1}{2}$ to 2 percentage points.

The relaxation of foreign capital controls had only a small impact on Danish interest rates and only on short-term bonds, since the liberalization was announced only after most of the reduction in Danish interest rates had already taken place. The same reasoning applies to the role fiscal policy played in bringing down interest rates through its effect on the government budget (Figure 4).

Figure 4. Denmark: Interest Rates, 1978–86

(In percent)

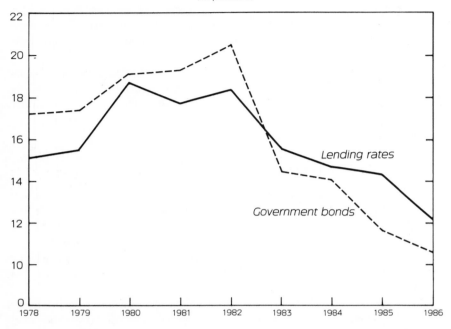

Source: Economic Council (1987).

During the period from October 1982 to May 1983, interest rates within the EMS (that is, German interest rates) were also reduced, but far less than the Danish rates. As a result, the differential between Danish and foreign long-term bonds was sharply reduced from 14 percent to a little less than 7 percent (Figure 5).

The argument that the reduction in the margin between Danish and foreign interest rates was the result of a highly expansionary monetary policy in Denmark has to be ruled out, because banks' liquidity with the central bank and the rest of the world decreased steeply in both 1982 and 1983 (OECD (1987)). A more likely explanation is that the credibility of the new exchange rate regime, supported by economic policy in general, increased dramatically during the period from October 1982 until May 1983.

The money supply of the general public increased by 25–30 percent as the difference between the yield on long-term bonds and the money market rate narrowed, and banks' holdings of long-term bonds increased rapidly. This asymmetric behavior on the part of the banks and the general public with respect to

Figure 5. Denmark: Nominal Long-Term Interest Rates, 1978–86

(In percent)

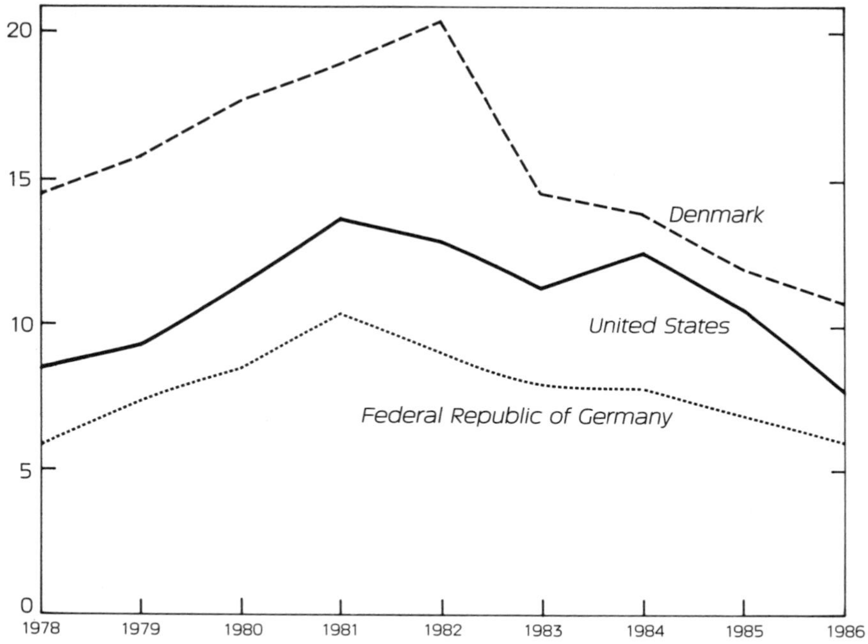

Sources: Economic Council (1987); and International Monetary Fund, *International Financial Statistics* (various issues).

deposits and the bond market can be attributed to differing expectations regarding changes in prices on the bond market. The increasing perceived credibility of the new exchange rate regime and supporting economic policies made the banks willing to finance larger bond holdings by an even smaller spread between the interest rate for long-term bonds and the short-term deposit rate. Consequently, the banks assumed a speculative position on the bond market as soon as the Government and Parliament signaled the change to a nonaccommodating exchange rate policy. However, the increase in the demand for money and deposits by the general public can also be explained to a large extent by the narrowing of the spread between interest rates, taking taxes into account (Christensen and Jensen (1987)).

The credibility of exchange rate and economic policy in general was the main reason for the banks' reduction of the long-term interest rate from 21–23 percent in October 1982 to 12–14 percent in May 1983. The banks took a speculative position on the bond market, thereby bringing down the interest rate, while the general public adjusted its portfolio to the differential between the prevailing interest rates.

Following the steep decline in 1982/83, the long-term yield fluctuated somewhat, but generally stayed around 14$\frac{1}{2}$–15 percent until the beginning of 1985. Following a breakdown in the biannual wage negotiations between the trade unions and the employers' organization in March 1985, legislation was passed authorizing wage increases of only 2 percent in each of the two subsequent years. Subsequent to the passage of the incomes policy by Parliament, the central bank reduced the money market rate by 2 percent, and by a further 1 percent effective August 1. The long-term bond yield dropped in stages from approximately 14$\frac{1}{2}$ percent at the beginning of 1985 to around 10 percent at the end of the year. The short-term rates also fell, but to a varying and slightly lesser degree. The lower level of interest rates and the associated capital gains contributed to an increase in domestic demand and the current account deficit in both 1985 and 1986.

The fall in Danish interest rates again reduced the margin between Danish and foreign rates. The difference between the yield on Danish and German long-term government bonds thus narrowed from 7 percent at the beginning of 1985 to 3 percent at the end of the year.

Even though the balance of payments deficit increased to DKr 29 billion in 1985, official international liquidity rose by about half that amount. Capital imports of the nongovernment sector contributed DKr 41 billion, although this amount was unevenly distributed throughout the year due to the phased reduction of Danish interest rates. For the year as a whole, however, net loans abroad by the government increased. Since the Treasury has easy and reversible access to external borrowing facilities, the monetary authorities presumably did not consider the international liquidity position to be adequate without official borrowing.

Interest rates were reduced in 1985, not because of an undesirable increase in foreign exchange reserves, but rather for domestic reasons. Therefore, even if the fall in interest rates contributed to the increase in the deficit on the current account, the reduction of the margin between Danish and foreign interest rates cannot be taken as evidence of a diminution or an elimination of the autonomy of Danish monetary policy (Vastrup (1986b)).

In 1986 and 1987 Danish interest rates did not follow foreign interest rates at all closely. As a combined result of monetary policy and a recovery in bond prices following uncertainty arising from a European Economic Community referendum in January 1986, bond yields began to rise in May 1986 from a low of 9 percent. Later in the year, the deficit on the current account reduced credibility, and yields rose to between 11 percent and 13 percent. The margin between yields on ten-year Danish and German government bonds fluctuated between 3.3 percent and 6.2 percent in 1986–87.

Some conclusions can be drawn from the reduction in Danish interest rates in 1982/83 and 1985. First, the reduction in 1982/83 was due to an increase in the credibility of the exchange rate policy in particular, and economic policy in general. [2] Second, the private sector did not react homogeneously to the increasing credibility of the new exchange rate regime. The banks reacted before the general public, with the consequence that the money supply rose. Third, the liberalization of the restrictions on external capital flows contributed only to a small extent to the reduction in interest rates in 1982/83. Fourth, the interest rate reduction in 1985 did not signal any lessening of the autonomy of Danish monetary policy, but was rather the result of a deliberately expansionary monetary policy.

The Autonomy of Danish Monetary Policy

The margin between Danish and foreign yields can sometimes be attributed to the reduced credibility of the fixed exchange rate regime and sometimes to deliberate monetary policy used mainly for domestic purposes. Accordingly, the degree to which the monetary authorities are able to pursue an independent monetary policy within the EMS depends on the specific circumstances. It has been argued that autonomy is not possible in a fixed exchange rate regime, but this argument depends on the assumption that a fixed exchange rate attains credibility either immediately or after a short learning process. [3] If credibility is assumed, perfect substitutability follows, and, with no transaction costs and no restrictions, a state of perfect capital mobility is implied. In small open economies, this assumption implies that the interest rate is exogenously given.

However, if shocks occur and some uncertainty with respect to credibility prevails, substitution is no longer perfect, and even small open countries with fixed but adjustable exchange rates will retain some monetary policy autonomy. Asymmetric behavior with limited changes in deposit and bond holdings is an indication of lack of perfect substitution. Under such circumstances, it is reasonable to assume that the degree of autonomy depends on the deviation of the actual from the desired value of all the main goals of the economic policy pursued—that is, unemployment, inflation, and the current account. Therefore, the degree to which the central bank may use monetary policy for domestic stabilization

---

[2]See also Andersen and Risager (1988), Christensen (1987), and Vastrup (1986a) for a similar interpretation.

[3]See the Economic Council's report for 1985 (Economic Council (1985)) for an exposition of this view. In the Economic Council's report for 1986 (Economic Council (1986)), the position had changed to the one presented here.

depends on the extent to which fiscal policy and incomes policy do not succeed in stabilizing the economy.

Since private capital flows normally occur when the central bank uses monetary policy for domestic purposes, a necessary condition is the willingness of either the central bank or the Treasury to use official reserves or foreign borrowing/lending to sterilize the private capital flows. Therefore, given some degree of autonomy, monetary policy should not necessarily be restricted only to the stabilization of official exchange reserves to ensure that private capital inflows are sufficient to finance a given deficit on the current account.[4]

III. Summary and Concluding Remarks

Despite a deficit on the current account (2–3 percent of GDP), external debt equal to 40 percent of GDP, and rising unemployment (but still low, compared with average unemployment in the rest of OECD Europe), the Danish experience with the general instruments of macroeconomic policy has generally been satisfactory.

The recession of 1979–82 demonstrated that a switching policy could produce strong results, even if they were somewhat delayed and primarily affected employment (and interest rates). Changes in domestic demand in 1979–81 and 1985–86 (and 1987) showed that, in the absence of a depression, proper demand management in an open economy like Denmark mainly affects the current account.

The experience of 1982–84 suggests that if both the international and the domestic economy are in a depression, an open economy might be operating under a Keynesian demand-constraint regime. But it is still true, as Neary (1980, p. 427) says, that "taking all possible regimes together, exchange rate policy was found to exert a more predictable influence on the level of employment than fiscal or monetary policy, whereas the reverse was true of the influence of these two sets of instruments on the trade balance."

The Danish case also shows that it is not reasonable to discuss the role of monetary policy in an open economy under the assumption of perfect substitutability between foreign and domestic bond yields. Therefore, the "monetary approach to the balance of payments" is not the proper framework. A "portfolio balance approach" seems more promising, because uncertainty about the future value of a fixed but adjustable exchange rate could invalidate the assumption of perfect substitutability.

---

[4]In OECD (1987), recent Danish monetary policy was unjustifiably criticized for not maintaining stable private capital inflows to finance a (given) part of the current account deficit.

If the central bank, in the absence of perfect credibility and substitutability, retains some autonomy in setting the domestic rate of interest, there may be good reason for not limiting monetary policy to the task of financing the current account with private capital flows. If public borrowing and lending on foreign capital markets were used for this purpose, monetary policy, along with fiscal policy, could be applied to domestic stabilization.

References

Andersen, Torben M., and Ole Risager, "Stabilization Policies, Credibility, and Interest Rate Determination in a Small Open Economy," *European Economic Review, Papers and Proceedings of the Second Annual Congress of the European Economic Association* (Amsterdam), Vol. 32 (March 1988), pp. 669–79.

Christensen, Anders Moler, and Hugo Frey Jensen, "Den danske penge-eftersporgsel, 1975-86," *Nationalkonomisk Tidsskrift* (Copenhagen), Vol. 125, No. 2 (1987), pp. 185–96.

Christensen, Michael, "On Interest Rate Determination, Testing for Policy Credibility, and the Relevance of the Lucas Critique: Some Danish Experiences," *European Journal of Political Economy* (Regensburg, Federal Republic of Germany), Vol. 3 (March 1987), pp. 369–88.

Economic Council, *Danish Monetary Policy in Transition* (Copenhagen: Economic Council, 1985).

————, *Danish Economy, November 1986* (Copenhagen: Economic Council, 1986).

————, *Danish Economy, May 1987* (Copenhagen: Economic Council, 1987).

Jensen, C.F., and J. Hald, "Valutaliberalisering og kapitalbevagelser," *Kvartalsoversigt, februar 1986* (Copenhagen, Danmarks Nationalbank, 1986).

Neary, Peter J., "Nontraded Goods and the Balance of Trade in a Neo-Keynesian Temporary Equilibrium," *Quarterly Journal of Economics* (Cambridge, Massachusetts), Vol. 95 (November 1980), pp. 403–29.

Organization for Economic Cooperation and Development, *OECD Economic Surveys: Denmark* (Paris: Organization for Economic Cooperation and Development, 1986).

————, *OECD Economic Surveys: Denmark* (Paris: Organization for Economic Cooperation and Development, 1987).

————, *OECD Economic Outlook*, No. 42 (Paris: Organization for Economic Cooperation and Development, December 1987).

Vastrup, Claus (1986a), "Hvor står dansk pengepolitic?" (Copenhagen: BRF).

———— (1986b), "Monetary Policy," *Monetary Review*, Danmarks Nationalbank (Copenhagen), Vol. 25 (May), pp. 17–19.

Comment

Giorgio Basevi

In his paper, Professor Vastrup examines two periods in Denmark's recent experience with economic policy. During the first period—from October 1979 to October 1982—the authorities could rely on at least two policy instruments: management of the exchange rate for external equilibrium (expenditure-switching policy), and management of aggregate demand (expenditure-reducing policy). In the second period, the new minority government took the exchange rate constraint implied by the European Monetary System more seriously. Thus, only aggregate demand management was left as an instrument, mainly through the tool of fiscal policy, since monetary policy was losing autonomy under the pressure of the exchange rate constraint and the liberalization of capital movements. On this latter point, however, the author holds a view that is at odds with the conventional one.

Notwithstanding the loss of instrument implied by the change in the exchange rate regime—or perhaps precisely because of it—the results seem to have been more successful in the second than in the first period, at least with respect to the reduction of inflation and the improvement in government finances. In fact, by tying their hands with a fixed exchange rate, the authorities might paradoxically have enlarged their room for maneuver. The apparent intent to discontinue using the exchange rate as a way to keep the country competitive might have been interpreted as a resolve not to allow the real value of the public debt to be reduced by means of inflation; such signals could have generated stabilizing expectations about the future behavior of the government with respect to both fiscal and monetary policy.

On the basis of these positive expectational effects generated by the decision of the authorities to discontinue using the exchange rate instrument while simultaneously liberalizing capital movements, the author posits a reinterpretation of the "new Cambridge school." According to this theory, fiscal policy is more effective in controlling external than internal equilibrium, and what is left of switching policy under a fixed exchange rate regime is relatively more effective in maintaining internal equilibrium.

I shall come back in a minute to the author's reinterpretation of this theory. But I first want to note that in contrast to his emphasis on expectational effects, the author has almost completely ignored the striking performance of the Danish authorities, who, under a minority government and within a few years, effected a sharp turnaround in the fiscal position. With what means and how, politically and economically, they could implement such a drastic change in policy remains a mystery, at least in Vastrup's paper. In any case, the success was remarkable not only in fighting inflation, but also, up to 1986, in promoting economic growth. As Table 1 shows, the Phillips curve seems to have flattened on the basis of these two variables—or in terms of inflation and the level of unemployment—during the period 1983–86.

Table 1. Denmark: Selected Economic Indicators, 1983–87

(Annual changes in percent, unless otherwise noted)

Indicator	1983	1984	1985	1986	1987
Current account (in percent of GDP)	−2.6	−3.4	−4.7	−5.1	−2.9
Public sector borrowing requirement (in percent of GDP)	−7.2	−4.1	−2.1	3.3	1.9
Gross domestic product	2.5	3.5	4.2	3.4	−0.2
Gross private investment (rate of growth)	5.0	12.0	11.5	14.9	−7.6
Consumer prices	6.8	6.5	4.9	3.6	4.1
Unemployment (in percent of total labor force)	10.1	9.9	8.7	7.6	7.7

Source: Commission of the European Communities

Table 1 depicts the impressive and rapid turnaround in the public sector borrowing requirement (PSBR), but it also shows that this improvement was not accompanied by an improvement in the current account of the balance of payments, which, in fact, deteriorated in the period 1983–86. Thus, the author's assertion that aggregate demand policy is relatively more effective when applied to external equilibrium can be viewed as a reinterpretation of the "new Cambridge school," whereby external equilibrium is defined not in terms of the current account but rather in terms of the overall balance of payments. Table 2 shows how the current account deficit was financed in the period 1981–86.

The improvement in the PSBR in 1983–86 was reflected not in the current account balance, but rather in net private capital inflows, at least up to 1985, as shown in Table 2. The improvement in net private capital flows was probably a consequence of the new confidence inspired by the authorities' decision to follow a more stringent exchange rate policy while at the same time liberalizing capital movements.

As a consequence of these successes, by 1987 the growth and investment performance of the economy had become quite modest. In the light of this

Table 2. Denmark: External Financing, 1981–86

(In billions of Danish kroner)

Financing	1981	1982	1983	1984	1985	1986
Current account deficit	12.3	19.2	12.8	17.8	29.1	34.6
Change in official reserves	−5.4	−2.5	7.2	−3.5	13.9	−14.1
Public capital flows	−8.9	−25.6	−17.4	5.7	−4.3	−36.7
Private capital flows	2.0	8.9	−2.6	−20.0	−38.7	16.3

Source: Organization for Economic Cooperation and Development

slowdown, it seems reasonable to ask why the author should agree with the Organization for Economic Cooperation and Development and the European Economic Community that Denmark's current account deficit should be reduced quickly and substantially. It would appear more appropriate for a small country like Denmark, having accepted a more or less fixed exchange rate regime vis-à-vis its main European trading partners and having liberalized its capital movements, to stick to all the rules of the game and not try to finance the current account deficit with large public borrowing abroad. Rather, the deficit should be financed with private capital inflows or changes in international reserves until such time as the inflows are reabsorbed through the classical adjustment mechanism. After all, for a country in a situation such as Denmark's, monetary policy retains little or no autonomous control over internal equilibrium—contrary to what the author tries unconvincingly to maintain; but monetary policy does become a powerful instrument for controlling the level of international reserves. Thus, the attempt to avoid losing reserves by borrowing abroad not only slows down the classical adjustment mechanism, but also reduces the government's credibility in being able to repay its accumulating foreign debt. It would seem to make more sense to leave the determination of the appropriate rate of growth of foreign debt to the private international markets.

Concentrating on reducing the external deficit after the government deficit has been successfully corrected is more appropriate for large countries such as the United States. For a small country like Denmark, already on the path toward losing autonomy over monetary policy, it is probably better to stop worrying about the current account.

Comment

Charles Bean

I first have to say that I found this an extremely interesting and thought-provoking paper. I knew that Denmark in the 1980s was a somewhat curious case, but I had not realized until I read this paper and looked at the data just how peculiar. Denmark's case is an odd one, because it really does seem to support the idea that fiscal retrenchment can be associated with an expansion in activity and a worsening rather than an improvement in the current account—what one might call the German view that the multipliers on fiscal expansion are negative because of the adverse effects of budget deficits on expectations.

The period Vastrup considers falls naturally into two parts: 1979–82 and 1983–86. In the first period, as Vastrup documents, there was an increase in government spending that was only partially matched by an increase in taxes. The intention was to increase demand while at the same time switching it from foreign to domestically produced goods, thereby sustaining activity in the face of "OPEC II" [second oil price hike by the Organization of the Petroleum Exporting Countries] without leading to a deterioration in the current account. In the event, the latter aim was achieved, but not the former. Growth fell and unemployment rose; and the general government financial balance fell from -1.7 percent of gross domestic product (GDP) in 1979 to -9.1 percent of GDP in 1982. Of course, some of the deterioration in the public sector finances was due to the decline in activity, but the adjusted deficit figures in Table 3 in Vastrup's paper (p. 92) confirm that there was a significant expansion in fiscal policy over this period.

After the formation of a new (minority) conservative administration in the second half of 1982, things changed. Government spending was held constant in real terms and therefore declined as a proportion of GDP, and taxes were steadily increased. At the same time, the government switched from a policy of continued devaluations within the European Monetary System to one of maintaining parity with the deutsche mark. This fiscal contraction, far from producing a fall in activity, led to a fall in unemployment, from a peak of 10.4 percent in 1983 to 7.8 percent in 1986. As a result of the fiscal contraction and sustained growth at about 3.5 percent a year, there was a drastic fall in the government financial deficit, so that balance was achieved by the end of 1985. However, as a reflection of the rapid growth in activity, the current account deteriorated markedly.

Can the massive slump in investment and consumption over 1979–82 be primarily attributed to adverse expectational effects from the fiscal expansion? Can the boom in private spending in 1983–86 likewise be attributed to beneficial expectational effects from the fiscal contraction? If the answer to both questions is yes, then the implication is for something like 125 percent crowding-out. Because the idea of expectational effects is so influential in certain quarters, it is worth discussing this possibility in detail. Such expectational effects certainly exist, but I refuse to believe they are of the required order of magnitude. There is nothing wrong that dividing by 10 cannot solve!

First, is it reasonable to attribute the slump in investment in 1980–81 to expectational effects? I think not. For a small open economy like Denmark whose long-term real interest rate is primarily determined by the rest of the world, the usual channel through which a "permanent" fiscal expansion produces a fall in bond yields and a rise in the long real rate is cut off. Another problem with the expectations story is that the timing is all wrong. The surge in investment in 1982 *predated* the introduction of the new fiscal measures, and the sluggish growth of investment in 1983 came after the introduction of the measures and after credibility had been established. The effects of OPEC II seem to be a plausible alternative candidate, and indeed, the slump in investment was roughly the same as that experienced in 1974–75.

Second, what about consumption? We are told that the savings ratio fell about 8–10 percentage points over 1982–86, and Table 1 (p. 90) suggests that it must have risen over the first period. Need these movements reflect expectational effects as Vastrup suggests (consumption-smoothing and backward-looking expectations go the other way)? I think the answer is no. Inflation accelerated between 1978 and 1980 and subsided between 1982 and 1985. We know from experience in, say, the United Kingdom that increases in inflation are associated with rises in the savings ratio as people react to the erosion of the real value of nominal assets by reducing consumption. My guess is that consumer behavior can be adequately explained without having to resort to expectational effects. (Incidentally, I would find the argument for important expectational effects more persuasive if moderately well-specified investment and consumption equations displayed large residuals at this time.)

I therefore think the key feature in an understanding of the Danish experience—which is only touched upon in Vastrup's paper—is the behavior of the labor market. How was the implied reduction in wage-push achieved so effortlessly? And, in particular, why was the March 1985 settlement of 2 percent, imposed unilaterally by the government, accepted by the unions without a struggle (I gather things have been unwinding since)? There are surely important lessons to be learned here.

Another important question is why the disinflationary process had so few adverse real effects. The process had three main components: fiscal consolidation; a pegging of prices via maintenance of the exchange rate; and a pegging of wages via incomes policy. This dual nominal anchor feature is reminiscent of the Israeli stabilization plan, which also seems to have been fairly successful. I think the reason that credibility was achieved so rapidly in the Danish case was that the new policies were put to the test very soon. The Danish authorities did not follow the devaluations by other Nordic countries, and this policy immediately and credibly signaled the government's intentions.

An interesting issue is whether the fiscal consolidation—although necessary for other reasons—was also necessary for the disinflationary program to work. In high-inflation countries like Israel, the answer is clearly "yes," because the loss in seigniorage must be made up somehow; but it is less clear that the same argument holds for Denmark where seigniorage is a minimal part of government revenues.

Incidentally, it is also worth noting that the Danish experience highlights the fact that current account deficits should not be something to worry about if they are associated with an investment boom and the deficit country is acquiring a real asset to offset its new financial liability.

I have few comments on the second part of the paper relating to monetary developments, which for the most part seem uncontroversial. Vastrup does make the interesting point that if the fixed exchange rate regime is less than 100 percent credible, then bonds denominated in different currencies will be imperfect substitutes. This leaves open the possibility that interest rate policy can be directed toward domestic ends while intervention is used to maintain the exchange rate. This view seems to suggest that a lack of credibility might be a good thing, because it adds another instrument to the authorities' portfolio. However, I am not sure that this is an appropriate conclusion, because the possibility of a realignment may provoke a speculative attack, which would reduce the room for maneuver on both the fiscal and monetary front. Working out the optimal degree of commitment to an exchange rate target under these circumstances seems to be an interesting topic for future research.

Fiscal Adjustment, Debt Management, and Conditionality

*Manuel Guitián**

A prominent feature of the recent global economic scene is fiscal disequilibrium. Over the past decade, the fiscal deficit as a percentage of gross national product (GNP) has roughly doubled for the world as a whole. Many countries exhibit large, growing, and persistent fiscal imbalances. While ten years ago a sizable proportion of countries had surpluses, these have by now become virtually nonexistent. Fiscal disequilibrium cuts across regions, levels of development, and indeed, countries with widely differing social and economic systems (J. de Larosière (1982, p. 81)).

In recent years the world has been witnessing an explosion in public debt. Whether one considers small or large industrial countries, developing countries, or socialist countries, all are experiencing large increases in public debt. In developing and socialist countries, the debt being accumulated is mostly foreign. In industrial countries, it is mostly, though not exclusively, domestic. In all cases the share of debt in the gross domestic product is growing (J. de Larosière (1984, p. 261)).

The paragraphs quoted above highlight two prominent features of the adjustment problems that have confronted a wide variety of country economies for an extended period of time. These are the prevalence of fiscal imbalances and the consequent accumulation of public debts. As such, the quotations provide a most appropriate setting for a paper aimed at a discussion of fiscal adjustment, debt management, and conditionality. Although these issues are examined in the paper mainly from the specific perspective of countries with large stocks of external public debts, it is important to keep in mind that their scope is broader. Indeed, as the quotations make clear, the twin problems of protracted fiscal imbalances and large increases in public debt—domestic, foreign, or both—cut across all categories of countries.

Adjustment problems tend to arise in various ways and for a variety of reasons. As a common characteristic, they exhibit frequently an unsustainable rate of

*The views expressed in the paper are the author's and not necessarily those of the International Monetary Fund.

domestic absorption of resources in the economy, typically in reflection of an excess of total demand for resources beyond the amounts that are available internally and those that can be secured from abroad on a sustained basis. But adjustment problems can also arise from the prevalence of inefficiencies in the use of existing resources or other distortions that limit the level or the rate of expansion of aggregate supply and that, as a result, keep the economy from operating at full capacity or from reaching its potential rate of growth or both.

The design of an adjustment strategy must be based on an accurate assessment of the nature and characteristics of the imbalance confronting the economy. This evaluation normally entails ascertaining aspects such as the causes of the imbalance—for example, whether it is due to external or internal events; or its character—for example, whether it is exogenous or endogenous; or its source— for example, whether it reflects demand or supply factors; or its probable durability—for example, whether it is permanent or transitory. An assessment of these various features of an economic imbalance can be critical for the formulation of an appropriate set of corrective policy measures; and the issues that arise in this broad context have been extensively analyzed elsewhere.[1]

For the purposes of this paper, however, an additional, though related, dimension of an imbalance needs to be stressed because of its particular relevance: the relationship that develops over time between the emergence of an imbalance in the economy that needs redressing and the consequent design and implementation of an adjustment effort to correct it. As they evolve, an imbalance and its correction can be seen as *flow* events, and the nature of their interaction can be crucial. This is because the extent to which an adjustment *need* and an adjustment *effort* are commensurate in magnitude and timing will determine whether or not the imbalance is being passed on from one period to the next. In other words, it will determine whether or not a flow imbalance is being converted into a stock maladjustment. It is clear that considerations of this nature will influence the various characteristics of an economic imbalance that were outlined earlier. For example, imbalances that at first sight would appear either temporary or exogenous, if allowed to persist, will most likely develop features of a permanent or endogenous character.

From the standpoint of the subject matter of this paper, the importance of the connection between these two types of flow events cannot be overstressed. The reason is that such connection captures the essence of the process that binds fiscal deficits together with the accumulation of public debt. This issue is at the center of the analysis developed in the paper, and its relevance has been made

---

[1]See, for example, Tanzi (1987a) and Guitián (1981 and 1987b) and the references cited in these works.

evident by developments in the international economy over the last ten or fifteen years. During that period, as highlighted by the quotations at the beginning of the paper, numerous instances can be found of cases where prolonged imbalances have been incurred which could only be sustained by resort to persistent borrowing, and which, thus, inevitably cumulated into large stocks of debt outstanding.

For an examination of these various issues, the paper is structured along the following lines. After this introduction, Section I analyzes the process of fiscal adjustment from the perspective of global macroeconomic balance as well as from the standpoint of efficiency in resource use. Section II focuses on debt management questions and, in particular, on their bearing on fiscal and balance of payments problems. Against this background, Section III reviews conditionality practices as they have evolved recently to address the specific problems confronted by large debtor countries. This review considers the implications for conditionality of the time dimension of imbalances that have persisted for extended periods and thus developed the complex characteristics of a stock-flow problem. Finally, Section IV draws together some concluding remarks concerning the importance of fiscal policy in the process of adjustment, the constraints that debt accumulation poses for economic management over time, and their relationship with evolving conditionality practices.

I. The Issue of Fiscal Adjustment

Economic policies in general, and fiscal policies in particular, are aimed (explicitly or implicitly) at a broad range of objectives of a diverse though typically interrelated nature. The combination of specific objectives pursued at any particular point of time is likely to be based on a combination of economic criteria with other considerations of a noneconomic nature. Both policy objectives and the reasons that prompt their pursuit are not immutable, and the emphasis or the priority placed on the attainment of specific aims inevitably varies over time. Nevertheless, a broad consensus has developed in most, if not all, countries concerning the basic constellation of objectives that appear worth pursuing from an economic standpoint. This constellation normally includes the attainment of a sound level and rate of growth of economic activity; the maintenance of an appropriate level of employment and the consequent avoidance of unemployment; an acceptable measure of domestic price and exchange rate stability; and a viable external payments position. As time elapses, social preferences evolve, and so do the dynamics of the constraints that constantly confront country economies in their struggle to attain particular policy objectives. In turn, this evolution of social preferences influences the relative importance that is attached to each of these broad aims over time. Accordingly, the standards of measurement of attainment of policy aims reflect the interplay between social preferences and the constraints that economies confront in the process of their fulfillment. But broadly speaking, the objectives listed above are generally accepted as legitimate aims of economic policy in virtually all economies.

Typically, these objectives have to be sought in conjunction with the pursuit of other goals that, as noted earlier, reflect a mixture of economic, social, and political considerations. Many of these considerations reflect in particular the importance each society attaches to issues such as the equity and distributional effects of economic policies. However, the scope for the attainment of a wide spectrum of policy aims is constrained by the prevailing and prospective balance that obtains between the resources required for that purpose and those that are available. It is not surprising, therefore, that an integral part of the process of economic policy formulation and decision making entails delicate choices concerning the mix of the various policy objectives as well as the relative speed of their attainment. Indeed, the appropriateness of those choices can be critical from the perspective of the feasibility of sustained implementation of the required policies.

These considerations, although of a general character, are nevertheless relevant in the context of fiscal policy. This is because persistent fiscal imbalances are often associated with the evolution of attitudes about the scope of government in the economy and in society at large. In most instances, those attitudes tend to be influenced more by the legitimacy of a wide variety of policy aims than by the feasibility of their attainment. Thus, the role and functions of government have expanded sharply in most economies in recent years.[2] In itself, an increase in the role of government in the economy does not necessarily entail the emergence of a fiscal imbalance. If society's choices about the role of government are matched by its ability and willingness to provide the resources required for the government to fulfill that role, imbalances need not arise. Experience shows, however, that in most instances social agreement on an expanding government role is both more expedient and far easier to attain than the social consensus required to finance the expansion on a sustained basis; as a result, there is an ever present need for fiscal adjustment.

Macroeconomic Aspects

In a broad sense, an effort of adjustment in a country entails in one way or another the alignment of the level and the rate of expansion of aggregate demand

---

[2]For further elaboration of these issues, see de Larosière (1982 and 1984) and, in particular, Mueller (1987), where a variety of explanatory hypotheses for the growth of government are assessed from a public choice perspective.

and expenditure in the economy with those of its potential productive capacity and income. The considerations outlined above, as well as experience, indicate that unsustainable demand expansions are frequently associated with imbalances in the fiscal accounts and more generally in the public sector finances; hence, the need for fiscal adjustment.[3]

A process of fiscal adjustment is bound to be influenced importantly by two critical factors: the *amount* of resources on which the government can count; and the *efficiency* with which it uses them.[4] These two factors interact in a variety of complex ways but, for expository purposes, it is convenient to discuss them separately.

From the standpoint of the amount of resources, a fiscal adjustment effort must ultimately be based on policy actions designed either to raise revenues to whatever level is necessary to finance fiscal expenditure on a sustained basis or to contain expenditure within bounds that are consistent with available revenues. In either or both of these ways, the aggregate demand-supply maladjustment to which the fiscal imbalance was contributing can be corrected. At this general level, the key issue at stake is the extent to which the government's resource demands are commensurate, on a durable basis, with its ability to raise revenues. This dimension of fiscal policy can be labeled the *macroeconomic aspect of fiscal management*, on the grounds that the focus of analysis is mainly addressed to the attainment and maintenance of global balance between the demands for and the availability of resources in the economy.[5]

Naturally, these fiscal policy aspects bear a close relationship to the broader domain of financial policies that influence credit, money, and borrowing flows in an economy both domestically and vis-à-vis the rest of the world. Such a relationship is derived from the consequences that divergences between the flow of fiscal outlays and receipts have for the government's borrowing requirement, both from domestic sources— with consequent effects for the amount of savings available in the rest of the economy—and from foreign sources—with important implications for the future availability of foreign exchange and savings in the economy.[6]

---

[3]Ever since formulation of the "Ricardian equivalence" proposition, the effects of fiscal policy on aggregate demand have been a subject of continuing interest and debate in the literature; see, for example, Barro (1974), Carmichael (1982), Feldstein (1982), McCallum (1984), and Masson (1985).

[4]An extensive examination of these questions in the broader context of macroeconomic policy management can be found in Guitián (1987b).

[5]This is the counterpart of what I have termed elsewhere in a broader context the fiscal aspect of macroeconomic management; see Guitián (1987b); in a similar vein, Tanzi (1987a) has referred to a macroeconomic approach to stabilization policy.

[6]These issues fall beyond the scope of this paper, but extensive analyses can be found in a variety of studies; see, for example, Guitián (1973 and 1981), International Monetary Fund (1977 and 1987), Frenkel and Mussa (1981), Calvo (1985), and Masson (1985).

Efficiency Aspects

Apart from their effects on the global resource balance of the government sector, the particular type and mix of policy measures undertaken to redress a fiscal imbalance can influence significantly the general performance of the public sector as well as of the economy as a whole. For example, the implications for the private economy of a particular government policy will vary depending on whether the fiscal adjustment is mainly focused upon expenditure control or whether it stresses instead revenue raising and collection. Adjustment based on curtailment of spending seeks to restore balance to the economy by lowering the share of government in aggregate demand.[7] In contrast, an adjustment based on the collection of additional revenues increases the government's uptake of incomes in the economy, which, other things being equal, will tend to lower the private sector's share in aggregate demand. But these are not the only differences that can arise from diverse fiscal policy mixes. Not only do these policy mixes vary in impact, but they also differ with regard to the certainty and speed with which they yield results. For example, measures of expenditure restraint and revenue-raising actions do not carry the same probability of yielding results of an equivalent magnitude over similar time intervals. As is the case with other economic agents, any action undertaken by governments to reduce spending carries more certainty in its impact on the fiscal imbalance than actions to raise revenues, which also depend on reactions elsewhere in the economy. Specifically, although it can be expected that actions undertaken to curtail expenditure will be reflected in a commensurate decline in the deficit, the same assurance need not obtain from actions intended to raise revenues.[8]

Fiscal policy can also be influential in enhancing productivity and efficiency in the economy. To this end, by affecting the efficiency and composition of spending, the quality of expenditure management can be critical. The effectiveness and durability of an effort to control government spending and, more generally, aggregate demand, will depend, among other things, on directing policy action toward the curtailment of unproductive outlays as well as toward the safeguard of efficient expenditure and, in particular, investment projects. A second area of importance is the quality of tax policy. In this context, the importance of an improvement in the structure of tax rates cannot be overstressed. By providing

---

[7]Spending in this argument refers to government outlays to purchase goods and services and does not include transfers, which are equivalent to negative taxes, a reduction in which will tend to lower private expenditure. I am indebted to Vito Tanzi for this clarification.

[8]The differential impact of diverse policy actions is not confined to the domain of the fiscal imbalance as such; see, for example, Khan and Lizondo (1987) for a discussion of the different effects of various fiscal policy actions on the exchange rate and competitiveness; see also Guitián (1976).

appropriate incentives toward efficient use and allocation of resources, such improvement can enhance productivity in the economy at large. A third area that can contribute to the effectiveness of fiscal policy is public pricing. This involves the issues of the economic appropriateness of administratively set consumer and producer prices and the related question of subsidies, which often loom large behind the prevalence of fiscal imbalances. These various elements of fiscal policy represent what may be called the *efficiency aspect of fiscal management*, which is of great importance not only for fiscal adjustment but also for the performance of the economy at large.[9] By raising productivity, fiscal policy thus affects aggregate supply and provides a critical support to the attainment of macroeconomic balance, as it contributes to bringing output to potential.

Sectoral Aspects

There are specific sectoral issues in which public sector policies play an important role and can influence the overall level of efficiency in the economy. The most important areas concern the public enterprises. In this connection, efficiency questions often arise that relate to the impact on the operations of these enterprises of decisions concerning pricing, investment, employment, and financial management. Even in an environment where an appropriate relative cost-price structure prevails, it is not uncommon to observe public enterprises being shielded from the influence of relative price changes by means of special tax treatment, subsidized transfers, or protection from foreign competition, with obvious costs for the taxpayer and the economy as a whole.

Key areas where distortions tend to arise include the prevalence of employment at levels that exceed those associated with the efficient operation of the enterprise. Situations of this sort represent a waste of resources that add unnecessarily to the costs of production and often carry undesirable distributional effects. Access to borrowed resources (domestically and from abroad) on terms that are not consistent with the yields of the investments undertaken by the enterprises also lead to inefficiencies that eventually burden the budget, the taxpayer, and the economy at large. Related to these issues are decisions in the fields of pricing and tariffs as well as financial management, which often are intended to address issues of a noneconomic nature and consequently are frequently determined by criteria that pay little attention to budgetary or efficiency requirements.[10]

---

[9]Tanzi (1987a) refers to these aspects of fiscal policy as the microeconomic approach to stabilization. For a broad elaboration of these various issues, see also International Monetary Fund (1987).

[10]For a discussion of these issues, see Johnson and Salop (1980) and International Monetary Fund (1986).

These various aspects of fiscal management (macroeconomic efficiency and sectoral) are mutually supporting. Indeed, lack of due regard to one of them may easily undermine the effectiveness of the other. In general terms, the conduct of fiscal policy, if it is to be effective in the adjustment process, needs to be based on measures that are both efficient and sustained. Otherwise, it can hardly be expected that their effects will be durable or significant. Thus, a global fiscal balance that has been attained by an inefficient or transitory policy package is unlikely to be maintained. When the need for fiscal adjustment is being assessed, attention is often focused on its size and speed: the size is given by the magnitude of the accumulated imbalance; the speed will be influenced by the resources at the disposal of the government. For the design of the adjustment effort, these are important questions. For its durability, however, the quality, efficiency, and sustainability of the policy action are the critical factors.[11]

II. The Issue of Debt Management

The discussion of fiscal policy in the paper so far has focused on its role in the performance of the economy under the assumption that fiscal imbalances would not be allowed to persist for long. Accordingly, the framework of analysis centered on relationships among flow variables, with little consideration being given to their linkages with stock accumulation. Indeed, for a significant period of time, this was also the perspective that characterized the treatment of fiscal policy in the literature. There can be hardly any doubt that the analysis of flow relationships has provided many important economic policy insights. Concentration on the flow aspect of those relationships, however, can detract attention away from the consequences for the medium- and long-term performance of the economy of fiscal imbalances that cumulate from one period to the next. Interest in the interaction between fiscal deficits and (domestic and foreign) debt accumulation has recently been revived in the literature. The resulting analyses have been instrumental in recalling the broader effects of fiscal imbalances and in restating the position that, when placed in a proper time perspective, certain short-term benefits perceived from fiscal expansion often prove to be more apparent than real.

Fiscal Deficits and Debt Accumulation

As noted in the previous section, fiscal deficits and the resulting public sector borrowing requirements place claims on resources that must be obtained either from within the economy or from abroad, or both. The process by which domestic resources can be secured has been extensively examined in the context

---

[11]For further discussion of the importance of the durability of fiscal policy actions, see Tanzi (1987a).

of the relationship between fiscal and monetary policies. [12] Typically, the pressure on domestic savings resulting from large public sector borrowing requirements will lead to increases in interest rates if the fiscal imbalances are accompanied by a tight monetary policy stance, or by domestic price rises (soon followed by nominal interest rate hikes as well) if they are accompanied instead by an accommodating stance of monetary policy.

The consequences of the various possible fiscal and monetary policy stances for output, price, and balance of payments developments will depend on the amount of idle resources and capacity in the economy. They will also depend on the extent, if any, to which the domestic financial policy mix brings about a containment of private sector demand to offset the expansionary impact of fiscal policy. Even though the need to undertake an adjustment effort will typically remain, the adjustment path in the economy will vary, depending on whether the fiscal imbalance is accompanied by an accommodating monetary policy. In these circumstances, the continued impact of an expansionary fiscal-monetary policy mix will put immediate pressure on output, prices, and the balance of payments. On the output and balance of payments fronts, the pressure may be released temporarily if the economy is operating below capacity and engages in foreign borrowing or uses its international reserves. Eventually, however, price increases will set in, nominal interest rates will rise and, as a result, the government borrowing requirement will be increasingly difficult to meet. [13]

The combination of an expansionary fiscal stance with a restrained monetary policy, however, will tend to contain the effects of aggregate demand on output, prices, and the balance of payments. But the public sector deficit will still require financing, which the authorities will typically have to secure by attracting savings (both domestic and foreign) by paying remunerative yields. In the process, the persistence of large public sector deficits will bring about rapid accumulation of public debt, thus converting what had begun as a flow imbalance into a potential stock problem.

There is ample evidence in the international economy of experiences along the lines summarized above. In general, those experiences have shown that the channels through which high fiscal deficits and rising public debts influence the economy are both varied and complex. A first and clear one is the rises in interest rates that are made necessary by the high absorption of savings, domestic as well as foreign. This may take place in an environment of more or less inflation and exchange rate depreciation, depending on the extent to which monetary policy accommodates or offsets the fiscal imbalance. In either case, however, the

---

[12]See, for example, International Monetary Fund (1977); see also International Monetary Fund (1987) and the references listed therein.

[13]See in this context the interesting analysis provided by Sargent and Wallace (1981) on the limitations of monetary policy even to attain inflation targets.

process is likely to distort incentives and worsen the performance of the economy in terms of output, employment, and growth.[14] A second channel is the impact of the rise in interest rates on the scope for prospective fiscal management as debt financing preempts future resources for debt servicing. A third and related channel is the consequences of the entrenchment of inflation and inflationary expectations, which, by stimulating indexation, further complicate the task of controlling inflation and, by imparting rigidity to the debt-servicing bill, can also reduce the effectiveness of fiscal management. This is because even though the provision of attractive returns can help assure the public sector of continued availability of private savings, over time the very need to pay such returns will absorb increasing amounts of fiscal receipts unless the public sector imbalance is eliminated on a sustained basis.

The intertemporal issues that arise when fiscal imbalances are financed mainly or exclusively by domestic debt issues will not be pursued in this paper. An ample literature is available on the topic, which focuses on the scope for debt financing of budget deficits and on the implications for fiscal and monetary policy of the continuation of such a process, as well as on the derivation of the conditions of its sustainability.[15]

Perhaps the general point that appears most relevant in the context of the present paper is the constraint that persistent fiscal imbalances and the consequent public debt accumulation in an economy impose for the scope and effectiveness of fiscal policy (and indeed to those of monetary policy as well) over time. These issues are becoming increasingly well recognized, a development that explains the focus that is currently placed on the appropriate concepts to measure the consequences of fiscal policy on the economy. In circumstances of relative stability and in which flow fiscal imbalances have not led to large accumulations of public debt, the overall fiscal deficit or the government's borrowing requirement is broadly used as a global indicator of the stance of fiscal policy in the economy.

However, as pointed out at the outset of the paper, in many economies imbalances have been allowed to persist for relatively long periods. The international economy has witnessed in recent years numerous instances of countries experiencing sustained pressures on resources for protracted periods of time. The pressures, as already noted, were either met by persistent borrowing and international reserve losses or resulted in domestic inflation.

---

[14]The argument is general if fiscal adjustment is not undertaken. However, it is conceivable that for a period of time a sufficiently restrictive monetary policy and the consequent relatively high interest rates induce capital inflows that permit the economy to continue expanding and even put upward pressure on the exchange rate. Without a restoration of fiscal balance, however, the process is unlikely to be sustained.

[15]See, for example, McCallum (1984), Masson (1985), Dornbusch (1986), and, in particular, Spaventa (1987), where numerous other references are provided.

With inflation under way and with inflationary expectations deeply entrenched, indexation mechanisms have become increasingly prevalent. From the perspective of the public finances, this has led to a growing debate about the relationship between fiscal deficits and inflation and their joint linkage with public indebtedness. Thus emerged the concept of the "operational balance" as an aggregate indicator to measure the impact of fiscal policy. This balance excludes the inflationary component of the budget deficit—that is, it consists of the traditional deficit net of the outlays related directly or indirectly to the phenomenon of indexation or, in other words, net of the portion of debt service that compensates public debt holders for actual inflation. [16] The rationale behind this inflation-adjusted budget balance is that the demand for government debt instruments is sufficiently stable, so that the public will be willing to hold the resources provided to maintain the real value of the stock of those instruments.

Where large fiscal imbalances have not been associated with an inflationary process of the magnitude typically required to provoke extensive indexation, public debts have accumulated perhaps to an even larger extent. It is quite clear that this growth of public debt would pose severe constraints to fiscal policy over time. In these circumstances, another concept for the impact of the budget on the economy soon surfaced: the "primary balance"—that is, the traditional budget balance excluding interest payments on the public debt. The case for focusing on this concept was based on a questionable distinction between government direct expenditure on goods and services and its outlays to service debt. Proponents of both the operational and the primary balance concepts stress the lack of government control on the inflation-determined component and the interest component of fiscal spending, respectively, as one of the reasons for their usefulness for policy purposes relative to that of the traditional overall budget balance concept.

The various analytical concepts of budget balance are relevant in different contexts, but they cannot substitute for one another. Concern with inflation control continues to establish the overall borrowing requirement as a key indicator. [17] This need not detract from the importance of the primary and operational balance concepts, which help shed light on the magnitude of the effective fiscal effort that may be required to restore fiscal balance after a period of sustained inflation and debt accumulation.

---

[16]Nominal budget deficits and inflation interact, in the sense that the former can lead to rises in the latter, and vice versa. This relationship has been termed "symbiotic" by Tanzi and Blejer (1985), though perhaps "parasitic" would have been a better label. On the concept of the operational balance, besides the above source, see Tanzi, Blejer, and Teijeiro (1987). Further discussion of budget deficit concepts can also be found in Chelliah (1987) and Tanzi (1987b).

[17]For the primary or the operational balance to play a role equivalent to the overall balance in this regard, each would need to be supplemented by a clear and firm commitment regarding inflation. An exchange of views with Vito Tanzi brought up this correspondence.

External Indebtedness and Fiscal Imbalances

External indebtedness assumed a brisk pace in the 1970s, and external debt continued to grow during the current decade. This is not surprising in view of the turns taken by the international economy during those periods. The characteristics and constraints of the international borrowing process have consequently been subject to intensive examination at the conceptual and the policymaking levels.[18] Developments leading to the emergence of widespread external debt-servicing difficulties in many debtor economies reflected a combination of external and internal factors. Adverse relative price changes, rises in interest rates, and declining export market prospects were all events in the international environment that did not favor debtor countries. In addition, economic management in these countries often proved to be lacking in the areas of public finances and exchange rate policy and generally with regard to efficient use of foreign resources. Among the various proximate domestic factors behind the rapid accumulation of external debt and the subsequent debt-servicing problems, the incurrence of persistent fiscal deficits has been identified as perhaps the most important.[19] This finding is of relevance for the design of the required adjustment effort.

In parallel with the analysis presented above on fiscal policy, external debt management can be viewed from the standpoint of its impact on macroeconomic balance—as it affects the level and composition of demand—as well as from the perspective of its effect on the efficiency and growth potential in the economy— as it influences the process of investment and capital accumulation in the country. On a global macroeconomic plane, the availability of foreign savings and the accumulation of external debt are means by which the flows of domestic expenditure and income can differ in an economy. From this vantage point, fiscal activities financed by recourse to external borrowing can be sustained only if those government activities are of the efficiency and productivity required to service the debt in the future. Experience with the accumulation of external public debt in numerous instances indicates that this has not always been the case. Instead, levels and patterns of government spending and, more generally, of aggregate demand developed in many economies that were financed by borrowing abroad, both of which became patently unsustainable as the availability of foreign savings declined.

---

[18]See, for example, Guitián (1981 and 1987a), McDonald (1982), Sachs (1984), Dillon and Lipton (1985), Tanzi (1985), Mehran (1985), Ize (1987), and Ize and Ortiz (1987).

[19]For a recent discussion of the origins of the debt problem, see Feldstein and others (1987). On the issue of the relationship between fiscal imbalances and external debt, see Wiesner (1985) and de Vries (1987).

There is a parallel here worth noting between domestic monetary policy and external debt management. When a fiscal imbalance emerges, as noted earlier in the paper, the possibility exists of its effects being contained by a tightening of monetary policy. In effect, this is equivalent to the government seeking to obtain resources from the rest of the economy at a price. This price, of course, is the acceptance of the structure of interest rates at which the government debt issues will be absorbed by the public. As long as this process continues, signals of imbalance, such as price and balance of payments pressures, will remain muted. The sustainability of the process, however, will depend on the government's ability to invest efficiently the borrowed resources, so that its debt can be serviced, on the one hand, and to contain future imbalances within the permissible bounds of the rate of increase in the demand for government paper, on the other.

A similar set of considerations underlies the process of foreign borrowing. During its incurrence, the availability of foreign savings can muffle the alarms that might have sounded on the inflation and international reserve fronts in the absence of external borrowing. Sustainability of the process of indebtedness, as already noted, will require efficient use of the resources. These considerations indicate the importance of ensuring consistency between fiscal and monetary policy as well as between them and external debt management.

Developments in external public indebtedness pose a number of issues, which may put the fiscal authorities in a quandary. There is, first, a need to earn or save foreign exchange in order to service the debt. The most likely means for the economy to earn the needed foreign exchange is the provision of appropriate incentives for the production of traded goods and services. In turn, expenditure cuts in the public sector will contribute directly or indirectly to saving foreign exchange outlays (and to releasing resources for exports). But again, the need for incentives and, in particular, for enhanced competitiveness is evident here. There is, in addition, a need for the government to raise from the economy at large the resources required for its debt service. This will typically call for increases in taxes, which may run counter to the incentives mentioned above. If there is scope for reducing inefficient government spending, the quandary may be simplified, but experience indicates that this is not often the case. In general, high and rising external public debt service obligations compete for resources with other uses and, rather than improve incentives for productive activities, they may in effect impair them.[20] This is a difficult policy dilemma, which underscores the importance of efficiency in the use of savings (both domestic and

---

[20]For an interesting discussion of this dilemma, see Krueger (1987). See also Dornbusch (undated manuscript).

foreign) and, to this end, of appropriate debt management (both internal and external).

Foreign Debt and the Structure of the Balance of Payments

Apart from its connection with fiscal policy and, more generally, with domestic financial management, the accumulation of external debt carries important implications for balance of payments analysis. The borrowing process, in general, is a vehicle to transfer command over resources from surplus to deficit sectors or economies. In a closed economy context, the domestic borrowing process channels resources from savers to investors, thereby helping the economy, with its given resource and technology endowment, to attain its potential level and rate of growth of output. In an open economy, the availability of foreign savings adds directly to the resources available in the system. If used efficiently, foreign savings can allow the economy to reach higher spending levels by making it possible for it to grow at higher sustained rates than otherwise.

Thus, linkages exist, via the current account of the balance of payments, among fiscal and monetary policies, foreign borrowing, the saving and investment balance, and the consequent long-run evolution of the economy. These considerations underscore the need for attention to be paid not only to the evolution of the overall balance of payments—that is, to international reserve management—but also to its composition or structure between the current and capital account components.

It should be noted that the prospective evolution of the current account can be strongly influenced by past foreign borrowing. This is because rising external borrowing, though it helps finance current account deficits, also pre-empts growing foreign exchange resources for the servicing of interest on the resulting debts. Thus, even when the stock of debt itself is not falling, current account prospects are affected by past borrowing. A declining stock of external debt would pose a more severe constraint on the current account, since it would have to generate the foreign exchange required to pay interest and also to provide for net repayments of principal.

On the capital account, an increasingly important issue concerns the structure of capital flows, of which debt constitutes only one—albeit extremely important—component. [21] Just as there is an equilibrium structure of the balance of payments, there must be an equilibrium structure of capital flows that conforms to portfolio balances in the respective economies. A particularly important dimension of this issue is the balance required between debt-creating and non-debt-creating flows, or, to put it differently, between flows that separate liability from asset accumulation (debt-creating flows) and those that tie the process of

---

[21] These issues have been discussed in some detail in Guitián (1985 and 1987a).

asset-liability accumulation together (non-debt-creating flows), as well as those that do not generate liabilities (aid flows). For the purposes of balance of payments management, particularly in large debtor countries, restoration of balance between equity, direct investment, debt, and other flows is of primary importance.

III. The Issue of Conditionality

The concept of conditionality is one of the important dimensions of the cooperative nature of the International Monetary Fund as an institution. It follows from the Fund's responsibility to assist members in overcoming their balance of payments difficulties by, among other things, providing them with access to Fund financial assistance. In order to fulfill this responsibility, the Fund had to develop procedures and reach understandings with members that would ensure temporariness in the use of the resources of the institution. To this end, the procedures and understandings developed by the Fund and its membership were based on the member's adoption and implementation of economic policies that would redress its adjustment problems in general, and its balance of payments difficulties in particular, over a reasonable period of time.[22] The expectation was that, by supporting the member's corrective policies with the institution's resources, the process of adjustment would be eased and, thus, a net benefit would be derived by the member that would not obtain in the absence of such financial support.

It is clear, then, that the nature of the problem confronting a member in need of Fund resources, together with the institutional requirement of ensuring that their use is revolving in character, determines to a large extent the necessary policy responses. Typically, the approach requires bringing the domestic absorption of resources in line with production—that is, balancing the amounts of resources demanded with those that are available. In addition, the approach often requires that such balancing be accompanied by resource reallocations to raise efficiency throughout the economy, in order to ease the balance of payments constraint on a sustained basis. The process of reaching understandings on policies to influence the balance as well as the allocation of resources in an economy is both complex and delicate. Not only are the required decisions difficult to make internally, but a question arises with regard to the proper scope of Fund intervention in the process.

---

[22]The nature and evolution of the conditionality practices of the Fund have been examined extensively in recent years. See, for example, Finch (1983), Guitián (1981 and 1983), and the studies contained in Williamson (1983).

Need for Appropriate Boundaries

The issue of the appropriate degree of participation by the Fund in economic policy decision making is not amenable to simple or categorical answers. It basically entails determining lines of demarcation between national and international considerations in the process of adjustment. In reflection of a variety of factors, views differ as to where such lines ought to be drawn. To begin with, there is a potential conflict between the desire for national policy autonomy and the limits to it imposed by the interdependence that links national economies.[23] When it arises, the conflict is dynamic and it influences the varying degrees of cohesion and divergence that prevail over time in international economic relationships.

The Fund's early approach to the drawing of proper boundaries is clearly illustrated in the practices of conditionality that evolved in the fiscal and debt-management areas. On the fiscal front, the general principle was the sufficiency of reaching a broad but quantified set of understandings on a global indicator of the impact of the government budget or, more generally, the public sector finances on the domestic economy and the balance of payments. Attention was focused on the overall deficit and its financing as a standard of measurement for the extent of the fiscal imbalance.

The implications of keeping the understandings between the member and the Fund confined to developments in this global variable are clear in terms of the lines of demarcation mentioned above: the member retained all its policy independence to decide on the specific measures that were to be undertaken to ensure the observance of the understanding; the decision on all the necessary actions was left to the process of internal policymaking. International considerations, in contrast, were confined to judgments on the outer limits of the magnitude of the fiscal imbalance and the speed of its adjustment—that is, the size of deficit reduction and the time within which it was to be accomplished. Thus, although a variety of policy mixes could be under discussion between the Fund and the member, the scope of the latter's commitment was limited to the commonly agreed scale and pace of reduction in the government or public sector deficit as a means to restore macroeconomic balance to the economy. Although this approach constituted the norm, there were instances where distortions had developed and where their removal would be necessary to eliminate the imbalance on a sustained basis. In those instances, understandings between the member and the Fund on specific actions to eliminate such distortions were also

---

[23]A comprehensive discussion of the opportunities as well as the constraints that arise from the existence of interdependence among national economies can be found in Cooper (1986); for an examination of these issues and the related subject of policy coordination in the context of the major industrial countries and of the European Monetary System, see Guitián (1988b and 1988c).

required. These broad considerations provided the basis for the bulk of the policy discussions undertaken between the institution and its members in the context of requests for access to Fund resources.

Although based on discussions of policies, the actual practices of conditionality focus on the process of monitoring policy implementation. From this standpoint, early procedures tended to concentrate on the sources of financing for the deficit and, in particular, on the extension of domestic credit to the public sector by the central bank or the domestic banking system. Thus, the typical fiscal policy undertaking in adjustment programs supported by Fund resources was often a commitment to confine domestic credit expansion to the government or public sector within an agreed quantified path. This commitment could be supplemented by understandings on the adoption of specific actions (for example, in the area of administered pricing policy) that would be undertaken to remove distortions.

These practices provided ample scope for independent national policy decision making and kept international considerations within strict and well-defined boundaries. It must be noted, however, that at the time, the code of conduct contained in the Articles of Agreement subscribed by members was based on the maintenance of par values for their currencies. The par value system in itself provided a clear constraint to national policy independence and, therefore, made it possible for conditionality practices to be relatively unobtrusive both with regard to policy instruments and policy objectives.[24]

The evolution of the international economy and the willingness (or lack thereof) of countries to take international considerations into account in their national economic policy decision making interact constantly, and their interplay affects the adjustment process. Consequently, within their invariable aim of easing adjustment, conditionality practices are always undergoing adaptation. The adaptations seek to keep the lines of demarcation between national policy autonomy and international interdependence sufficiently flexible to maintain cohesion within the international financial system at large.

As noted above, this process of continuous search for appropriate boundaries and its practical translation into conditionality practices is influenced by the nature of the code of international conduct that countries agree to uphold. The more flexible such a code is, the more difficult it is to draw boundaries that keep international considerations in the background. Other factors that influence the

---

[24]A review of these early practices of conditionality are found in Guitián (1981); a discussion of those practices on the fiscal front has been recently provided by Tanzi (1987a). An examination of the boundaries between national and international interests with regard to policy instruments and objectives is contained in Guitián (1987b). For reviews of fiscal adjustment experiences in programs supported by the Fund, see Beveridge and Kelly (1980) and Kelly (1982).

adaptation of conditionality are the ever evolving views as to the appropriate set of objectives on which there is a legitimate international interest.

Important changes have taken place on both of these fronts since the abandonment of the Bretton Woods par value system. Accordingly, conditionality practices have evolved in a variety of ways, and adaptations have taken place with respect to the length of the adjustment period (which was extended, for example, in the context of the extended facility); the procedures on access to Fund resources (which were made more ample by means of the enlarged access policy); and the adjustment policies to be undertaken by members that request Fund resources (which have focused increasingly on the issue of efficiency and the durability of the adjustment effort).[25]

In this process, an interesting evolution has taken place with regard to the drawing of boundaries between national and international spheres of interest. To the extent that members have access to larger amounts of Fund resources for longer periods of time, additional leeway is available for national policy implementation. From this standpoint, on the one hand, the scope for national policy independence with regard to the size and speed of adjustment have tended to increase. On the other hand, emphasis on efficiency has required both concentration on specific policy actions and understandings on concrete policy mixes, which have tended to limit the range of national policy choices in this regard. Thus, a shift in certain aspects of the boundaries has actually occurred. In earlier periods, the international presence was at its clearest in the determination of the size and speed of the adjustment effort (which—then as now—depended on the amount and maturity of Fund resources, and which at that time were lesser and shorter), and it was at its most unobtrusive in the area of specific measures and concrete policy mixes. Recently, national autonomy has been given more leeway in the former domain—as the amount of resources has risen and their term lengthened—in exchange for a broader international presence in the latter—as the range of policy-mix choices has narrowed.

Temporal Aspects of Adjustment

These developments in conditionality practices are related to the discussion in earlier sections of the paper concerning flow and stock imbalances. In turn, the characteristics of the imbalances that recur in the international economy are influenced by the undertakings that countries are willing to accept as participants in the international system.

It can be argued that there is a common thread between the requirements of the par value system (a fixed exchange rate regime), the characteristics of

---

[25]A description of adaptations in conditionality and its various instruments through the early 1980s is contained in Guitián (1981).

conditionality (its scope and pervasiveness), and the specific terms of access to Fund resources (amounts and maturity). A firm commitment to a fixed exchange rate presupposes an unequivocal constraint on domestic policies, which provides a simple but effective indicator of the development of imbalances (pressure on international reserves). Thus, such imbalances can be detected and acted upon at an early stage, a sequence of events that has obvious implications for conditionality and access to Fund resources. When the imbalance is confronted promptly, its magnitude and potential for causing further distortions are relatively limited. This implies that policy conditions can be broad in nature and that the supporting amount of Fund resources can be relatively small and remain outstanding for a relatively brief period. In this setting, it is only natural to view imbalances as a flow problem—made evident by an overall balance of payments deficit, the elimination of which is the central policy objective—and their correction as entailing use of a limited amount of resources for a short period of time.

Since the abandonment of the par value system, the international economic system has moved toward flexible exchange rate arrangements, and thus, the thread tying all these elements and events together has become less obvious. To begin with, the constraints on national economic policies, though still present, are somewhat looser. While there are benefits that flow from the more flexible arrangements, there are also costs. One of those costs is of particular relevance in the context of this discussion. Whereas in the previous regime domestic imbalances soon found their way into the external constraint and therefore brought the country and the international community together promptly, imbalances now can persist for long periods before the external constraint prompts a response.[26] More complex and to some extent less clear indicators are involved in the process of evaluation of the imbalance. Thus, what begins as a maladjustment of flow variables can become a stock imbalance through accumulation of debt and arrears (domestic as well as foreign), often in a setting of persistent inflation.

This sequence of events also has implications for conditionality and for access policy, both of which have consequently been adapted. Policy conditions and the supporting amount of Fund resources have continued to reflect the nature and characteristics of the imbalance. The size of the latter, typically large, determines that policies to deal with it will have to be well-defined and sustained; the amount and maturity of access will have to be commensurate; and with the implicitly longer adjustment process, policy objectives other than the balance of

---

[26]In particular, exchange rate flexibility provides a measure of insulation to the economy from the balance of payments constraint. Thus, a domestic imbalance can prevail for a relatively long time before a policy response becomes imperative.

payments will need to be taken into consideration. Thus, the complexity of the process of demarcation of national versus international boundaries in economic policy has increased and, with it, the need for a firm consensus behind conditionality practices and procedures that stress the requirements of interdependence.

Evolving Approaches

The recent experience in the international economy provides ample evidence of the extent to which protracted flow imbalances can develop into serious stock disequilibria, which, in turn, can render the system at large subject to severe strains and tensions. Conditionality practices evolved in the direction of promoting cohesion within the system by bringing together the various interests at play. Important initiatives were taken to cope in particular with the problems confronted by large debtor countries.

The principle behind those initiatives was relatively straightforward: the debtor country in question undertook to implement a sustained adjustment effort, which would be supported by an arrangement with the Fund; besides providing its own resources, the Fund, in turn, undertook a catalyst role to enlist the support of major creditor countries and other sources of capital flows such as the commercial banks. The initial focus of the strategy to deal with the problems posed by external indebtedness in the international economy was on the design and implementation of a substantial adjustment effort on the part of the debtor country and on the assurance of the flow of external finance from official and private sources on the requisite *scale*. But international attention soon turned also to the *terms* of external financing so that they would be consistent with the prospects of adjustment and recovery. In many respects, the dimensions of conditionality thus became more complex. Besides setting the guideposts of the international interest in the process of national policy formulation and thus constraining national policy independence, Fund conditionality also sought to set the amount and terms of support required from the other parties in the system, thus also constraining their freedom of action to reflect international considerations. An important measure of symmetry was thus being developed—albeit with setbacks in practice—with regard to the efforts required from debtors— that is, adjustment—as well as from creditors—that is, financing.[27]

In effect, the financial arrangements of the Fund provided the instrument of cohesion required to bring debtors and creditors together. As imbalances continued to prevail, pressures developed as debtors and creditors sought to protect their perceived interests and it became increasingly difficult to arrange timely

---

[27]For a detailed description of these evolving approaches, see Guitián (1987a). Another area where a measure of symmetry is indeed desirable is that of surveillance; for a brief discussion of the relationship between surveillance and conditionality, see Guitián (1985).

concerted financing arrangements. In the circumstances, the Fund has continued to adapt its conditionality practices to maintain cohesion among members and sources of capital by seeking to establish a reasonable balance in the assignment of responsibilities. The original concerted lending approach has therefore been refined to include a large variety of financing modalities, so as to adapt the process to specific country characteristics and prospects as well as to the requirements of the various international sources of financing.[28]

The present requirements of the international economy are such that the search for efficiency and symmetry appear of paramount importance. Efficiency in adjustment, a necessary condition for growth, will require the adoption and maintenance of policies by debtor countries that eliminate distortions, that are transparent and well-defined, and that thus provide a clear basis for economic decisions.[29] The search for efficiency and the attainment of policy objectives beyond those relating to the balance of payments will inevitably influence conditionality practices, if only because the number of policy instruments will have to be commensurate with the number of objectives pursued.

At the same time, an important measure of symmetry will have to be achieved between the exercise of conditionality and the fulfillment of the Fund's surveillance responsibilities. This symmetry is required to ensure that balance obtains between individual country adjustment efforts, flows of international financing, and the stability in the world economic environment. It is clear that efficient economic policies in borrowing countries are an essential requirement for the resolution of debt-servicing difficulties. But it is also increasingly evident that such a requirement will not be sufficient unless accompanied by appropriate adjustment in other countries as well. Policy consistency in the industrial world is of the essence in this context to provide a setting for stable and balanced expansion of activity, trade, and capital flows in the international economy.

IV. Concluding Remarks

Experience with the adjustment process indicates that fiscal and public sector financial imbalances often lie behind economic and balance of payments difficulties.[30] This common feature of difficulties in the economies of Fund members

---

[28]A parallel approach is being developed that might be termed a concerted aid strategy to assist low-income members overcome protracted balance of payments problems. Their efforts to this end can be supported by a new structural adjustment facility that the Fund began to operate in 1986 and that is currently in the process of enhancement.

[29]The limits of economic policies to guarantee economic objectives, particularly the attainment of endogenous real variables, should not be overlooked, however; for an elaboration of this issue, see Guitián (1988a).

[30]Imbalances, of course, can arise from exogenous factors such as an unfavorable world economic environment, terms of trade changes, and the like. The arguments in the text, however, focus only on those generated domestically.

has been discussed in terms of the effects on their macroeconomic balance as well as on general and specific aspects of efficiency and the longer-term evolution of the economies in question. If allowed to persist, fiscal imbalances soon contribute to the accumulation of debt, which then imposes its own dynamics on the adjustment process. As a consequence, growing constraints bind economic policy management, and adjustment efforts become progressively difficult to undertake and sustain. The resulting imbalances acquire characteristics of a distributional nature both internally and externally, on which consensus becomes increasingly hard to obtain, and thus complicate the orderly functioning of the adjustment process. These considerations lie behind the increasing focus that conditionality places on the quality and sustainability of fiscal adjustment, as well as on the consequences of the accumulation of large stocks of public debt for fiscal and macroeconomic management.

Several important inferences can be drawn for conditionality practices from recent events in the international economy. A first inference is that, to be effective, conditionality needs to be based on a mandate given to the Fund and supported by a firm consensus among the membership. Over time, the firmness of this consensus and the scope of the mandate change and, with them, the characteristics of conditionality; it is important to note, however, that despite these changes, conditionality is critical to the safeguard of the cooperative character of the organization and that its appropriate implementation cannot but strengthen it.

A second inference is that the consensus is likely to require a clear definition of the scope of responsibility of the Fund as an institution. This definition will need to make clear the extent of its involvement in the process of national policymaking in countries seeking access to Fund resources (conditionality as such). It will also have to comprehend the extent of its influence on the policies of other members, in particular the large ones (surveillance). The separation of these two areas of Fund responsibility is becoming increasingly difficult as the membership moves the institution toward the assumption of a broader role in the resolution of issues (including certain aspects of those related to external indebtedness) that extend beyond those that can be described as typical balance of payments problems.

A third inference—which is a corollary of the previous two—is that the Fund can only be as effective as its members' attitude allows it to be. From this standpoint, fluctuations in the institution's effectiveness can typically be related to varying support from its membership.

A fourth inference is that neither Fund conditionality nor its surveillance can substitute for domestic policy decisiveness. On the contrary, domestic policy determination can go a long way in enhancing the effectiveness of the Fund in its various responsibilities.

A final inference worth underscoring is the relationship between members' willingness to abide by a well-defined code of international conduct and the characteristics of Fund operations and functions. The more internationally minded members are and the firmer and clearer is the code of conduct by which they are willing to abide, the less obtrusive the role of the Fund will need to be. The more scope for national policy independence members wish to retain and correspondingly, the less binding their code of conduct is, the more difficult the implementation and safeguard of international norms of behavior become and with them, the fulfillment of the responsibilities of the Fund. In this respect, the Articles of Agreement and the support (financial and otherwise) that members are willing to provide the Fund constitute good standards of measurement for their commitment to the international system.

References

Barro, Robert J., "Are Government Bonds Net Wealth?", *Journal of Political Economy* (Chicago), Vol. 82 (November–December 1974), pp. 1095–1117.

Beveridge, W.A., and Margaret R. Kelly, "Fiscal Content of Financial Programs Supported by Stand-By Arrangements in the Upper Credit Tranches, 1969-78," *Staff Papers*, International Monetary Fund (Washington), Vol. 27 (June 1980), pp. 205–49.

Calvo, Guillermo A., "Macroeconomic Implications of the Government Budget: Some Basic Considerations," *Journal of Monetary Economics* (Amsterdam), Vol. 15 (January 1985), pp. 95–112.

Carmichael, Jeffrey, "On Barro's Theorem of Debt Neutrality: The Irrelevance of Net Wealth," *American Economic Review* (Nashville, Tennessee), Vol. 72 (March 1982), pp. 202–13.

Chelliah, R.J., "Growth-Oriented Adjustment Programs: Fiscal Policy Issues," in *Growth-Oriented Adjustment Programs*, ed. by Vittorio Corbo, Morris Goldstein, and Mohsin Khan (Washington: International Monetary Fund, 1987), pp. 365–86.

Cooper, Richard N., *Economic Policy in an Interdependent World: Essays in World Economics* (Cambridge, Massachusetts: MIT Press, 1986).

Corbo, Vittorio, Morris Goldstein, and Mohsin Khan, eds., *Growth-Oriented Adjustment Programs* (Washington: International Monetary Fund, 1987).

de Larosière, J., "Restoring Fiscal Discipline: A Vital Element of a Policy for Economic Recovery," *IMF Survey* (Washington), Vol. 11 (March 22, 1982), pp. 81–87.

————, "The Growth of Public Debt and the Need for Fiscal Discipline," *IMF Survey* (Washington), Vol. 113 (September 3, 1984), pp. 261–67.

de Vries, Margaret Garritsen, *Balance of Payments Adjustment, 1945 to 1986: The IMF Experience* (Washington: International Monetary Fund, 1987).

Dillon, K. Burke, and David Lipton, "External Debt and Economic Management: The Role of the International Monetary Fund," in *External Debt Management*, ed. by Hassanali Mehran (Washington: International Monetary Fund, 1985), pp. 31–52.

Dornbusch, Rudiger, *Dollars, Debts, and Deficits* (Cambridge, Massachusetts: MIT Press, 1986).

————, "The World Debt Problem: Anatomy and Solutions," (unpublished manuscript, a study prepared for the 20th Century Fund, undated).

Feldstein, Martin, "Government Deficits and Aggregate Demand," *Journal of Monetary Economics* (Amsterdam), Vol. 9 (January 1982), pp. 1–20.

————, and others, *Restoring Growth in the Debt-Laden Third World: A Task Report to the Trilateral Commission*, Triangle Papers, 33 (New York: The Trilateral Commission, 1987).

Finch, C. David, "Adjustment Policies and Conditionality," Chap. 4 in *IMF Conditionality*, ed. by John Williamson (Washington: Institute for International Economics, 1983).

Frenkel, Jacob A., and Michael L. Mussa, "Monetary and Fiscal Policies in an Open Economy," *American Economic Review, Papers and Proceedings of the Ninety-Third Annual Meeting of the American Economic Association* (Nashville, Tennessee) Vol. 71 (May 1981), pp. 253–58.

Guitián, Manuel, "Credit Versus Money as an Instrument of Control," *Staff Papers*, International Monetary Fund (Washington), Vol. 20 (November 1973), pp. 785-800; reprinted in *The Monetary Approach to the Balance of Payments: A Collection of Research Papers by Members of the Staff of the International Monetary Fund* (Washington: International Monetary Fund, 1977), pp. 227–42.

————, "The Effects of Changes in the Exchange Rate on Output, Prices and the Balance of Payments," *Journal of International Economics* (Amsterdam), Vol. 6 (February 1976), pp. 65–74.

————, *Fund Conditionality: Evolution of Principles and Practices*, IMF Pamphlet Series, No. 38 (Washington: International Monetary Fund, 1981).

————, "Fund Programs for Economic Adjustment," in *The Fund and China in the International Monetary System: Papers Presented at a Colloquium Held in Beijing, China, October 20–28, 1982*, ed. by A.W. Hooke (Washington: International Monetary Fund, 1983), pp. 96–114.

————, "Ajustamento Económico e Interdependencia: Desafio à Condicionalidade," in *Ajustamento e Crescimento na Actual Conjuntura Económica Mundial*, ed. by José da Silva Lopes (Washington: International Monetary Fund, 1985), pp. 57–78.

———— (1987a), "External Debt Management and the International Monetary Fund," in *Issues in North American Trade and Financing*, ed. by R. Tremblay (Montreal: North American Economics and Finance Association, January 1987), pp. 5–10.

———— (1987b), "Adjustment and Economic Growth: Their Fundamental Complementarity," in *Growth-Oriented Adjustment Programs*, ed. by Vittorio Corbo, Morris Goldstein, and Mohsin Khan (Washington: International Monetary Fund), pp. 63–94.

_____ (1988a), "Comment" ["Three Views on Restoring Growth"], in *Inflation Stabilization: The Experience of Israel, Argentina, Brazil, Bolivia, and Mexico*, ed. by Michael Bruno, and others (Cambridge, Massachusetts: MIT Press), pp. 399–404.

_____ (1988b), "Comment" ["Empirical Evidence of Policy Coordination Among Major Industrial Countries Since Rambouillet Summit of 1975," by Gunter GroBer, pp. 110-35], *Economic Policy Coordination*, moderator, Wilfrid Guth (Washington: International Monetary Fund), pp. 142–48.

International Monetary Fund, *The Monetary Approach to the Balance of Payments: A Collection of Research Papers by Members of the Staff of the International Monetary Fund* (Washington: International Monetary Fund, 1977).

_____, *Fund-Supported Programs, Fiscal Policy, and Income Distribution*, Occasional Paper No. 46 (Washington: International Monetary Fund, 1986).

_____, *Theoretical Aspects of the Design of Fund-Supported Adjustment Programs*, Occasional Paper No. 55 (Washington: International Monetary Fund, 1987).

Ize, Alain, "Fiscal Dominance, Debt, and Exchange Rates," IMF Working Paper 87/52 (mimeographed, International Monetary Fund, August 17, 1987).

_____, and Guillermo Ortiz, "Fiscal Rigidities, Public Debt, and Capital Flight," *Staff Papers*, International Monetary Fund (Washington), Vol. 34 (June 1987), pp. 311–32.

Johnson, Omotunde, and Joanne Salop, "Distributional Aspects of Stabilization Programs in Developing Countries," *Staff Papers*, International Monetary Fund (Washington), Vol. 27 (March 1980), pp. 1-23.

Kelly, Margaret R., "Fiscal Adjustment and Fund-Supported Programs, 1971–80," *Staff Papers*, International Monetary Fund (Washington), Vol. 29 (December 1982), pp. 561–602.

Khan, Mohsin S., and Saúl Lizondo, "Devaluation, Fiscal Deficits, and the Real Exchange Rate," *World Bank Economic Review* (Washington), Vol. 1 (January 1987), pp. 357–74.

Krueger, Anne O., "Debt, Capital Flows, and LDC Growth," *American Economic Review, Papers and Proceedings of the Ninety-Ninth Annual Meeting of the American Economic Association* (Nashville, Tennessee), Vol. 77 (May 1987), pp. 159–70.

Masson, P. R., "The Sustainability of Fiscal Deficits," *Staff Papers*, International Monetary Fund (Washington), Vol. 32 (December 1985), pp. 577–605.

McCallum, Bennett T., "Are Bond-Financed Deficits Inflationary? A Ricardian Analysis," *Journal of Political Economy* (Chicago), Vol. 92 (February 1984), pp. 123–25.

McDonald, Donogh C., "Debt Capacity and Developing Country Borrowing: A Survey of the Literature," *Staff Papers*, International Monetary Fund (Washington), Vol. 29 (December 1982), pp. 603–46.

Mehran, Hassanali, ed., *External Debt Management* (Washington: International Monetary Fund, 1985).

Mueller, Dennis C., "The Growth of Government: A Public Choice Perspective," *Staff Papers*, International Monetary Fund (Washington), Vol. 34 (March 1987), pp. 115–49.

Sachs, Jeffrey, *Theoretical Issues in International Borrowing*, Princeton Studies in International Finance, No. 54 (Princeton, New Jersey: Princeton University Press, 1984).

Sargent, Thomas J., and Neil Wallace, "Some Unpleasant Monetarist Arithmetic," *Federal Bank of Minneapolis Quarterly Review* (Minneapolis, Minnesota), Vol. 5 (Fall 1981), pp. 1–17. This article is reprinted as Chap. 5 in Thomas J. Sargent, ed., *Rational Expectations and Inflation* (New York: Harper and Row, 1986).

Spaventa, Luigi, "The Growth of Public Debt: Sustainability, Fiscal Rules, and Monetary Rules," *Staff Papers*, International Monetary Fund (Washington), Vol. 34 (June 1987), pp. 374–99.

Tanzi, Vito, "Fiscal Management and External Debt Problems," in *External Debt Management*, ed. by Hassanali Mehran (Washington: International Monetary Fund, 1985), pp. 65–87.

———— (1987a), "Fiscal Policy, Growth, and Design of Stabilization Programs," in *External Debt, Savings, and Growth in Latin America*, ed. by Ana María Martirena-Mantel (Washington: International Monetary Fund).

———— (1987b), "Discussion" ["Growth-Oriented Adjustment Programs: Fiscal Policy Issues," by R.J. Chelliah, pp. 365–86], in *Growth Oriented Adjustment Programs*, ed. by Vittorio Corbo, Morris Goldstein, and Mohsin Khan (Washington: International Monetary Fund).

————, and Mario I. Blejer, "Política Orçamental numa Economia com Inflação Elevada e Dívida Elevada," in *Ajustamento e Crescimento na Actual Conjuntura Económica Mundial*, ed. by José da Silva Lopes (Washington: International Monetary Fund, 1985), pp. 121–39.

————, Mario I. Blejer, and Mario O. Teijeiro, "Inflation and the Measurement of Fiscal Deficits," *Staff Papers*, International Monetary Fund (Washington), Vol. 34 (December 1987), pp. 711–38.

Wiesner, Eduardo, "Latin American Debt: Lessons and Pending Issues," *American Economic Review, Papers and Proceedings of the Ninety-Seventh Annual Meeting of the American Economic Association* (Nashville, Tennessee), Vol. 75 (May 1985), pp. 191–95.

Williamson, John, ed., *IMF Conditionality* (Washington: Institute for International Economics, 1983).

Comment

Ricardo Arriazu

The words "adjustment programs" and "stabilization programs" have been frequently—and also loosely—used to describe at least three different types of disequilibrium adjustments. In general, they describe programs aimed at: (1) the reduction of inflation rates; (2) the reduction of external current account deficits (deficits that reflect excesses of domestic aggregate demand in relation to output); and (3) the reduction of balance of payments deficits.

Although disequilibria that are reflected in inflation and deficits in the current account and the overall balance of payments often tend to be closely related, this is not always the case. In fact, all possible combinations of the performance of these economic indicators can be the result of specific economic policies.

For example, balance of payments deficits associated with current account surpluses and price stability will almost certainly be the response, under fixed exchange rates, to portfolio changes associated with increased holdings of foreign exchange involving no net wealth changes. However, persistent inflation associated with current account and balance of payments surpluses will tend to be the response to a policy of persistent devaluation of the domestic currency (crawling peg), which generates inflationary taxes in excess of nominal fiscal deficits. Attribution of other possible combinations of results to specific economic policies is left to the reader.

The relationship between economic performance and policy is recognized by Manuel Guitián early in his paper: ". . . an adjustment strategy must be based on an accurate assessment of the nature and characteristics of the imbalance confronting the economy" (p. 113). Nevertheless, most of his paper deals with cases where current account deficits are registered jointly with balance of payments deficits and inflationary pressures, because this is the most typical combination of disequilibria for countries confronting serious imbalances.

It is important to note that when these three indicators register the results described in the previous paragraph, the sources of the imbalances tend to be exclusively of domestic origin, reflecting excessive domestic absorption in relation to output. Furthermore, as Guitián also points out, in most cases the imbalances originate in fiscal deficits. This point can be illustrated with the use of a slightly modified absorption identity:

$$X - M = (T - G) + (Y - E - T),$$

where

$X =$ exports of goods and services

$M =$ imports of goods and services

$X - M =$ current account of the balance of payments

$T =$ taxes, including the inflationary tax or the devaluation tax depending on the unit and purpose of the measurement)

$G =$ public sector expenditures

$T - G =$ public sector budget imbalance

$Y =$ national income, measured in the corresponding unit of account

$E =$ private sector expenditures

$Y - E - T =$ private sector budget imbalance.

This identity clearly shows that current account disequilibria are mirror images of imbalances in either the public sector budget, the private sector budget, or both. Current account deficits are the counterpart of domestic expenditures in excess of income. Experience tends to indicate that, in most cases, current account deficits are the mirror image of fiscal deficits. In only a few cases, such as Chile in the late 1970s and, recently, the United Kingdom, are these deficits the counterpart of private sector budget imbalances.

In the design of economic policy measures aimed at the solution of some of the problems described above, it is vitally important—as recognized by Guitián—to understand clearly the characteristics of the basic imbalances behind the problems. Thus, not only must the type of imbalance be described correctly, but also the economic sector where these imbalances originate must be identified. This latter requirement, in turn, calls for total consistency in the measurement of the different sectoral imbalances.

Economic data in most countries are based on widely accepted criteria, and with the exception of countries confronting inflationary pressures, may be considered generally consistent. For countries where inflation has been a daily experience for decades, as well as private holdings of foreign assets and capital outflows—even under strict capital movement controls—economic data and, therefore, measurements of imbalances tend not to be reliable.

The absorption identity can be of help in an illustration of this point. Most countries measure their external accounts for balance of payments reasons in terms of an international unit of account (in most cases, dollars), whereas they measure the same transaction for national accounts purposes in volume terms. At the same time, the public sector budget is measured in terms of a nominal domestic currency (even though it is also frequently transformed into "constant" national currency for the purpose of comparing the time path of budget imbalances in an inflationary environment). The private sector budget, however, is never measured in this way, even though some of its components are published in the form of flows of output, income, consumption, and investment.

It should be immediately clear to the reader that measuring the different sectoral imbalances in different units of account does not help in determining the true characteristics of the imbalances to be corrected; and that the transformation of nominal flows into "real flows" in the public sector budget is not a good substitute for uniform units of account or for an accurate measurement of the effects of inflation on financial assets.

Inflation and the Measurement of Fiscal Imbalance

The following example examines the basic distortions that inflation introduces in the measurement of fiscal imbalances. In this example, the public sector budget of a country with an assumed structure of taxes, expenditures, and debt is examined under three different inflationary conditions: price stability; prices increasing at a rate of 50 percent a year; and prices increasing at 100 percent a year. In the last two cases, monthly inflation rates are assumed to be stable throughout the year.

The basic data for financial assets and liabilities used in the example follow approximately the financial structure of heavily indebted countries like Brazil or Mexico. In the case of Argentina, the stock of domestic debt is smaller as a consequence of a stronger run out of the domestic currency. Interest rates approximately reflect current rates, even though during the last few years, real rates on domestic assets have tended to be higher in real life.

Basic Data

Gross national product (GNP)	100
Net external debt	50
Interest-bearing domestic debt	20
Non-interest-bearing domestic debt	10
Total net financial wealth	−80
International interest rates	8 percent a year
Real domestic interest rates	10 percent a year
Nominal domestic interest rates	inflation + 10 percent

In addition to these data, it is necessary to make a few policy assumptions related to the policies to be followed in the field of exchange rate and debt management, as well as those referring to structural factors (fiscal lags) and the reaction of economic agents to inflation. The assumptions are: (1) the country is small and a price taker; (2) all goods are internationally traded; (3) the exchange rate policy is full indexation to inflation; (4) nominal tax adjustments are 90 percent of inflation rates; (5) nonfinancial public sector expenditures are constant in real terms; (6) domestic interest-bearing debt is constant in real terms;

(7) domestic non-interest-bearing debt declines in real terms as inflation increases; (8) gross external debt is constant in real terms; and (9) changes in reserves are used as an adjustment variable.

Table 1 shows the time path of the domestic interest-bearing debt and the corresponding interest payments flows for the year as a whole. This table clearly shows the effects of inflation on nominal interest payments.

Table 1. Interest Payment Flows on Domestic Debt

	Annual Rate of Inflation			
	50 percent[1]		100 percent[2]	
Month	Debt at Beginning of Period	Nominal Monthly Flows	Debt at Beginning of Period	Nominal Monthly Flows
1	20.000	0.852	20.000	1.358
2	20.687	0.882	21.189	1.439
3	21.398	0.912	22.449	1.624
4	22.134	0.943	23.784	1.615
5	22.894	0.976	25.198	1.711
6	23.681	1.009	26.697	1.813
7	24.495	1.044	28.284	1.921
8	25.337	1.080	29.966	2.095
9	26.205	1.117	31.748	2.156
10	27.108	1.155	33.636	2.284
11	28.040	1.196	35.636	2.488
12	29.004	1.236	37.755	2.564

Note: Figures are arbitrary, reflecting approximations to cases such as Mexico and Brazil. The figures were selected so that 100 = GDP before inflation.

[1]At 50 percent inflation, the nominal monthly interest rate is 0.04261 percent.

[2]At 100 percent inflation, the nominal monthly interest rate 0.06791 percent.

Table 2 shows income and expenditure flows under different inflationary environments. In each case, the flows are presented for two periods: the last month of the period, and the year as a whole, under the assumption of a constant monthly rate of inflation. As this table shows, as inflation increases, the following things happen: (1) taxes decline in real terms, owing to so-called fiscal lags (Olivera-Simone-Tanzi effect); (2) external interest payments are maintained in real terms, owing to the exchange rate indexation policy; and (3) real interest payments on the domestic debt rise significantly in response to the corresponding increase in the nominal interest rate.

The combination of these three events is reflected in a sharp deterioration in the nominal fiscal balance, which turns from a surplus (1 percent of GNP) to a significant deficit (almost 14 percent of GNP).

Table 2 is incomplete, because it does not include the financing of the imbalances. In Table 3, the structure of the financing of the public sector deficit is

Table 2. Public Sector Budget: Nominal Flows

Economic Indicator	Annual Rate of Inflation					
	0 percent		50 percent		100 percent	
	Last Month of Year	Year as a Whole	Last Month of Year	Year as a Whole	Last Month of Year	Year as a Whole
Taxes	3.333	40.000	4.804	49.028	6.232	57.048
Nonfinancial expenditures	-2.750	-33.000	-4.125	-41.386	-5.500	-48.997
Primary balance	0.583	7.000	0.679	7.643	0.731	48.061
Interest payments	-0.500	-6.000	-1.736	-17.118	-3.231	-28.780
External debt	-0.333	-4.000	-0.500	-5.016	-0.667	-5.939
Domestic debt	-0.167	-2.000	-1.236	-12.402	-2.564	-22.841
Total financial needs	-0.083	-1.000	1.057	9.775	2.400	20.729
Memorandum items:						
GNP	8.333	100.000	12.500	126.411	16.667	140.472
Budget deficit (in percent of GNP)	1.0	1.0	-8.46	-7.79	-14.99	-13.96
Adjustment of nominal value of external debt	—	—	25.000	—	50.000	—

Note: Figures are arbitrary, reflecting approximations to cases such as Mexico and Brazil. The figures were selected so that 100 = GDP before inflation.

Table 3. Financing of the Public Sector Deficit: Nominal flows

Economic Indicator	Annual Rate of Inflation					
	0 percent		50 percent		100 percent	
	Last Month of Year	Year as a Whole	Last Month of Year	Year as a Whole	Last Month of Year	Year as a Whole
Total financing needs	−0.0830	−1.000	1.057	9.775	2.499	20.729
External debt	—	—	—	—	—	—
Domestic liability						
Non-interest-bearing	—	—	0.432	4.413	0.793	7.466
Interest-bearing	—	—	0.097	10.000	2.245	20.000
Changes in reserves	0.0830	1.000	0.332	4.638	0.539	6.736
Memorandum items:						
Changes in reserves (in foreign currency)	0.0830	1.000	0.248	3.755	0.269	4.724

Note: Figures are arbitrary, reflecting approximations to cases such as Mexico and Brazil. The figures were selected so that 100 = GDP before inflation.

shown under the same inflationary assumptions. This table should be interpreted in the following way. The country's financing needs, which are shown in the first line of the table, were obtained from the flows in Table 1. Since inflation also influences the nominal demand of economic agents for different financial assets, this element should be reflected in the economic policy assumptions. The assumptions used here reflect the desire of economic agents to maintain a constant real stock of interest-bearing debt instruments and a declining real stock of non-interest-bearing debt instruments. Under a fixed exchange rate, any difference between the financial needs of the public sector and the flow demand for financial assets of the private sector is adjusted through changes in reserves.

In Table 3, accumulation of reserves is shown to increase with inflation, a result that seems incompatible with the absorption identity. A careful evaluation of the data, however, shows that this is not the case, as can be seen in Table 4.

Table 4. Fiscal Imbalance, Inflationary Taxes, and Reserve Changes

(End-of-period nominal stocks)

Economic Indicator	Annual Rate of Inflation		
	0 percent	50 percent	100 percent
Assets	1.000	5.633	9.446
Reserves	1.000	5.633	9.446
Liabilities	80.000	119.413	157.466
Domestic			
Non-interest-bearing	10.000	14.413	17.466
Interest-bearing	20.000	30.000	40.000
External	50.000	75.000	100.000
Nominal net financial wealth	−79.000	−113.780	−148.018
Inflation-adjusted net			
financial wealth	−79.000	−75.853	−74.009
Changes in net financial wealth			
At old prices	1.000	4.147	5.991
At new prices	1.000	6.220	11.982

Note: Figures are arbitrary, reflecting approximations to cases such as Mexico and Brazil. The figures were selected so that 100 = GDP before inflation.

Table 4 depicts the country's financial structure after the fiscal flows of the period and the changes in net financial wealth measured in terms of the new prices and the old prices have been taken into account. As this table shows, net financial wealth has improved somewhat during the period, a result that can only be consistent with a fiscal surplus. This improvement is consistent with the reserve accumulation shown in Table 2, and also exhibits the same tendency to increase with inflation. This apparent contradiction arises because Table 2, which is based exclusively on flows, does not take into account the decline in the real value of the domestic debt derived from inflation (the so-called inflationary tax).

A brief analysis of these figures allows us to draw the following conclusions. There are several definitions of fiscal imbalances, and each has its particular usefulness. The most useful definitions are: (1) nominal flow imbalances (Table 2), which are a counterpart of the financing needs of the public sector; (2) total nominal deficit, which is the counterpart of the nominal changes in net financial wealth; (3) inflation-adjusted deficit, which is the counterpart of the "real" changes in net financial wealth (that is, the correct measurement of imbalances from a net wealth point of view; (4) dollar-adjusted deficit, which is a counterpart of variations in net financial wealth measured in dollar terms and is useful in the measurement of imbalances leading to current and balance of payments disequilibria; and (5) zero-inflation deficit. This last concept, which measures the size of fiscal imbalances under the assumption of price stability, is perhaps the most important measurement for assessing the characteristics of a disequilibrium for adjustment purposes. It should not be used in combination with the inflation-adjusted concept, which attempts to measure the size of the imbalance after all the distortions introduced by inflation have been eliminated, whereas the zero-inflation deficit includes all these distortions and, in addition, includes under revenues the amount of inflationary tax collected. In a sense, the zero-inflation deficit is an ex-ante concept that measures the magnitude of the adjustment required to eliminate inflationary and external sector pressures, whereas the inflation-adjusted deficit is an ex-post concept that incorporates the real resource transfers originating in inflation.

Inflation tends to increase the nominal flow deficit. These increases tend to be large; the larger the interest-bearing domestic debt, the larger the fiscal lag. Inflation also tends to be higher, the larger the size of the zero-inflation deficit, the smaller the non-interest-bearing debt, the larger the fiscal lags, and the faster the run out of a currency.

Reconciliation of nominal flow figures with the changes in nominal net financial wealth is feasible, but it requires elaborate measurements of the inflationary tax and other inflation-induced distortions. Table 5 shows, as an example, these calculations for the year as a whole, under the assumption of a 50 percent rate of inflation.

In this table, the gross inflationary tax was measured not only in relation to the original stock of non-interest-bearing domestic debt (10 x 0.5), but also in terms of the monthly flow demand for this asset. The effects of inflation on taxation (fiscal lags) were measured by comparing the amount of perceived taxes in the

Table 5. Changes in Net Financial Wealth, Inflationary Taxes, and Nominal Flow

Component	Change
Changes in net financial wealth at new prices	**6.220**
Zero-inflation surplus at new prices	1.500
Gross inflationary tax	5.870
Fiscal lags	−1.137
Cross effects and interest compounding	−0.010

Note: Figures are arbitrary, reflecting approximations to cases such as Mexico and Brazil. The figures were selected so that 100 = GDP before inflation.

case of full indexation with the flows shown in Table 2. The zero-inflation surplus corresponds to the financial needs figure under the heading "zero inflation," measured at the new prices. The last item ("cross effects") originates in the compounded effects of real interest rates and inflation.

Gross, Net, and Effective Net Inflationary Taxes

The analysis in the previous paragraphs shows that there are at least three relevant concepts associated with inflationary taxation.

Gross inflationary tax corresponds to the concept traditionally used in the literature. It measures the decline in the real value of public sector non-interest-bearing debt. It is normally measured in terms of liquid monetary assets (M1), but from a fiscal point of view should be measured in terms of the public sector debt. It should include not only the initial stock but also the effects of inflation on the real value of the flow demand of this instrument. In circumstances when negative real interest rates prevail, the measurements should also include these effects.

Net inflationary tax is defined as the difference between the gross inflationary tax and all the other effects of inflation on the public sector budget (fiscal lags, effects on real interest rates, etc.). It should be clear that changes in net financial wealth equal zero-inflation budget plus net inflationary tax.

Net effective inflationary tax measures the effects of inflation on the financing possibilities of the public sector. It is equal to the net inflationary tax minus the "runout of domestic debt instruments." As economic agents try to avoid paying the inflationary tax, the decline in the real demand for domestic debt instruments reduces the financing possibilities of the public sector. In the extreme case when the net effective inflationary tax turns negative, even though inflation will tend to improve the net financial wealth of a country, the improvement will be of no help in satisfying the financial needs of the public sector. In these circumstances, inflation is a very inefficient adjustment mechanism, since the financing needs will grow faster than the financing sources and will be initially reflected in reserves losses and eventually in hyperinflation.

Negative net effective inflationary taxes will tend to be present in countries with persistent inflationary pressures where the stock demand for public sector debt instruments is very low and fiscal lags tend to be very large.

Comment

Richard Portes

As in so much of recent macroeconomics, the stock-flow distinction lies at the heart of this excellent treatment of the macroeconomic basis of International Monetary Fund (IMF) adjustment programs for indebted less-developed countries. In particular, the relations between fiscal deficits, domestic public debt, external debt, and debt service must be elucidated. This requires a clear intertemporal perspective as well as an understanding of the complexities of actual adjustment programs.

The precise characteristics of adjustment will determine whether a current flow imbalance translates over time into a stock maladjustment, carrying its own consequences for flows. Some of the relevant issues have been analyzed by Buiter (1985) for developed countries—mainly the United Kingdom and the United States—and in the book edited by Giavazzi and Spaventa (1988)—mainly on the Italian case. I shall not repeat the arguments there and shall therefore focus on the less-developed countries, although I fully agree with Manuel Guitián that the problems are quite general in application.

Guitián stresses the need to balance available and required resources. This is surely where we must start. The first qualification I would make, however, is that the intertemporal budget constraint stressed here should not be taken as a rigid criterion for assessing fiscal stance, or rather a fiscal rule. Let us define the latter as a time path for government revenues and expenditures, or in simpler terms, a time path for government deficits and surpluses. The path may be fully specified, period by period, in a manner defined by an open-loop adjustment rule.

Consider now a fiscal rule, so defined, that respects the intertemporal budget constraint. It may still not be sustainable. First, even if the expected growth rate exceeds the expected real rate of interest, subsequent shocks may reverse that relationship—as indeed occurred in the early 1980s. Second, the tax burden determined by the rule may not be collectible. Third, the expenditures specified in the rule—for example, on the armed forces or on transfer payments—may not be enough to keep the government in power. Finally, if the tax burden implied by the rule involves some seigniorage element, its inflationary consequences may be unstable, a point to which I shall return below.

Conversely, a fiscal rule that violates the intertemporal budget constraint may nevertheless not be unsustainable. Debt can be inflated away, to the extent that it is denominated in home currency; this is of course less likely for a developing country than for a highly industrialized country. But the developing countries have other options that are perhaps more likely: they may repurchase their debt at less than its face value; or, in the extreme case, they may repudiate.

A sustainable fiscal rule, respecting the intertemporal budget constraint, may still encounter liquidity constraints if the capital market is imperfect. Cohen (1985) calculated an "index of solvency" for indebted countries that suggested that only a few were "insolvent," even on relatively pessimistic assumptions regarding long-run growth rates and real interest rates. Nevertheless, many have since had to reschedule. Often the rescheduling has involved substantial changes in macroeconomic policies toward "adjustment," although on this ("solvency") definition of the intertemporal budget constraint, there was no need to adjust. The problem, of course, is that these countries cannot under current conditions maintain the levels of borrowing required by these "sustainable" long-run paths; one might suggest that this was the fundamental weakness of the Baker Plan.

Guitián points out that a stock imbalance feeds back on flows. Until recently, a particular aspect of this relation has been neglected: the relation of external debt service to domestic fiscal flows. Financing an increased burden of debt service requires as its domestic counterpart an increase in the government's primary surplus, selling more domestic debt to the public, or raising seigniorage revenues. But increasing taxes or cutting expenditures will often hit investment rather than consumption, as the recent experience of many highly indebted countries suggests. Selling more domestic debt, where the capital market is sufficiently developed to permit it, will normally raise real interest rates, again with undesirable consequences for investment. And there are well-defined limits to seigniorage revenues—as inflation accelerates and velocity rises, the real value of seigniorage will ultimately fall.

The paper makes a point about policy that I would query. First, it is suggested that for some time at least, a country could counteract the effects of a loose fiscal stance by applying a tight monetary policy. But not all countries can apply Reaganomics successfully! The Sargent-Wallace argument gave rise to several models that can generate higher inflation as a consequence of temporary monetary restraint, and the cases of Israel in 1979 and Turkey in 1984 indicated that the theory may have some empirical content.

Perhaps more important for a country with a very limited capital market, the central bank may be the only significant source of finance for the government deficit. If the Treasury has no alternative but to require the central bank to monetize the deficit, and there is no de facto separation of powers, the growth of the central bank's domestic assets is no longer a choice variable but is rather determined by the public sector deficit. The distinction between fiscal and monetary policies then becomes meaningless, and Guitián's proposal cannot be operational.

I believe that for many of the highly indebted countries, the problems raised above will make it impossible for them to succeed with any adjustment in the medium term—that is, sufficiently to maintain full debt service and obtain renewed access to voluntary external finance. No conditionality will be able to bring this about. The only alternative is then some form of debt relief—voluntary or forced reduction in the debt overhang. "Debt fatigue" is becoming insupportable, and the debt burden now inhibits investment, both for the reasons sketched above and because debt service acts as a tax on the yield of investment. It thereby reduces the likelihood of successful adjustment.

To implement debt relief, I would propose substantial reliance on market-based procedures, with large-scale purchases of debt at discounted prices, often by the debtors themselves. This brings us back to the title of this conference and the relation between fiscal policy, adjustment, and financial markets. How to expand the existing secondary markets for bank debt, how they could behave in these circumstances, and how prices on these markets are related to domestic policies are questions requiring further conferences.

References

Buiter, Willem, "Guide to Public Sector Debt and Deficits," *Economic Policy: A European Forum* (Cambridge), Vol. 1 (November 1985), pp. 13–79.

Cohen, Daniel, "How to Evaluate the Solvency of an Indebted Nation," *Economic Policy: A European Forum* (Cambridge), Vol. 1 (November 1985), pp. 139–67.

Giavazzi, Francesco, and Luigi Spaventa, eds., *High Public Debt: The Italian Experience* (Cambridge: Cambridge University Press, 1988).

Comment

Salvatore Zecchini

Manuel Guitián's paper has the undoubted merit of presenting in a condensed and general form the complex issues of fiscal adjustment that the International Monetary Fund (IMF) has had to cope with in the past decade. Fiscal imbalances are not the only cause of the severe economic imbalances that industrial and developing countries have experienced in the 1980s. But fiscal adjustment is at the center of any approach to the correction of these imbalances, no matter what the main source of the imbalance is, because it encompasses more fully than other macroeconomic policies three degrees of effects. Fiscal adjustment can contribute in a major way to the control of domestic demand expansion, while managing the impact of this control on the efficiency of resource allocation and on the distribution of income among income earners and the population at large.

Guitián's presentation of the fiscal adjustment issues is so comprehensive and far-reaching that it can be shared by most, if not all, of us. The purpose of my contribution to this discussion is therefore to spell out briefly some of the more controversial issues that have arisen in the design and assessment of the fiscal adjustment efforts that have come under the scrutiny of the Fund.

The perspective that the IMF takes in addressing the issue of fiscal adjustment is basically that of helping the country to achieve external balance. This is also one of the underlying themes of Guitián's paper. However, the relationship between fiscal deficit and external deficit is not a one-to-one relationship, whereby the correction of the first leads more or less automatically to the adjustment of the others, as some schools of thought have argued and as the IMF staff has tended to assume in program design. In fact, some IMF members that had upper credit tranche arrangements with the Fund in the period 1982–85 redressed their external current account imbalance without achieving the targeted correction in the fiscal area. Furthermore, other countries overperformed in terms of fiscal correction but did not achieve their objective of external balance. If we were to plot on a diagram the improvements of these countries in their external current account as a percent of gross domestic product (GDP) against the improvements in their fiscal account, the result would be a scatter of outcomes spread out at some distance from the 45-degree intercept that would support a direct relationship between the two sets of results.

Therefore, if this relationship is not so direct, one must look for the other factors that mediate between and explain the link between the two imbalances. In this respect, some useful insight can be derived from an analysis of sectoral balances between savings and investment in the framework of the flow of funds. Through this approach, we may find some interesting explanations for certain country experiences. For instance, in the case of Italy, how was it possible that the high and widening budget deficit of 1979–85 was not translated into a widening current balance of payments deficit. If, for simplicity, we consider only two sectors in the economy—the general government and the private sector—we can see that between 1979 and 1980 the widening of the external account was mainly due to a decline in net saving accumulation by the private sector. In contrast, between 1981 and 1984, when Italy experienced a gradual increase in the deficit of the public sector, its impact on the external deficit was more than offset by a rise in net savings of the private sector. As a result, the current account turned into a surplus in 1983, while the general government deficit continued to increase. Actually, the private sector, and particularly private fixed investment, had to bear a large portion of the burden of external adjustment, which had negative repercussions on the longer-term development of the economy.

The importance of an analysis of the savings-investment balances for the major sectors of any economy when an adjustment program is being designed or the surveillance function of the Fund is being implemented is underscored by several other factors. One might include among these factors the strong reluctance of some major industrial countries to include this analysis among the indicators used in the policy coordination exercise undertaken by the Group of Seven countries. I prefer to consider another argument that has recently become quite fashionable in academic circles—that is, the so-called Ricardian equivalence theory.

It is generally believed that budget deficits are generally one of the causes of excessive domestic absorption, accelerating inflation, displacement of private investment, and rising deficits in the current balance of payments. However, some economists have recently argued that according to Ricardian equivalence, this chain of cause and effect does not materialize under certain circumstances. Specifically, if there is an interdependence between private and public decisions to save, an increase in the public deficit is matched by a rise in private saving in anticipation of future taxation. The result would be a lack of responsiveness of total domestic savings to changes in the fiscal stance and, consequently, a limited role for fiscal policy in the adjustment strategy.

This line of reasoning does not seem to be supported by the statistical evidence. Recent econometric tests carried out by the IMF (Haque and Montiel (1987)) suggest that in 15 out of 16 major developing countries with IMF programs, the Ricardian equivalence proposition can be rejected at a comfortable level of statistical significance. This strengthens the belief that without fiscal correction, no viable adjustment is possible independently of the specific cause of the imbalance in the economy.

Guitián rightly emphasizes the vicious circle that has emerged between flow imbalances and stock maladjustment; the accumulation of public debt is both the result of a series of major budget deficits and the cause of further deficits in the future. Furthermore, the sheer magnitude of the stock of debt can shape the course of adjustment and the development of the economy.

However, although the importance of this stock-flow interdependence should not be underestimated, the intractable debt problem facing many developing countries is also the result of two largely exogenous factors—namely, the rise in real interest rates in world markets, and the sharp reversal in the terms of trade of the indebted countries. The climb in real interest rates was mainly determined by monetary conditions in the major industrial countries and, particularly, by the mix of macroeconomic stabilization policies pursued in the first half of the 1980s. The worsening of the terms of trade appears to be mainly the result of a weakening of demand and prices in commodity and energy markets in the early 1980s.

Overall, the fiscal imbalances of these countries can be traced back to a variety of factors and are reflected in a wide range of distortions in the economy. If one considers the multifaceted relationship of causes and effects, it becomes evident that the approach to fiscal adjustment followed by the Fund in the first half of the 1980s was too narrow in scope and, consequently, not able to produce durable results. The IMF guidelines on conditionality provide the framework for the approach to fiscal correction and have as their main goal rapid progress toward a sustainable balance of payments. Problems associated with attaining a more systemic control over inflation, limiting the impact of stabilization measures on the long-term growth potential, and restoring equilibrium between the stock of external debt and the debt-servicing capacity of a debtor country were not of primary concern for the Fund and the deficit country in the design of the adjustment strategy and performance criteria. Instead, the primary concerns were the size of the fiscal deficit and the speed of its reduction, since these were the relevant variables in the traditional model used by the IMF staff. In essence, in this model, given a predetermined demand for money, the impact of a change in the fiscal deficit on domestic credit expansion leads to the targeted changes in the current balance of the external account.

Guitián correctly stresses the evolution of the approach to conditionality that has occurred since 1985, which has been characterized not by a change in the guidelines but by a broadening of their interpretation. In this evolution, emphasis has been shifted away from the quantity of deficit correction to the quality of overall fiscal adjustment. Although Guitián does not delve into the causes of this evolution, this is an interesting area to explore. A major factor behind the change in emphasis has been the mixed success of Fund-supported programs, together with increasing signs of adjustment fatigue, as evidenced by social tensions in countries that are still far from a viable fiscal or external position. In fact, since 1983 most of the slippages in the implementation of adjustment programs occurred in the area of public finances; and even in those cases where compliance was satisfactory, the improvements were more temporary than structural. This outcome is hardly surprising, since the public budget is the main ground where the conflicting claims on the national income by the various segments of the population have to be reconciled, and where the authorities face the most rigid constraints on the political side.

The shift in emphasis toward the qualitative aspects of fiscal adjustment involves, first, a more penetrating analysis of the implications of changes made in the revenue and expenditure sides of the budget to achieve targeted objectives; and, second, a more profound modification of public intervention in the economy. Both actions are likely to elicit strong opposition from the authorities involved, unless they are aimed at other objectives, besides correction of the external balance, that are considered valuable from a social point of view. The principal additional objectives favored by authorities have been the maintenance of a satisfactory growth rate over both the medium term and the short term, and a lasting solution to the external debt overhang, possibly through debt relief. To these objectives the Fund has added better control over domestic inflationary impulses, an objective that countries with a long history of high inflation have not valued adequately. The widening of the number of objectives in the fiscal strategy requires a corresponding enlargement in the number of fiscal instruments and, consequently, the assignment of different roles to interventions in the budget deficit, the expenditure side, the revenue side, and the financing of the deficit. Let us briefly consider these aspects.

With respect to the deficit, the Fund has introduced the concepts of primary and operational balances into its conditionality, as, for example, in the case of the program with Mexico. Introducing these definitions was justified by the assumption that interest payments or the inflationary component of interest payments have a low impact, compared to other public expenditures, on other economic imbalances, particularly in sustaining inflation. Furthermore, it was believed that the reabsorption of these components of the deficit would take place over a longer period and would benefit from the easing of inflation as well as of conditions in the financial markets. However, a program that focuses on such narrow definitions of the deficit may run the risk of being based on unrealistic assumptions about the inflationary process in the country under consideration. Therefore, it would be advisable to use these definitions only in instances where other parts of the adjustment program are committed to a strong anti-inflationary stance.

An interesting innovation in some programs—such as the recent ones carried out in Argentina and Brazil—has been the use of "heterodox" measures, as opposed to "orthodox" demand management via macroeconomic policies. These heterodox measures, which include temporary price-wage freezes or compulsory de-indexation, were aimed at obtaining a quick reversal of inflationary expectations and at boosting public confidence in the complementary macroeconomic strategy. The rationale was that improvements in private expectations could help minimize output losses due to fiscal stabilization. In practice, the heterodox approach proved to be successful only over a very short period, since it was not supported by more fundamental adjustments in the fiscal and monetary stance (see Blejer and Cheasty (1987)).

Among the countries undertaking adjustment programs, the weakest performance in the fiscal areas has been recorded on the expenditure side. The contribution of expenditure restraint to the reduction of domestic absorption has been much lower than the contribution of revenue-raising measures. Furthermore, capital expenditure, and investment programs in particular, has borne the brunt of the expenditure stabilization, with implications for the growth potential of the economy. At the same time, little progress has been made in limiting transfers to public enterprises or the parastatal sector, or in improving their efficiency or gaining better control over extrabudgetary expenditures.

The Fund has contributed in part to this outcome, since its approach has basically been concerned with reducing only the size of the claim of the public sector on domestically produced resources. The transition from a quantitative to a qualitative approach will require instead an analysis of the impact of the expenditure structure on long-term growth and inflation and will call for some form of conditionality on the composition of expenditure. Such an approach implies the development of microeconomic analysis as a basis for achieving macroeconomic balance in the development process. In undertaking this endeavor, the IMF should not fall prey to the frequently used assumption that any expansion of public expenditure represents a suboptimal use of domestic resources and should therefore be resisted. After all, the government sector provides, among other things, social goods that are preconditions for any economic development process. However, the Fund should encourage the authorities to scrutinize more closely the costs and benefits stemming from groups of expenditure items, as a means to strengthen the economic system. Moreover, the Fund should require that the authorities exert more control over the expenditure decisions of all public entities, and particularly the local ones.

In Fund-supported programs, tax measures have played an important role in raising revenues for the purpose of fiscal stabilization, but efforts to improve tax administration have been less successful. In the area of taxation, the Fund should work more purposefully toward achieving optimal taxation under the specific conditions of the country concerned. For instance, taxes that have a highly inflationary impact or that lessen incentives to expand production should be avoided.

Guitián's paper also touches upon a crucial issue that has received increasing attention since 1985—the interaction between the financing of the budget deficit and the management of external debt in countries with an excessive accumulation of external debt. Guitián stresses the need to restore a balance between debt-creating and non-debt-creating financial flows. This has implications for the structuring of economic activities that are carried out directly or indirectly by the public sector. Specifically, those activities in which public interest priorities do not override economic goals should be restructured so as to attract foreign capital in the form of direct investment or equity participation. Furthermore, the decision of the public sector to borrow abroad should be consistent with a sustainable relationship between the marginal productivity of the resources invested in the country and the marginal cost of borrowing. When the second exceeds the first, it is most likely that a debt overhang will emerge in the not-too-distant future.

Another issue that has not received enough attention in the Fund's use of conditionality is the interaction between exchange measures and fiscal stabilization. For countries with a relatively high stock of foreign indebtedness, the usual IMF recommendation to depreciate the exchange rate has brought about an increase in the burden of debt servicing for the budget. Likewise, the conversion of foreign debt into equity implies the replacement of external debt with domestic debt. If, in this process, the debtor country does not benefit from a substantial discount over the face value of previously held debt, and if domestic interest rates are relatively high, the final result will be a net increase in the budget expense for debt service. Therefore, better coordination is needed between external and fiscal measures.

As can be seen from the issues discussed above, improving the quality of fiscal adjustment within the framework of IMF conditionality implies a deeper involvement by the Fund in domestic policy decisions that governments have usually regarded as their exclusive domain. As Guitián points out, "the issue of the appropriate degree of participation by the Fund in economic policy decision making is not amenable to simple or categorical answers" (p. 127). However, two basic considerations have to be borne in mind. First, most of the qualitative aspects that have been discussed here fall within the domain of economic policies over which the Fund exercises its surveillance function under Article IV, Section 1. Second, the cooperative nature of the IMF can justify the exchange of a more penetrating conditionality for the provision of financing in an amount that is necessary to support structural improvements in an economy but is not voluntarily provided by the markets. If a country is willing to undertake a major effort to correct systemic weaknesses in the economy, then the Fund has to allow more time for adjustment and, consequently, more financing because of the persistence of external deficits over longer periods. This is also the fundamental rationale behind the enhancement of the structural adjustment facility for low-income countries.

This approach should not be available to the low-income countries alone; rather, it should be extended to all IMF members. To this end, two main conditions must be fulfilled. First, the magnitude of Fund resources should be raised to match the current scale of national products and external trade in the world economy. Second, the objective of promoting orderly economic growth, as spelled out in Article IV, Section 1, should be explicitly incorporated in the existing guidelines for conditionality.

References

Blejer, Mario I., and Adrienne Cheasty, "High Inflation, 'Heterodox' Stabilization, and Fiscal Policy," IMF Working Paper 87/88 (mimeographed, International Monetary Fund, November 18, 1987).

Haque, Nadeem U., and Peter Montiel, "Ricardian Equivalence, Liquidity Constraints, and the Yaari-Blanchard Effect: Tests for Developing Countries," IMF Working Paper 87/85 (mimeographed, International Monetary Fund, December 16, 1987).

Credit Constraints and Investment Finance: Some Evidence from Greece

J. Dutta and H.M. Polemarchakis

Credit management has important effects on the availability of investible funds for the private sector; it is quite often the cornerstone of financial reforms aimed at increasing investment, and hence, industrial growth rates. In this paper, we examine the potential impact of interest rate policies on investment in the mining and manufacturing sector of Greece.

Financial markets in Greece are not well developed. The virtual nonexistence of markets for bonds and equity results in a situation where the private sector depends on bank credit as its only source of external finance. Bank credit is heavily subsidized, so that both deposit and lending rates set by the Bank of Greece have been predominantly negative in real terms since 1973.

As a result, one would expect credit availability to be restricted, and private industrial investment to be constrained, by the shortage of funds. However, survey data from firms in the private manufacturing sector, as reported in Deleau (1987), do not support this expectation. Most individual firms surveyed do not perceive a shortage of funds as restricting investment. In effect, even negative real interest rates do not provide an effective subsidy. This would appear to be somewhat of a puzzle. The "naive" explanation implies that the rate of return on capital has been persistently negative across firms and types of productive activity; but this explanation is a difficult one to maintain consistently.

We argue here that the puzzle arises only if we think of bank credit as the sole source of long-term finance. Consider a firm that operates in a credit-controlled environment; in addition to borrowing, the firm can finance its borrowing with corporate savings (retained profits). If borrowing is rationed repeatedly, the firm will use profit retention as a source of finance to optimize on its investment outlay. We should visualize this firm as optimizing jointly over its investment budget and profit-retention rate, taking into account the credit ceiling and debt-servicing costs.

The model of credit-constrained investment financing has rather different implications than does a more naive model where firms react passively by setting their investment budget equal to the credit ceiling. In the first place, this argument accounts for the apparent lack of perceived fund constraints that shows up in firm surveys; it simply reflects the fact that firms optimize in their retained-earnings decisions. We estimate from aggregate data that a dollar's worth of increased credit availability will finance $0.96 of dividend payments, and only $0.04 of increased investment outlay. That credit availability is not perceived to be a major constraint on investment should be interpreted as follows: firms would not turn down increases in offered credit at the prevailing interest rates. Yet, they would use most of this new borrowing to substitute for retained earnings, and only a negligible part to finance increased investment.

It is easily demonstrated, at a formal level, that a firm that is experiencing borrowing constraints will not, in general, equate the return on capital with the interest rate, which entails different qualitative effects of interest rate changes on investment outlay. To contrast this approach with a naive argument, consider firms whose investment decisions are passive relative to borrowing constraints. Figure 1 describes the ex-post investment function in an economy where all firms

Figure 1.   Investment Function Without Corporate Savings

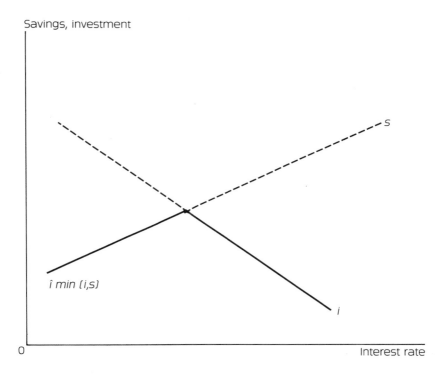

Savings, investment

î min (i,s)

i

S

0   Interest rate

equate their investment budgets with the level of borrowing. The savings
function, s, determines the amount banks can lend to firms; and i is the ex-ante
investment function. The ex-post investment function $\hat{i}$ is the minimum of ex-
ante savings and investment. At low interest rates, $\hat{i}_r > 0$.

Figure 2 demonstrates the ex-post investment function of firms that choose
financing methods optimally, relative to a credit constraint. Household savings,

Figure 2. Investment Function With Corporate Savings

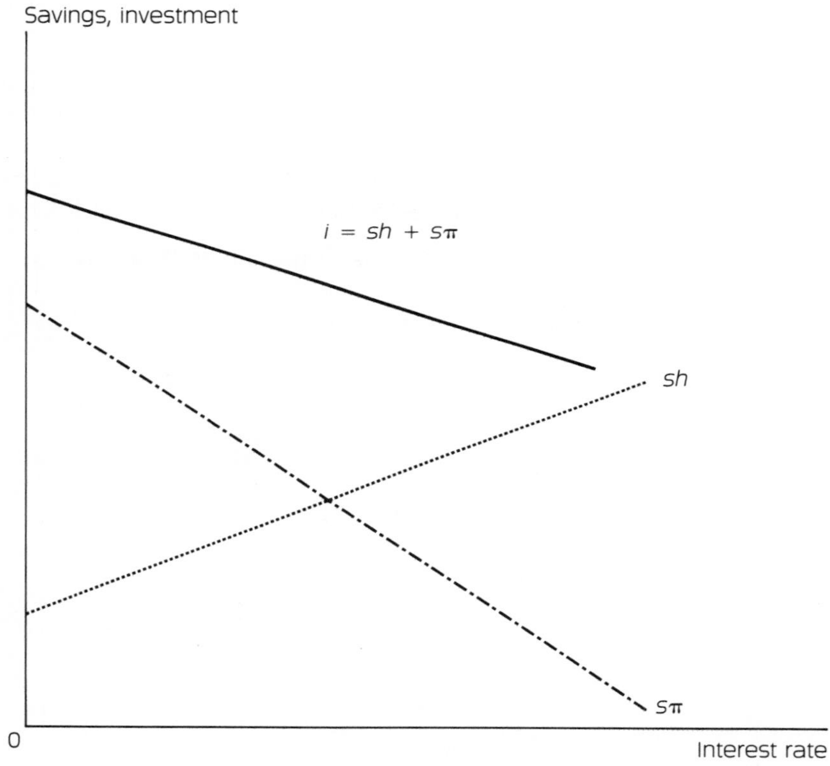

sh, is the amount that banks can lend. Corporate savings out of profits is a
function, $s\pi$, which is unambiguously decreasing in r. Investment, both ex ante
and ex post, equals $i = sh + s\pi$. It follows that $i_r < 0$ whenever $sh_r + s\pi_r < 0$.
Our point estimates suggest that this is true for investments in the Greek
manufacturing sector, even for real interest rates as low as –10 percent.

For our argument to be empirically convincing, we need to establish that
corporate savings are at once a major and a discretionary component of invest-

ment finance. Figures 3, 4, and 5 illustrate some evidence to this effect. In
Figure 5, we notice, first, that the proportion of investment financed by retained

**Figure 3. Greece: Investment and Corporate
Savings — Mining and Manufacturing, 1964–86**

(In billions of Greek drachmas)

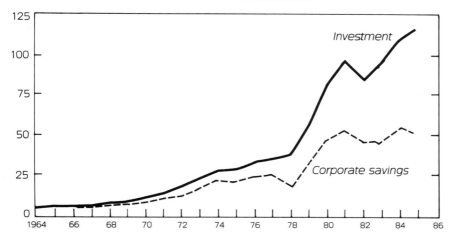

**Figure 4. Greece: Real Investment and
Corporate Savings (1970 Prices), 1964–86**

(In billions of Greek drachmas)

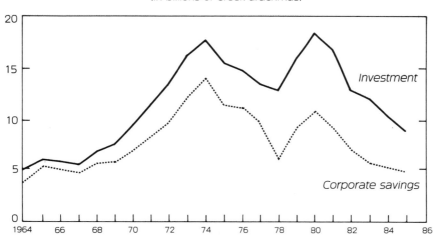

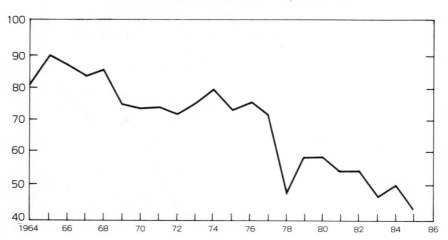

Figure 5. Greece: Corporate Savings as a
Percentage of Investment, 1964–86

earnings has varied substantially from above 80 percent in the mid-1960s to below 50 percent in the mid-1980s. In Figures 3 and 4, we see that the time path of corporate savings displays properties very similar to that of investment; this apparent parallel movement points to its importance as a discretionary source. An important indicator, apparent in Figure 5, is the long-term decline in the role of corporate savings in financing investments. Others, including Tsoris (1984) and Deleau (1987), have noted that the indebtedness of Greek manufacturing firms is high and increasing. Our argument associates this rise with declining profitability and consequent cutbacks in real investment outlay.

The empirical analysis suggests that one of the major determinants of this decline in profitability is the long-term increase in product-wage rates in manufacturing, a natural outcome of government policy measures aimed at increasing workers' standard of living. The questions that should be addressed in this context deals with the design of financial reforms in the presence of redistributive measures.

A related set of questions, which we do not address here, deals with the role of interest rate subsidies in the nonexistence of securities markets, which, to a great extent, must be traced to institutional factors, including the legal framework supporting the rights of investors. However, the availability of subsidized credit can support and perpetuate the existing structure of "family-based" enterprises, which do not need to dilute control in order to increase their capital base with equity finance.

We think that questions about the lack of equity financing are important precisely because of redistributive policy. If equity were a predominant source of finance, real wage increases would generate very different spillover effects on the investment activities of firms. A policy aimed at taking advantage of these effects must focus financial reforms on securities markets, rather than debt markets, which appear to be of limited effectiveness anyway.

I. Modeling the Investment Decision

The Firm—Credit Constraints

We consider a firm that has a given technology, using capital, k, and labor, ℓ, to produce an output, x. Each period, the firm faces a product price, a wage rate, and a price for the investment good. Investment decisions have to be made one period in advance, since capital needs time to build. Each period, the firm starts with a given capital stock; it decides on its level of employment and, hence, on total output; in addition, it has to decide on the amount of investment, i, so that next period's capital stock is $k' = i + (1 - \delta)k$, with δ as the one-period depreciation rate for capital.

Investment is financed by one of two means: long-term borrowing from the banking sector; or retained profits by the firm (corporate savings). We will assume, for simplicity, that all borrowing in period t has to be fully repaid in period $t + 1$, so that the repayment period equals the time required for building productive capacity. We focus on a situation where interest rates are managed, so that real interest rates are low relative to the possible rate of return on capital; this implies that at the announced rate of interest, the firm is constrained in its borrowing, and can only borrow an amount b, a credit ceiling set by the bank; if it wishes to invest more than this, it must finance the additional amount from retained earnings.

The firm is owned by shareholders, who are paid dividends; profits of the firm are either retained to finance new investment or paid out as dividends. In particular, we abstract from working capital needs, as well as constraints on short-term borrowing. In each period, the shareholders have to decide simultaneously on the dividend payout rate and the level of investment, taking into account the credit ceiling faced by the firm. In fact, since the bank informs the firm about its borrowing limits, investment and dividend payouts are outcomes of the same decision.

The following identities summarize the basic structure of the problem:

$$\pi = x - w\ell - \bar{b}(1 + \bar{r}), \tag{1}$$

$$x = f(k, \ell), \tag{2}$$

$$k' = (1 - \delta)k + i \tag{3}$$

$$qi = b + \pi - d, \tag{4}$$

where the product price is normalized to equal 1; q is the relative price of investment goods; w is the real wage rate; r is the real (long-term lending) rate charged by the bank; b is the credit ceiling; π, d, and i are real profits, dividends, and investments, respectively. Variables determined in the previous period are denoted by an overbar ($-$) and in the following period by a prime symbol ($'$).

The production function f is increasing and concave in both arguments, and displays constant returns to scale. We assume, further, that shareholders care only about real dividend payments, so that x can be thought of as a composite consumption good.

It may be useful to think of the firm's decision as being taken in two steps; it begins a production period with a given capital stock. The firm, which is a price taker in the product and capital markets, first chooses a level of employment. In doing so, it maximizes profits, so that the marginal productivity of labor is equated to the product wage rate. Once profits are realized, the firm has to make a second decision—to split profits into dividends and corporate savings. At this point, the firm needs to know, in addition, the credit ceiling set by the bank, and to anticipate the real wages and the real interest rate it will face next period; once this is known, the shareholders know the (expected) contribution of retained earnings to profits next period, so that they choose to trade off dividends today for profits tomorrow. In the following section, we indicate the nature of this optimization problem and the determinants of investment financing.

Optimization and Dividend Decisions

A representative shareholder derives utility from dividend income; the shareholder's objective function is summarized as a two-period utility function:

$$u(d) + v[\pi' + q'(1 - \delta)k'], \tag{5}$$

where both u and v are increasing and concave in their respective arguments. The two-period representation can be justified either as representing shareholder myopia, or as a representation of a longer-term optimization problem via the value function.

Since the firm operates by maximizing profits each period, it must be true that

$$f_\ell = w \tag{6}$$

which we can rewrite as

$$x - w\ell = h(k,w),\tag{7}$$

with $h_k > 0$; $h_w < 0$. The function h is simply the potential operating profits achievable by the firm with a given capital stock and facing a given real wage rate in the labor market. It follows that realized profits are operating profits minus effective debt-servicing costs:

$$\pi = h(k,w) - \bar{b}(1 + \bar{r}).\tag{8}$$

The budget constraint facing the representative shareholder is thus defined by equation (8), and, in addition

$$k' = (1 - \delta)k + (b + \pi - d)/q.\tag{9}$$

The firm now chooses its payout policy to maximize equation (5), subject to equations (8) and (9); the optimal payout rule can be written either in terms of dividends or in terms of real retained profits, which is just the residual. Thus, optimal retained profits will be

$$s\pi = \pi - d = s\pi[\pi, k, q, \rho', w,' b(1 + r)].\tag{10}$$

Notice that in order to implement this decision, the firm has to know the product wage rate next period, the inflation rate for its own output, and the inflation rate on capital goods $\rho' = (q'/q) - 1$; in the actual estimation procedure, we use both the "perfect foresight" as well as a "rational expectations" specification to examine the responsiveness of investment decisions.

Comparative Statics

The function h defines potential operating profits at a given capital stock and wage rate; from the linear homogeneity (constant returns to scale) of the production function, it follows that the rate of return on capital is constant for a given wage rate.

Writing this return as $r(w)$, a decreasing function of w, we have

$$h(k,w) = r(w)k.\tag{11}$$

Realized profits next period are then

$$\pi' = r(w')[(1 - \delta)k + (s\pi + b)/q] - b(1 + r').\tag{12}$$

The effective return on investment expenditure each period is

$$r^* = r[(w')/q] + \rho'(1 - \delta) - 1.\tag{13}$$

It follows that for $r^* < r$, if the effective rate of return on investment is less than the real interest rate, the firm will disinvest and, in particular, will not borrow;

since our interest is to model a situation where the interest rate subsidy is effective and the credit ceiling does in fact bind, we assume that

$$r < r^*. \tag{14}$$

A shareholder thus maximizes

$$u(\pi - s\pi) + v[(1 - \delta)k + (1 + r^*)s + (r^* - r)b] \tag{15}$$

and the first-order conditions are

$$u' = (1 + r^*)v'. \tag{16}$$

Totally differentiating both sides, we obtain

$$\tau(d\pi - ds\,\pi) = (1 + r^*)[(1 - \delta)/r(w)d\pi \\ + (r^* - r)db + (1 + r^*)ds\,\pi], \tag{17}$$

with $\tau \equiv u''/v'' > 0$. It follows that

$$ds\,\pi = \frac{\tau - (1 + r^*)(1 - \delta)/r(w)}{\tau + (1 + r^*)^2}d\pi - \frac{(1 + r^*)(r^* - r)}{\tau + (1 + r)^2}db \\ \equiv s_1 d\pi - s_2 db. \tag{18}$$

The firm's propensity to save, s_1, is less than 1. The negative impact of increased credit availability on corporate savings can be understood as follows: if the real rate of return is relatively constant, and higher than the unit cost of debt servicing, firms would like to borrow to finance their entire investment plans. To the extent they cannot, corporate savings finance the gap; whenever they are allowed to borrow more, they can use current profits to finance a higher dividend payout. Notice that $s_2 < 1$, as long as $r > -1$; and further, that $s_2 > 0$ if and only if $r^* > r$, as we have in fact assumed. The hypothesis $r^* = r$ (firms are not constrained in their borrowing) is thus easily testable, either with aggregate data or with cross-sectional analysis.

The coefficient s_2 indicates the extent to which bank credit in fact subsidizes investment. Notice that for $\tau = 0$,

$$\frac{1}{(1 - s_2)} = \frac{(1 + r^*)}{(1 + r)},$$

which gives us a point estimate of the markup of profitability over the interest factor.

II. Data Analysis and Empirical Evidence

In the last section, we modeled the internal decision making by a firm that determines the corporate savings component of its investment; the firm takes into account the fact that it can only borrow up to a preset credit limit and then determines its total investment budget as borrowing plus own savings. The fact that it is constrained in borrowing alters the nature of its optimal investment. We showed that corporate savings are a decreasing function of total debt-servicing costs and, hence, of the real interest rate and of the credit ceiling, even if the real interest rate is zero or negative.

Empirical Implications

This model has important implications for the empirical analysis of the investment decision. In the simplest version of a constrained (or disequilibrium) investment model, the reduced form is derived as follows: total investible funds equal available savings, domestic and foreign, which is an increasing function of the real interest rate, as well as of variables such as disposable income, y; investment expenditure of the firm is a decreasing function of the real interest rate, and depends, in addition, on other factors affecting firm profitability, summarized as z. The equilibrium interest rate, $r_e = r(y, z)$ equates savings to ex-ante investment; if the government (or the banks), which manages the interest rate, offers an interest rate different from r_e, and in particular, below r_e, the capital market is in disequilibrium, and actual investment is constrained by the availability of savings. This can be written as

$$s = s(r; y) \tag{19}$$

$$i = i(r; z) \tag{19a}$$

$$\hat{i} = \min\left[s(r; y); i(r/z)\right] = \hat{i}(r; y, z), \tag{19b}$$

where i is the ex-ante level of investment, and $\hat{i}$ the actual, or ex-post level. Clearly, if r, the administered interest rate, is below r_e, actual investment is less than intended; and for this regime, the model predicts, empirically, that $\hat{i}$ is increasing in r and in y. Increasing the real interest rate will loosen the credit constraint on industry, and increase the availability of investible resources. This argument is a simplified version of the model familiar both from the literature on "fixed prices" (see, for example, Malinvaud (1980) and (1985)), as well as on interest rate management (see, for example, International Monetary Fund (1987), which cites the well-known McKinnon-Shaw argument).

This argument envisages, on the one hand, firms that formulate their investment decision a priori, and are then repeatedly faced with a credit ceiling. On the other hand, firms that operate in a perpetually credit-constrained environment are likely to take this ceiling into account when making their investment plans, and organize their investment and financing decisions on this basis. The model of the previous section describes the nature of the constrained investment decision. To write the comparable reduced form for this model, we decompose total private sector savings into two components: household savings, sh, and corporate savings, $s\pi$. This distinction is important precisely because interest rates are managed, which drives a wedge between the return on debt—that is, the bank rate—and the return on capital. Household savings responds to r, the bank rate, as well as to personal disposable income, y. (Strictly speaking, y should include income from sources other than profits.) All household savings are held as bank deposits, which can be lent out to firms to finance investment; if reserve requirements are ignored for the moment, this represents the credit ceiling set by the banking sector as a whole. Firms finance investment with borrowing and with corporate savings; corporate savings depend on current profits, the credit ceiling, and the bank rate, as well as on factors z, which determine the rate of return on capital internal to the firm; ex-ante constrained investment is equal to available credit plus corporate savings:

$$sh = sh(r;y) \tag{20}$$

$$b \leq sh \tag{20a}$$

$$s\pi = s\pi[b(1 + r), \pi, z] \tag{20b}$$

$$i = b + s\pi. \tag{20c}$$

When the credit constraint is binding—that is, $b = sh$, we can write the investment function in reduced form as

$$i = sh(r;y) + s\pi[sh(1 + r); \pi, z]. \tag{21}$$

It follows that

$$i_{(1+r)} = shs\,\pi_{b(1+r)}$$
$$+ (1 + r)sh_{(1+r)}s\,\pi_{b(1+r)} + sh_{(1+r)}. \tag{22}$$

Evidently, i_r can be negative; and is strictly decreasing in y. Denoting $\varepsilon(sh)$ as the interest elasticity of household savings, and (i) as the interest elasticity of private investment, we have

$$\varepsilon(i) = \alpha\{\varepsilon(sh) + s\,\pi_{b(1+r)}[1 + \varepsilon(sh)](1 + r)\}, \tag{23}$$

with α the proportion of total private savings held by households; it can be seen that at $r = 0$, $\varepsilon(i)$ is negative if

$$\varepsilon(sh) < -s\,\pi_{b(1+r)}/(1 + s\,\pi_{b(1+r)}). \tag{24}$$

impact of a relaxation of credit ceilings. If this change is autonomous (for example, if it is funded by a net capital inflow), the net effect is to increase investment by a factor of $(1 - s_2)$, which can be estimated from a direct estimate of equation (18). However, if the change is induced by an increase in real interest rates, the net effect has to incorporate the effect of increased debt-servicing costs faced by the firm; and, as equation (23) shows, this is likely to reduce total investment. We estimate $s\pi_{b(1 + r)}$ and $\varepsilon(sh)$, and from there, the implied interest elasticity of investment.

On Data and Trends

For the present, we concentrate on patterns of investment in the aggregate mining and manufacturing sector. All data are from the Organization for Economic Cooperation and Development's *OECD Economic Surveys: Greece* (OECD (various years)), which, in turn, are computed from raw data provided by the Bank of Greece. One of the problems is that direct data for corporate savings (either levels or rates) are not available; from 1967 onwards, the National Income Accounts of Greece include business savings in the category of private sector and household savings—that is, the residual after consumption and public savings. According to the OECD, "[t]he relatively small decline in private savings seems to conceal two divergent trends. Household savings appear to have increased since 1980, whereas business savings have fallen markedly" (OECD (1986), p. 36).

We estimated the corporate savings component as the increase in nominal gross capital formation in mining and manufacturing, minus the increase of long-term lending by the banking and financial services sector; clearly, this estimation makes two implicit assumptions: first, that the financing of long-term investment projects is obtained either from the banks or from corporate savings (including any possible interfirm credit); and second, that all long-term lending is in fact spent on gross investment. There is some empirical basis for the first kind of assumption. Tables 1 and 2 below portray recent data on the financing of investment in the Greek economy; Table 1 gives the sources of financing for aggregate investment, and Table 2, the sources of external finance for the private sector.

Tables 1 and 2 demonstrate that the only source of financing available to private firms other than bank loans is foreign capital; we have ignored this component in calculating corporate savings. Apart from being of a small order of magnitude, some of this capital inflow is in the form of ownership, and likely to be closely approximated by a proportional factor of corporate savings.

Table 1. Greece: Investment and Its Financing, 1981–85

(In percent of resources available for investment)

Resource	1981	1982	1983	1984	1985
Net lending from abroad	24.4	20.7	23.5	29.5	39.5
Private sector savings	109.7	110.3	105.1	107.3	105.5
Public sector	−34.1	−31.0	−28.5	−36.8	−45.0

Table 3 shows the average long-term lending rates for industry, the inflation rate in product prices, and the ex-post real interest rate. As evident from this table, real interest rates have been largely negative from 1972 on.

Figures 3–6 show trends in the calculated corporate savings component over time, real and nominal and relative to investment and to revenue. The negative trend in the corporate savings rates is clearly discernible in Figures 5 and 6. Figures 7 and 8 show trends in variables that are exogenous to the investment decision, factor prices, and the real cost of borrowing.

Table 2. Greece: Private Sector Financing, 1982–84

(In percent of total)

Resource	1982	1983	1984
Bank credit	86.9	80.2	79.3
Short term	46.0	38.9	42.1
Long and medium term	40.9	41.3	37.2
Security issues, net	00.2	00.3	00.7
Net capital inflows from abroad	12.9	19.5	20.0
Real estate	9.7	13.3	14.2
Business	3.1	5.7	4.4
Other	0.1	0.5	1.4

Empirical Analysis

We estimate the parameters of the corporate savings function in two versions. In the first version, we estimate directly the linearized version of the reduced form specified by equation (10), or equivalently, equation (20b). This yields a point estimate of the parameter $s_{b(1+r)}$; whereas direct estimation of equation (20) yields estimates for the interest elasticity of savings—that is, $\varepsilon(sh)$. We can use this to simulate the interest elasticity of investment expenditure at different real interest rates.

In the second version, we use the approximation suggested by equation (18). The long-run, or steady-state, corporate savings decision depends on profits and

Table 3. Greece: Interest Rates, 1961–85

(In percent)

Year	Lending Rate	Forward Inflation	Real Interest Rate (ex post)
1961	7.500000	1.458097	5.955072
1962	7.500000	1.676595	5.727380
1963	7.500000	1.766801	5.633663
1964	7.500000	3.009296	4.359513
1965	7.500000	3.483105	3.881692
1966	7.670000	1.628697	5.944485
1967	8.000000	−0.213671	8.231258
1968	8.000000	2.569604	5.294352
1969	8.000000	4.384100	3.464033
1970	8.000000	1.800001	6.090372
1971	8.000000	3.339899	4.509489
1972	8.000000	18.251000	−8.668848
1973	8.830000	22.588400	−11.223250
1974	10.830000	9.114801	1.571921
1975	11.000000	12.860600	−1.648583
1976	11.000000	11.235400	−0.211624
1977	11.000000	8.568705	2.239407
1978	11.580000	18.165800	−5.573356
1979	13.580000	24.328400	−8.645168
1980	17.250000	22.959200	−4.643166
1981	18.500000	18.965100	−0.390954
1982	16.500000	21.091500	−3.791760
1983	18.500000	20.162700	−1.383708
1984	18.500000	18.104900	0.334533
1985	18.500000	25.250700	−5.389751

Note: The inflation rate refers to prices of manufactured goods. The long-term lending rates were taken from Deleau (1987).

the availability of credit; the estimation yields a point estimate of s_2, and, hence, the long-run response of investment to changes in credit availability, as $(1 - s_2)$; this also gives us an approximation of the interest subsidy factor. We then model the deviation from the steady-state corporate savings level as an adjustment process, affected by anticipations of the real wage rate and the interest rate. Even though constraints on the availability of data preclude more ambitious modeling at the moment, there is strong evidence that these deviations (or equilibrium errors) have some persistence over time, even though they dissipate in the long run. This means, for example, that a large increase in the real wage rate leads to a cutback in current investment expenditures, and this negative

Figure 6. Greece: Corporate Savings as a
Percentage of Revenue, 1964–86

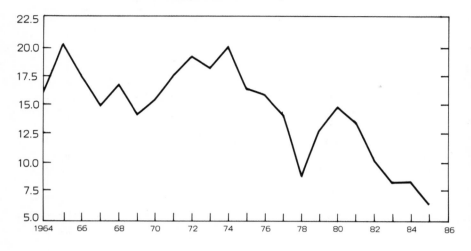

Figure 7. Greece: Real Wages

(Index, 1970 = 1)

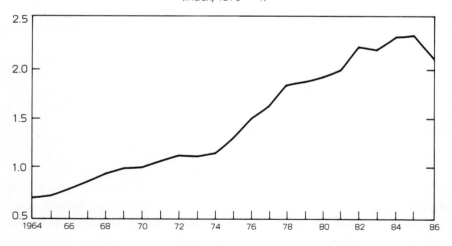

effect persists for a few periods, leading to investment cutbacks in subsequent periods as well.

Table 4 reports the results of the analysis of the corporate savings function. We used real revenues (that is, value added deflated by a product price index) to

Figure 8. Greece: Relative Price of Capital Goods

(Index, 1960 = 1)

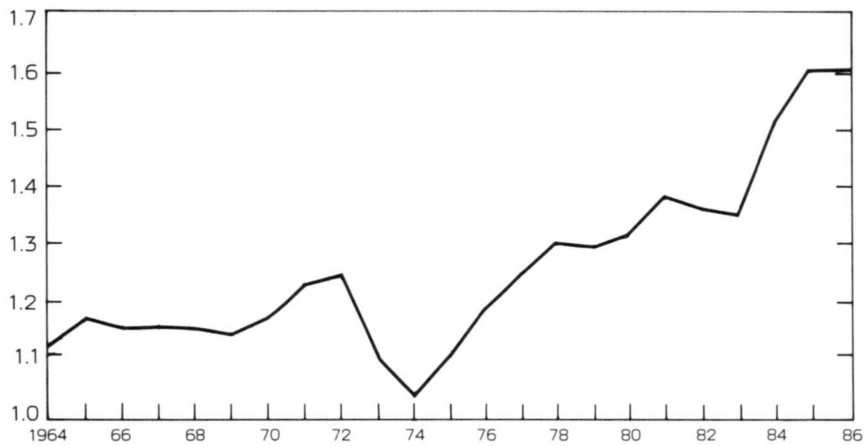

approximate profits, because of the unavailability of reliable data on sector-specific profits in the private sector. A first-order moving average term is incorporated to account for possible effects generated by capital accumulation, since real investment is endogenous. As it turns out, this is not statistically significant. Equation (25) estimates the relation with the assumption of perfect foresight; equation (26) reports the results of a "rational expectations" assumption, so that real wages and ex-post real interest rates are correctly anticipated on average, given current information. The estimation technique is instrumental variables (IV); the current real wage rate and real interest rate are used as instruments.

Equation (25)—that is, the perfect foresight hypothesis—yields a point estimate of 0.4309 for $s\pi_{b(1+r)}$, whereas the rational expectations hypothesis (equation (26)) yields 0.3089. In both versions, initial estimation with ρ (capital goods inflation) showed that its coefficient was statistically insignificant from zero.

To complete this version, we estimate an equation representing the interest elasticity of credit availability; that is, the responsiveness of long-term lending by banks to the mining and manufacturing sector to variations in the real interest rate (Table 5). We estimate in log linear form to get direct point estimates for $\varepsilon(sh)$; as in Table 4, we estimate the perfect foresight (equation (27)) and rational expectations (equation (28)) versions. In both versions, the interest elasticity parameter is not significantly different from zero, even though we will use the

Table 4. Greece: The Corporate Savings Function—Estimates for 1962–86

Corporate Savings Function	Coefficients							
	c	rev	$b(1 + r)$	w'	q	MA	R^2	D-W
Equation (25) OLS (t-ratios)	0.1754 (3.95*)	0.2570 (5.87*)	-0.4309 (1.89**)	-0.0486 (1.96**)	-0.148 (3.39*)	0.18 (0.68)	0.87	1.94
Equation (26) IV (t-ratios)	0.1433 (1.48*)	0.3021 (7.35*)	-0.3089 (2.33*)	-0.0820 (3.35*)	-0.1120 (1.06)	0.10 (1.09)	1.81	1.87

Note: The dependent variable is corporate savings in the mining and manufacturing sectors. All variables are deflated by the product price index. OLS denotes ordinary least squares; IV denotes instrumental variables; c refers to the constant term; rev denotes post-tax revenues; b denotes long-term borrowing from banks; w' is the (forward) index of manufacturing wages; q is the index of capital goods prices; MA is the one-period moving average; R^2 denotes the coefficient of determination; and D-W is the Durbin-Watson statistic; * denotes significance at 95 percent; and ** denotes significance at 90 percent.

Table 5. Greece: Credit Availability—Estimates, 1964–86

Long-Term Borrowing (log b)	Coefficients				
	c	log (y)	log (1 + r)	R^2	D-W
Equation (27)	−5.4760	2.0690	0.4077	0.79	1.73
OLS (t-ratios)	(12.85*)	(5.64*)	(0.20)		
Equation (28)	−5.4360	2.0342	0.1376	0.71	1.72
IV (t-ratios)	(3.75)	(3.67)	(0.02)		

Note: Dependent variable is the log of total long-term borrowing; OLS denotes ordinary least squares; IV denotes instrumental variables; c refers to the constant term; y denotes personal disposable income; r denotes the deposit rate by banks; R^2 denotes the coefficient of determination; D-W denotes the Durbin-Watson statistic; and * denotes significance at 95 percent.

point estimates to simulate the interest elasticity of ex-post investments. We have used the log of personal disposable income for the income variable.

Table 6 reports results of simulations for $\varepsilon(i)$, the interest elasticity of total investment, with $\alpha = 0.33$. This is actually the sample average for bank lending as a proportion of total investment.

As is evident from Table 6, the interest elasticity of total investment is negative, even at real interest rates as low as −10 percent, for both sets of point estimates. We had essentially the same results when simulations were done for actual rather than average levels of r and of α; these are not reported here but yielded negative estimates for the entire period 1964–86.

It may be useful to compare these results with a direct estimate of the interest elasticity of investment in the private manufacturing sector. To do this, we estimate the reduced form in log-linear form; the estimates are reported in Table 7 below. We included, as before, the log of personal disposable income, which affects credit availability; in addition, we included a measure of real wage increases, $d\log(w)$; the coefficient of this turns out to be positive, which possibly captures the "income effect" of real wage increases on investment. In addition, it appears that investment "overreacts" to current inflation; equation (29) demonstrates the fact that inflation has a positive effect on real investment over and above its effect on the real cost of debt servicing.

The estimate of the interest elasticity of investment is −1.94, which is considerably higher in absolute value than our simulations in Table 6. We had used the point estimates for the interest elasticity of bank credit, even though this was statistically insignificant; setting this equal to zero yields estimates of $\varepsilon(i)$ much closer to the estimate here: the average value is −1.654 for the sample period.

Table 6. Simulations for $\epsilon(i)$
Estimated Interest Elasticity of Investment

Real Interest Rate	(1)	(2)
−0.10000000	−0.04561265	−0.05895918
−0.05000000	−0.05562118	−0.06475735
0.00000000	−0.06562972	−0.07055553
0.05000000	−0.07563825	−0.07635371
0.10000000	−0.08564679	−0.08215188
0.15000000	−0.09565532	−0.08795006
0.20000000	−0.10566386	−0.09374824
0.25000000	−0.11567240	−0.09954641
0.30000000	−0.12568093	−0.10534459
0.35000000	−0.13568947	−0.11114277
0.40000000	−0.14569800	−0.11694094
0.45000000	−0.15570654	−0.12273912
0.50000000	−0.16571508	−0.12853730

Note: Column (1) uses ordinary least squares point estimates (equations (25) and (27)); column (2) uses instructional variables point estimates (equations (26) and (28)); for both columns, $\alpha = 0.33$.

For the second empirical version, we estimated the "steady-state" relation between real corporate savings, profitability, and borrowing as shown in Table 8.

This estimation yields a point estimate for s_2 of 0.9591; thus, the effect of an autonomous increase in credit availability on investment is measured as 0.0409. In addition, the size of the estimated coefficient suggests that, on average, the private sector expects a large effective subsidy rate on its borrowing—the point estimate is 24.4, with the approximation of $\tau = 0$.

Table 9 reports a simple dynamic version of the process of adjustment. Suppose $cs^*(t) = i^*(t) - b(t)$ is the "steady-state" level of intended investment; and $dcs(t)$ is defined as the discrepancy between actual and intended levels of corporate savings. We model the current discrepancy as responding to past levels of discrepancies (following from the dynamic error-correction rule) and to current shocks. We restrict the dynamic specification to a first-order autoregression, whereas current values of q and (expected) real wages represent shocks in factor prices. We are unable to employ an appropriately richer specification because of the small number of observations.

Equations (31) and (32) underline the relative importance of persistence in deviations from the steady state via the autoregressive term. At this point we have basically 19 points of data, whereas the estimation of "error-correction" models of adjustment to equilibrium needs much larger parameterizations, and a correspondingly large data set. We use this last version as essentially indicative

Table 7. The Investment Function

Investment	c	log(rev)	log(y)	log(1 + r)	dlog(w)	log(1 + inf)	MA(1)	MA(2)
Equation (29)	-0.161	-1.882	-1.201	-1.94	2.519	0.996	0.17	-0.06
OLS	(0.27)	(5.112)	(3.246)	(2.689)	(3.921)	(2.201)	(0.55)	(0.18)

Note: Dependent variable is the log of investment expenditure in the mining and maufacturing sectors; OLS denotes ordinary least squares; c refers to the constant term; rev is post-tax revenues; y denotes personal disposable income; r is the lending rate; w is the index of manufacturing wages; inf denotes inflation (percent change in consumer price index); MA(1) refers to the first-order moving average; and MA(2) refers to the second-order moving average. $R^2 = 0.947$; the Durbin-Watson statistic = 1.94.

Table 8. Greece: Corporate Savings—The Long Run, 1963–86

Long-Run Corporate Savings Function	c	rev	b	MA(1)	MA(2)	R²	D-W
Equation (30) OLS (t-ratios)	0.1457 (1.45)	0.1772 (2.29*)	−0.9591 (4.86*)	0.82 (2.21*)	0.20 (0.46)	0.81	1.93

Coefficients

Note: The dependent variable is corporate savings; OLS denotes ordinary least squares; c refers to the constant term; rev denotes post-tax revenue in the mining and manufacturing sectors; b denotes long-term borrowing; MA(1) is the first-order moving average; MA(2) is the second-order moving average; R² denotes the coefficient of determination; D-W is the Durbin-Watson statistic; and * denotes significance at 95 percent.

Table 9. Greece: The Adjustment Process for Corporate Savings

Change in Corporate Savings	c	dcs(-1)	w'	w''	q	$(1 + r)$	R^2	D-W
Equation (31) OLS (t-ratios)	0.1583 (1.88**)	0.3991 (1.79**)	-0.0126 (1.24)	—	-0.0214 (0.54)	-0.1125 (1.70**)	0.53	1.87
Equation (32) IV (t-ratios)	0.1616 (2.16*)	0.3785 (1.85**)	—	-0.0190 (2.54*)	—	-0.1342 (2.01**)	0.53	1.87

Note: The dependent variable is change in corporate savings; OLS denotes ordinary least squares; IV denotes instrumental variables; c refers to the constant term; dcs(-1) denotes change in corporate savings, lagged one period; w' is the (forward) index of manufacturing wages; w'' is the (current) index of manufacturing wages; q is the index of capital goods prices; r denotes the lending rate; R^2 denotes the coefficient of determination; D-W denotes the Durbin-Watson Statistic; * denotes significance at 95 percent; and ** denotes significance at 90 percent.

in nature, which can be set up as a framework to measure the longer-run effects of changes in real wages and in real interest rates.

III. Conclusions

We analyzed the investment decisions of firms subject to a borrowing constraint. It is widely believed that the low and, in particular, negative lending rates maintained by the banking sector in Greece have generated severe constraints on the availability of credit, and this may have accounted for the actual decline in real investment in the manufacturing sector.

If borrowing is indeed the major constraint on investment expansion, we should expect to observe an increase in corporate savings rates and, hence, a decline in the ratio of borrowed funds to total investment. This, in fact, is not what happened. Aggregate data clearly demonstrate the rise in the "debt/ investment" ratio; analysis of cross sectional data (at the two-digit level of classification) by Tsoris (1984) bears out that for the period 1958–81, there was an increase in this ratio, on average. Most of this increase was accounted for by major declines in the retained earnings rates of a few industries, which are precisely the ones that reported secular declines in their profitability rates.

This analysis suggests that interest rate management will be of limited effectiveness in increasing investment. We say "limited," because, at the aggregate level, the empirical exercise predicts a negative effect, even though a more detailed analysis of industry-specific data would show up the differential effects on individual industries. When firms are credit-constrained, the rate of return on capital, r^*, is in general not equal to the interest rate, and the size of this discrepancy can also vary quite substantially between industries. As a result, the effect of interest rate increases can differ, at the margin, across industry groups, and quite substantially so.

The analysis here entailed that the interest elasticity of investment depend on the interest elasticity of household savings. Our estimates of this parameter are small and statistically insignificant. Giovannini's (1985) findings were more or less the same with a large cross-country study. One caveat should be kept in mind: it is presumed that the real interest rates in our study were significantly lower than the "world" rate. If the increase in the domestic rate allows it to catch up with the world rate, there should be a (discontinuous) jump in credit availability, at least in theory, because of the inflow of foreign capital; presumably, $\varepsilon(sh)$ is infinite at this point. Alternately, we may think of this analysis as locally valid for r^* less than the world rate.

In an earlier paper, van Wijnbergen (1983) also suggested that increases in the bank rate need not increase investment in the "medium run." This argument was based on the supply of loanable funds. If households can lend directly to firms—in other words, if an unorganized money market provides secondary financial intermediation—the total funds available for investment can actually decrease if they go through banks that have to observe reserve requirements. Our argument is based more directly on the ex-ante investment decisions of firms; among other things, the short-run effect will in fact persist, and does not peter out in a "long-run" analysis.

This solution, of course, begs the question of why profitability rates have been decreasing, in spite of a fairly long period of declining investment. The analysis shows that the long-term increase in the product-wage rates must be one of the important factors, by virtue of both its statistical explanatory power in alternative parameterizations as well as its persistence over a fairly long period. The increase is a consequence of directly redistributive policies followed by a succession of governments. A major policy instrument has been expansion in public sector employment at rising real wages.

The interesting questions that this analysis opens up relate to optimal, or effective, financial reform methods that complement redistributive policy. In particular, we know, at least in theory, that in the presence of full equity markets, an increase in the wage bill can generate positive income effects on investment. It is possible that the transition to perfect capital markets can be more effectively achieved with reforms in equity, as opposed to debt markets, when accompanied by redistributive policies.

References

Deleau, M., "Industrial Investment in Greece: Analysis and Recommendations" (Athens: Ministry of National Economy, 1987).

Giovannini, Alberto, "Saving and the Real Interest Rate in LDCs," *Journal of Development Economics* (Amsterdam), Vol. 18 (August 1985), pp. 197–217.

International Monetary Fund, *Theoretical Aspects of the Design of Fund-Supported Adjustment Programs*, Occasional Paper No. 55 (Washington: International Monetary Fund, 1987).

Malinvaud, Edmond, *Profitability and Unemployment: Based on the Marshall Lectures Given at the University of Cambridge, 1978* (Cambridge: Cambridge University Press, 1980).

————, *The Theory of Unemployment Reconsidered* (New York: Blackwell, 2nd ed., 1985).

Organization for Economic Cooperation and Development, *OECD Economic Surveys: Greece* (Paris: OECD, various years).

Sargan, J.D., "The Consumer Price Equation in the Post War British Economy: An Exercise in Equation Specification Testing," *Review of Economic Studies* (Edinburgh), Vol. 47 (January 1980), pp. 113–35.

Tsoris, Nicholas D., *The Financing of Greek Manufacture*, Centre of Planning and Economic Research Studies No. 8 (Athens: Centre of Planning and Economic Research, 1984).

van Wijnbergen, S., "Interest Rate Management in LDC's," *Journal of Monetary Economics* (Amsterdam), Vol. 12 (September 1983), pp. 433–52.

Comment

Mario Arcelli

Since the beginning of my academic career, when I translated Professor Papandreou's book, *Economics as a Science*, into Italian, my estimation of Greek economists has been very high. I must say that the paper presented by Dutta and Polemarchakis fully lives up to my expectations, being a fine piece of economic and econometric analysis. Therefore, I feel honored to have been invited by the International Monetary Fund to comment on it. At the same time, I feel a bit uneasy about having to talk about Greek fiscal policy, which is hardly mentioned in the paper and can therefore be referred to only indirectly.

Dutta and Polemarchakis state in their paper that lending rates set by the Bank of Greece have been predominantly negative in real terms since 1973. Credit rates have been subsidized, and administrative controls on credit have been imposed. As a result, they say, one would expect credit availability to be restricted and private industrial investment to be constrained by the shortage of funds. However, survey data from Greek firms in the private manufacturing sector indicate the opposite. According to Deleau (1987),[1] most individual firms do not perceive a shortage of funds.

For the authors, this appears to be a puzzle, since it implies that even negative real interest rates do not provide an effective subsidy. Therefore, in order to solve the apparent puzzle, they provide us with an elaborate model of the process of investment decision making by Greek firms that attempts to reconcile the facts.

One should note before commenting on the model that conditions in the Greek economy are changing quickly, so that the Dutta-Polemarchakis analysis appears to be more relevant to past experience when interest rates were subsidized and there were credit ceilings than to the future. As the Annual Economic Report of the European Economic Community (EEC) for 1987–88 observes:

> Substantial progress has been made in reforming the financial system. Preferential interest rates for certain categories of operators have been abolished. The general level of interest rates, which previously had been lower than the rate of inflation, has

---

[1]M. Deleau, "Industrial Investment in Greece: Analysis and Recommendations" (Athens: Ministry of National Economy, 1987).

been raised and commercial banks have been granted a degree of freedom in fixing their lending rates. The strict administrative rules and regulations governing the administration of credit have been made more flexible and efforts have been made to place treasury bills and medium-term paper with private non-banks. Continuation of these efforts, together with the creation of an efficient non-bank financial market, should facilitate the implementation of monetary policy and contribute to the modernization of the financial system, which is essential for the development of the country.[2]

So much for the future. Coming back to the Dutta-Polemarchakis paper, one is faced with the problem of explaining why, in spite of negative real rates of interest, firms have not tried to borrow more at these rates and do not appear to have been constrained by financial shortages in their investment choices. The authors argue that bank credit is not the only source of investment finance and that firms use profit retention as the source of residual finance for their investment outlay. Corporate saving reveals itself to be the most important source of investment financing and might explain, according to Dutta and Polemarchakis, the puzzling apparent lack of perceived fund constraints. Corporate saving provides additional funds, which in many cases substitute for external financing; the choice between the two channels of investment financing would be consistent with an optimization process for finding the source of financing. The model of credit-constrained investment financing proposed by the authors is different from a simple model where firms react passively by setting their investment budget equal to the credit ceiling. In the Dutta-Polemarchakis model a firm derives its investment budget, its profit retention rate, and its dividend payout simultaneously, taking into account the credit ceiling and debt-servicing costs. Any firm behaves as a profit maximizer, and a representative shareholder maximizes a utility function in the two variables: dividend income and anticipated profits, which are inversely related to debt-servicing costs. Corporate saving, which is given by real retained profit, adds up to credit to provide investment financing. Increasing the credit limit would go, partly, toward increasing the dividend payout ratios.

In the Greek experience, according to the estimation of the model, the effect of an autonomous increase in credit availability on investment is measured by a coefficient equal to 0.0409. This result can be read as a proof of the relative lack of constraints on investment.

At this point, several possible explanations of the facts could be offered that have not been explored, or at least mentioned by the authors. One explanation could be provided by developments in investment in Greece over the past several years. Growth in gross fixed investment in real terms in plant and equipment was

---

[2]Commission of the European Communities, *Annual Economic Report, 1987–88* (Brussels, October 21, 1987), p. 105.

−8.2 percent of gross domestic product (GDP) in 1983, −0.9 percent in 1984, 4.4 percent in 1985, −6.5 percent in 1986, and 2.2 percent in 1987; whereas total investment growth was negative in each of those years except 1985. It is therefore not surprising that firms have not perceived any shortage of funds, even with credit ceilings. The growth path of investment has been slow (negative), because the rates of profitability have been declining as a consequence of strong increases in real wage rates and, in the more recent period, as a consequence of the stabilization policy. Of course, the empirical data can be reconciled with the results of the Dutta-Polemarchakis model, but it is not necessary to resort to such an optimizing process to explain the lack of shortage of funds for investments.

Another possible explanation is that the choice of investment projects might have been restrained by a high degree of uncertainty about the future, which required a compensating premium higher than that granted by a negative real interest rate. In such circumstances, entrepreneurs prefer to finance investment with corporate saving rather than engaging in ambitious projects with borrowed funds, which carry the risk of worsening the firm's financial structure and profitability. In this case, retained profits are not a residual source of investment financing. It is not so clear, at least to me, from the figures given in the text, that corporate saving is a residual source of financing.

Other possible explanations for the lack of a perceived shortage of investment funds include the absence of competitive market conditions and nonoptimal investment decisions.

It would be interesting to know whether the authors' choice was dictated by their evident preference for an elegant economic model or by their collection of convincing empirical evidence of generalized optimizing behavior by firms. The assumption of perfect foresight or of rational expectations concerning real wages and real interest in order to analyze the corporate savings function remains questionable—at least, to me.

But let me now return to some of the results of the model within the perspective of fiscal policy. It appears from the estimation of the model that a relaxation of the credit ceiling that was not induced by higher interest rates would lead to some improvement, if modest, in investment.[3] This result, as I said earlier, can be read as a proof that firms did not suffer from investment financing constraint. In addition, real interest rates were negative. Would Dutta and Polemarchakis then accept the conclusion implicit in the previous statements,

---

[3]A relaxation of the credit ceiling that was induced by higher interest rates would encourage household saving, and the net effect on investment would be negative.

that in Greece private investment was not crowded out by public sector expenditure? How to reconcile this conclusion with the fact that for a number of years the public sector in Greece has been expanding rapidly with a significant increase in public debt?

One could argue, on the one hand, that persistent high deficits in the current account of the balance of payments, which ranged from 4.7 percent of GDP in 1983 to 4.1 percent in 1984, 8.2 percent in 1985, 5.4 percent in 1986, and 4.2 percent in 1987, provided an additional source of real resources. Capital inflows from abroad have certainly helped to sustain an unstable path. But, on the other hand, if viewed from a structural perspective, the basic problem facing the Greek economy from 1980 to 1985 appears to have been the continuing decline in productive investment, brought about by high wage rate growth and an unfavorable climate for industrial activity associated with a wide-ranging regulation of markets. The fall in actual and expected profitability can therefore explain the negative rate of growth of productive investment.

The expansion of public expenditure has not been positive in this context, if one embraces the hypothesis that unemployment in Greece was of a classical rather than a Keynesian nature, following Malinvaud's (1985) classification. [4] One passage in the paper seems to support this interpretation. Noting the decline in profitability growth rates, the authors say that their empirical analysis "suggests that one of the major determinants of this decline . . . is the long-term increase in product-wage rates in manufacturing . . . " (p. 162).

Elements of repressed inflation were also present. The situation was made more complex in Greece by the deficit on the current account of the balance of payments, and by the rate of inflation—after fluctuating around 20 percent for a number of years, consumer prices were growing at a rate of 25 percent at the end of 1985.

Greek economic policy in the last few years, starting in 1985, has been quite appropriate; it is based on the prescriptions of a stabilization plan, supported by the EEC, designed to achieve an improvement in the balance of payments through a deliberate cutback of domestic demand, in order to stabilize the level of the external debt.

Wage policy, the key instrument for restraining domestic demand, was based on a system of degressive indexation focused on a targeted inflation rate and excluding the effects of import prices. In addition, only moderate growth was permitted for farm incomes. The strict incomes policy led to a 10 percent reduction in real wages in the period 1986–87.

---

[4]Edmond Malinvaud, *The Theory of Unemployment Reconsidered* (New York: Blackwell, 2nd ed., 1985).

Since the end of 1985, according to the EEC's Annual Economic Report for 1987–88, the government has been working on a phasing-out of price controls. This policy, combined with the moderate growth of wage costs and a consistent exchange rate policy, has contributed to a significant improvement in the financial position of enterprises, which is expected to lead to a significant upturn in productive investment. Thus, in view of the scale of the adjustment of real wage incomes in the past two years, wage policy can no longer be the main instrument for managing demand.

To avoid a deterioration in the balance of payments, reducing the public sector deficit will have to be the prime instrument of demand management. This will be difficult, EEC experts warn, since the social security deficit is tending to increase, and incomes policy will not contribute to the moderation of the public sector wage bill to the same extent as in the two years prior to 1987–88.

I will not discuss further the economic policy suggested for 1988, but it appears evident that the Greek economy is now on a better path than in past years. We must, however, be grateful to Dutta and Polemarchakis for their effort to clarify important issues of investment financing and firm behavior in past years. Their model is also important as an analytical tool.

Comment

Christian de Boissieu

This paper deals only incidentally with fiscal policy in a brief reference to the subsidized interest rates prevalent in Greece prior to the recent process of financial liberalization. Its main purpose is to study the behavior of firms facing a quantitative credit constraint and to analyze the role of corporate savings as a means to loosen this constraint and to disconnect the pace of capital accumulation from the constraints concerning credit. Since this paper analyzes the optimizing behavior of firms facing some additional constraint ("additional" in comparison with a general equilibrium solution), it also represents an application of second-best theory to the field of finance and investment.

To summarize some of Dutta and Polemarchakis's arguments, I find it useful to refer to the following diagram, which features different regimes for firms' financing structure.

Diagram 1. Financing Structure

		Self-financing	
		Yes	No
Credit rationing	Yes	A	B
	No		

The horizontal rows give information about the situation on the credit market, whereas the vertical columns concern the possibility or the impossibility of self-financing by firms. There are four possible regimes. The core of the argument presented in the paper under review is the following.

In a B-regime, the adjustment is on the saving function, which, in this situation, is the short side of the loanable funds market. Therefore, actual investment is an increasing function of interest rates, since the rise in interest rates induces more saving (in this B-regime, we only have to consider household savings, since there is no room for corporate savings). The B-regime gives the same conclusions as the McKinnon-Shaw model.

In an A-regime, corporate saving has to be considered. In this regime, the short side of the loanable funds market is now the investment function. As a result, actual investment is a decreasing function of interest rates, with the two effects working in the same direction: that is, the traditional Keynesian "profitability effect," and a "liquidity effect," by which a rise in interest rates diminishes, other things being equal, firms' liquidity and the possibility of self-financing.

All this means in Dutta and Polemarchakis's paper is that self-financing explains the switching from one regime to the other. The discussion presented above concerns only the first row of the diagram. I think it is crucial to answer the following two questions. First, can we assume or confirm the existence of credit rationing? The authors do not insist on this point. Some extra information (I shall come back to this point later) would be useful in the case of Greece as it is for other countries. Second, if there is some credit rationing, where does it come from? It may be the consequence of transitory or permanent credit ceilings, or it may be the consequence of rational behavior by commercial banks. Since credit ceilings have been permanent for a long time in Greece, and since the authors present no reference to the well-known literature on the rationality of credit rationing, I am guessing that they have the first interpretation in mind.

Like most southern European countries (and like France until the end of the 1970s), Greece is an "overdraft economy." According to Hicks, "In a pure overdraft economy where firms kept no liquid reserves, they would be wholly dependent, for their liquidity, on the banks."[1] On more empirical grounds, indirect finance procedures (that is, financial intermediation) are predominant, and capital markets play a residual role. This has been the case in Greece, as suggested by the figures given by the authors, but recent efforts to promote new financial instruments and higher real interest rates will encourage the development of direct finance. For structural reasons extensively developed by work at the Bank of France between 1975 and 1980, overdraft economies incorporate specific features, such as a high degree of rigidity in nominal interest rates; the

---

[1]John Hicks, *The Crisis in Keynesian Economics* (Oxford: Blackwell, 1974), p. 54.

prevalence of indirect monetary control (credit ceilings); and the quasi-certainty that commercial banks will be refinanced at the central bank (which implies a causation between the money stock and the monetary base that is the opposite of the usual causation implied by money multiplier models). This paper is a useful contribution to the literature on the overdraft economy, which highlights micro-economic aspects, in particular the optimal corporate savings decision (and dividend policy) in an intertemporal model with a permanent credit constraint.

The authors propose for Greece a loanable funds theory of investment, including a hierarchy between the sources of financing, which is close to a lexicographic order. It can be called a loanable funds theory, since, during the period, the amount of investment is determined by the sum of the credit limit and retained profits. There is a lexicographic order for the financing, since retained profits intervene as a means of financing when the credit constraint is binding, and not before. This analysis raises several questions.

Is it realistic to assume that the credit constraint is always binding? Even in an economy with permanent credit ceilings and real returns on capital goods well above (structurally negative) real interest rates, we may observe an excess supply of credits at current interest rate levels (instead of an excess demand) due to such developments as low real growth and low expected demand for goods. Then, as I said earlier, it would be interesting to use extra information to determine whether credit ceilings are binding or not. The French experience with credit ceilings showed that penalty rates on parallel credit markets and short-run movements in the transaction velocity (or a related measure) can sometimes be used as relevant proxies for the state of equilibrium or dis-equilibrium on the credit market. It would be valuable to have some of this information for Greece.

Positive leverage due to the positive gap between real return on capital and real interest rates may justify the lexicographic order between external financing (from banks) and internal financing. But this argument must be weighted by the opposite Kaleckian argument of "increasing risk." In the model, internal financing is complementary to external financing because the credit constraint is effective. My feeling is that, within the credit ceiling, firms may trade off between the two types of financing, taking into account the respective costs (including the opportunity cost of self-financing) and the risk structure.

Instead of focusing on the influence of interest rates on investment, it would be more relevant to study the impact of profitability (that is, the difference between the real rate of profit and real interest rates) on investment. In Greece, before the adoption of the stabilization program in October 1985, the profitability of physi-cal capital was low, and therefore "classical" unemployment represented a high proportion of global unemployment. The main objective of the stabilization program was to raise, through wage disindexation, the share of profit in national income and to restore profitability—that is, to raise increases in the real rate of profit above the rise in real interest rates caused by disinflation and financial liberalization.

In the model which is proposed by Dutta and Polemarchakis, commercial banks are rather passive. This assumption seems correct for stylizing the functioning of a financial system that is traditionally "overdetermined"; the Greek monetary authorities used to fix interest rates and the volume of credit. Notwithstanding this structural phenomenon, it would perhaps be difficult but enlightening to articulate the macroeconomic constraint on credit (introduced by the monetary authorities), and the microeconomic rationing behavior of commercial banks, mainly based on the assessment of borrowers' default risk.

In theory and in the empirical estimates, nonlinearities may play an important role, due to the existence of many thresholds. The authors estimate with great ingenuity the effect of an autonomous increase in credit availability, and its split between investment and dividends. The respective weights of the two influences may vary with the level of the capital stock and the relative factor cost (real wages over real interest rates) and the attainment of lower or upper thresholds for these variables. There is also a puzzling gap between the economic analysis and the empirical result. Is it consistent to assume that the credit constraint is binding and restraining capital accumulation, and to show that, according to the data, when it is relaxed, 96 percent of the relaxation is used for dividend payments, and only 4 percent for investment financing?

This paper is a contribution to the analysis of spillover effects from the credit market to the market for capital goods. For a firm facing a credit constraint, the ways to circumvent, at least partially, such a constraint are numerous. For example, firms may resort to external financing. In an overdraft economy, the bond market and the stock market can be used only marginally. Three potential degrees of freedom are available: (1) capital inflows from abroad; the figures show that they represent an increasing proportion of the external financing of Greek private firms (20 percent in 1984); the tightness of exchange controls conditions the use of this channel; (2) trade credit (studies for various Organization for Economic Cooperation and Development (OECD) countries suggest that trade credit is endogenous to the stance of monetary policy); and (3) commercial paper procedures, which may exist even without a formal commercial paper market.

Firms may also resort to internal financing—that is, increases in profitability and corporate savings due to wage disindexation (which is very important in Greece since the adoption of the stabilization program) and increase in prices (for price-making firms).

The authors favor adjustments through profitability and the corporate savings decision. The lesson I draw from the French experience of credit constraints is that we need to develop microeconomic models explaining the choices firms make between alternative ways to circumvent credit constraints. Those models, incorporating traditional constraints and extra constraints concerning the external environment (such as exchange controls), will present second-best solutions adapted to quantitative constraints on certain types of financing. These solutions, dependent on relative costs and interest rate risk, among others, may be a combination of internal and external financing (and of the different channels within each category), rather than one-dimensional. For instance, I suspect that given such a permanent credit constraint as Greece has experienced, informal commercial paper procedures may have developed between firms, in order to finance not only short-term investments but also a part of long-run investments. Since trade credit and commercial paper have a direct impact on the velocity of money, even piecemeal information about the evolution of transaction velocity (or some proxy of this velocity, like the rate of turnover of deposits) could be relevant.

The paper includes puzzling relationships between credit and saving. In the model that leads to empirical estimates, the credit ceiling set by the banking sector is endogenous, and determined by household savings collected by the banking sector. The analysis leaves the world of the overdraft economy and focuses on a system with pure financial intermediation, without net money creation. If the credit ceiling is set by the banking sector on a voluntary basis—that is, without being imposed by the central bank—the model must add to the existing equations other equations representing rational behavior by banking firms, given their assessment of borrowers' default risk. If the credit ceiling is imposed by the monetary authorities, we are more perplexed: what can be the justification for a credit ceiling policy in an economy where financial intermediaries only transfer private savings, and where there is no net money creation to fill the gap between ex-ante saving and investment? The consistency of the interesting analysis presented by Dutta and Polemarchakis would be, I think, enhanced by a treatment of the relationship between stocks and flows, in particular, between credit and saving, which would be better adapted to the financial system they are studying in this paper.

Comment

Augusto Graziani

The purpose of Dutta and Polemarchakis's paper is to examine the the impact exerted by credit policies (and more specifically by interest rate management) on investment decisions taken by firms in the mining and manufacturing sectors in Greece. The analysis is cast in macroeconomic terms, in that the authors analyze the mining and manufacturing sectors as a whole.

The authors argue that credit policy is important, because, in the case of Greece, in addition to retained profits, bank credit is a major source of investment finance. In fact, they state that finance coming from domestic financial markets has been practically nonexistent. At the same time, they disregard the effects of capital inflows from abroad, which leaves *invested profits* as the only source of long-term finance. On the liquidity side, they neglect altogether the possible presence of money creation due to government deficits. In their model, there is therefore only one source of liquidity—namely, *credit creation by banks*.

The authors assume, both on the theoretical and the empirical level, that private investment is financed by two possible sources only: *long-term bank borrowing* and *retained profits*, or corporate saving (equation (20c), p. 168). Consequently, the main problem firms are confronted with is to determine the optimal mix of the two possible sources of finance, on the assumption that one of them, namely bank credit, is rationed and that investment decisions themselves depend on the rate of interest.

The authors assume that total household savings are kept as bank deposits. Banks, which are considered as *financial intermediaries*, are assumed to collect deposits and to lend liquidity out to firms, which use it for financing investment.

Empirical investigation leads the authors to the conclusion that investment in Greek industry has been mostly financed by retained profits and only marginally by long-term bank credit. In their view, any increase in bank credit is likely to produce an increase in dividend payments rather than in investment levels. This result, the authors conclude, contradicts the widespread idea that investment activity is severely constrained by credit rationing.

The analysis of corporate profits as a source of investment finance is not objectionable. The authors correctly emphasize the importance of internal finance, and its dependence on the level of interest charges and consequent

193

financial burdens. However, the consideration of bank credit as a second possible source of investment finance is apt to raise more serious questions.

One question arises from the authors' definition of banks as financial intermediaries, whose principal activities are collecting savings and financing investment. In a theoretical model, there is no problem with defining banks as brokers. This means that the very moment savings are deposited with a bank, liquidity is lost to savers and passed on to firms. In this case, liquidity is actually transmitted from savers to investors, and banks act as real intermediaries.

However, this definition of banking activity becomes illegitimate when it is applied to an analysis of historical data. In present-day practice, bank deposits are in the form of accepted means of payment, and the opening of a deposit implies no loss of liquidity to the depositor. This also implies that any time a bank finances a firm, the bank is not transmitting to it liquidity collected elsewhere, but is actually creating new liquidity without destroying any previously existing liquidity. It is certainly true that a single bank, by collecting deposits, acquires new reserves. But the whole banking system acquires no new reserves just from the movement of deposits from one bank to the next; the only way the system gets extra reserves is to borrow them from the central bank (or acquire them as a consequence of a government deficit). Even if banks could really finance investment (and, as we shall see, this is a very dubious point), they would definitely not finance it by means of liquidity gathered by collecting deposits.

Another implication of the fact that deposits are a means of payment is that as a rule savers do not keep the whole of their savings in bank deposits. (Of course, this can be legitimately assumed. But the implications of a similar assumption should not be forgotten—namely, that if total yearly savings were added to bank deposits, the quantity of money would be increasing each year by the whole amount of households' savings.) Rather, households tend to consider their bank deposit as a cash balance whose amount is variable, and they will add to it only when its current level deviates from whatever is considered optimum.

Firms borrow from banks in order to finance current production costs. The amount of borrowing therefore depends on production levels and production costs. If we consider firms as a whole, disregarding internal transactions, and assuming a closed economy and no government sector, the amount of borrowing coincides with the wage bill. It has no closer connection with the level of investment than it has with the level of consumption or of government expenditure. Once firms have been financed for the whole amount of their current costs and the wage bill has been paid, two extreme cases can be envisaged.

In the first case, households spend the whole of their money income either on the goods market or on the financial market, where they buy securities issued by firms. In this case, the amount of bank borrowing is always equal to the wage bill. Each period, new liquidity is borrowed from banks, while at the same time an inflow of the same amount comes in from sales of goods or from issues of securities.

In the second possible case, households regularly add a fraction of their income to their bank deposits. In this case, the liquidity that goes back to firms is lower than the liquidity paid out as wages, and the amount firms have to borrow from banks becomes higher and higher over time.

In the first case, bank credit can be defined as short-term credit, not because it is temporary, but because of its nature as a "revolving fund." In the second case, in each period a fraction of bank credit drops out of the revolving fund, and firms need what might be called permanent or "long-term" bank credit.

In both cases however, the function of bank credit is to finance cash balances held by agents (in the simplified case under examination, where intrafirm transactions are disregarded, total cash balances are held by households), and has nothing to do with investment. The amount of bank credit outstanding is related to the wage bill, to the payments system prevailing in the market, and to households' demand for cash. (In a pure credit economy, with no central bank and no legal tender, the amount of bank credit will cover the total money stock.) In any case, bank credit is not related to investment decisions or to the requirements of investment financing. Given the wage bill, firms might decide either to run down investments to zero and to produce only consumer goods, without reducing by one penny the amount of their bank debt; or to double investment expenditure by correspondingly reducing the production of consumer goods, without increasing their bank debt.

Although bank debt has no relation to investment, it is closely related to the demand for money. Given the wage bill, any increase in the demand for cash will increase the long-term bank debt of firms, even if investment is constant. In the extreme opposite case in which liquidity preference is zero (all money income of households is immediately spent on goods or securities), firms would have no bank debt, whatever the level of investment. Since bank debt depends on the demand for money and not on investment, a high level of bank debt does not mean that investment is particularly high or that sources of finance other than bank credit are lacking.

Since the function of bank credit is to finance the overall costs of production (or to supply cash balances required by agents, which is the same thing) and not to supply investment finance, investment can only be financed on the financial market or with firms' profits. If, as in the case of Greece as described by Dutta and Polemarchakis, financial markets are practically nonexistent and if foreign capital is disregarded, retained profits are the only possible source of investment finance. If banks were to finance investment, they could not do so by supplying credit, but by buying capital goods themselves, something they could only do by using profits earned from banking activities. But this is again a special case of investment being financed through corporate profits.

The above considerations can be restated in a somewhat simplified way in terms of standard macroeconomic theory. The investment plans of an individual firm can be financed by bank credit. But at the moment investment is performed (a new plant is built, or new capital goods are produced), liquidity made available by banks becomes income for the recipients of investment expenditure. The increase in income will continue until additional savings equal additional investments. Therefore, in any ex-post situation, investment is always financed by saving no matter what form it takes, whether domestic or foreign (equal to a deficit in the trade balance). In any case, it is not bank credit, no matter how the initial investment expenditure has been financed.

Because investment, like any other kind of expenditure, can (and probably must) be initially financed by bank credit, whereas final financing can only be supplied by saving, no empirical analysis of statistical data will ever find that investment has been financed by bank credit. This is another way of repeating the old Keynesian truth that in any ex-post situation savings and investment are necessarily identical.

It is of course possible, or even probable, that more generous bank credit may make possible a higher level of investment expenditure. Availability of bank credit can therefore remove a constraint, or even be a stimulus to higher investment, which will bring about a higher level of money (or possibly real) income. But once investment is performed, two things will happen: the higher investment will be matched by higher saving; and bank credit will be equal to the existing money balances and, although satisfying the current demand for money, will not be financing investment.

Since the function of bank credit is to supply ex-ante financing to cover overall costs of production, no direct correlation can exist between bank credit and investment. It is perfectly legitimate to assume, as the authors do, that bank credit is spent wholly or partially on investment projects. But since ex-post investment finance is necessarily supplied by savings, no empirical relationship between investment levels and the amount of bank credit can be found in statistical data.

Of course, if the relationship between the money stock and nominal income is stable, and if the investment multiplier is also stable, bank credit will be positively related to investment. But no matter how successful, any similar statistical test will always be measuring the demand for money and not the financing of investment. Any attempt to test the existence of a direct relationship between bank credit and investment is devoid of any theoretical basis.

Financial Regulation, Implicit Taxes, and Fiscal Adjustment in Italy

Franco Bruni, Alessandro Penati, and Angelo Porta*

Italy has a rapidly growing public debt, which exerts a pervasive influence on the working of its financial markets. Heavy administrative controls have been imposed on both domestic and international flows of funds. In recent years, fiscal adjustment has become more difficult because of a huge increase in real interest rates, which has followed in the wake of a process of financial deregulation.

This paper is concerned with the relation between government deficit and direct controls on financial markets. Section I presents an accounting framework to analyze the increase of Italian public debt during the last ten years; in particular, it estimates the impact of changes in interest rates and the amount of seigniorage collected by the Treasury.

Sections II and III examine the administrative controls that have been used to sustain the private sector's demand for government bonds and monetary base, and thus to collect implicit taxes to help finance the deficits. These sections also describe the recent trend toward liberalization. Section IV analyzes the relation between the "tax from controls" and the well-known concept of "inflation tax." Section V looks at the stock market and discusses the consequences of controlling international capital movements on the cost of raising equity capital by the corporate sector and the implications for the working of the crowding-out mechanism. Section VI contains some concluding comments on the possible effects of financial deregulation and its impact on the process of fiscal adjustment.

---

*Franco Bruni was principally responsible for Sections I and IV; Alessandro Penati, for Section V; and Angelo Porta, for Sections II and III. However, the authors retain joint responsibility for the entire paper and for any errors. The authors gratefully acknowledge the comments from participants in the seminar. The authors also gratefully acknowledge financial support from Consiglio Nazionale delle Richerche.

I. Accounting for Italian Public Debt Growth

During the last 12 years, the real value of the Italian public debt held outside the central bank increased at an average annual rate of about 10.5 percent; its ratio to gross domestic product (GDP) is now around 78 percent (93 percent including the part held by the central bank), having increased at a rate of around 3.5 percentage points a year.

This growth of public indebtedness is probably unsustainable.[1] To analyze its impact on financial markets, it is useful to divide it into three parts: first, the contribution of the public sector *deficit net of interest* expenses; second, the average *real ex-post interest rate* paid to private sector holders of the debt; and third, the negative contribution of the *Treasury's seigniorage* obtained by borrowing from the central bank. Both the second and the third components have to be computed net of the Treasury's interest payments on its balances with the central bank,[2] which in Italy approximately correspond to the payment by the central bank of a 5.5 percent interest rate to the banking system on its compulsory reserve deposits.

Table 1 shows this breakdown of the rate of growth of real public debt. Table 2 presents the equivalent breakdown of the increase in the debt-to-GDP ratio, where the real growth rate of the denominator is subtracted from the real interest rate component. (See Appendix for an explanation of the simple algebra used for the calculation.)

The analysis can go deeper if the Treasury seigniorage is also broken down. Seigniorage is obtained when the deficit is financed via the central bank's issue of the monetary base. New injections of these issues will find their place in the private sector portfolio for three reasons. First, a certain amount of inflation will develop, cutting the real value of the pre-existing base. Second, an increase in the real demand for money base can take place as a consequence of a change in real income and/or in the velocity of circulation of the base. Third, the composition of the monetary base can change, with an increase in the portion issued to finance the Treasury. Thus, for a given real demand for total monetary base, the private sector will accept a larger amount of the Treasury base when the other

---

[1]In the theoretical literature on the sustainability of public debt growth, Galli (1985) and Spaventa (1987a) have written on Italy's problems; specific discussions of the Italian case and relevant figures can be found in Spaventa (1984); Cividini, Galli, and Masera (1987); and Spaventa (1987b). A general review of theoretical and policy problems can be found in Buiter (1985).

[2]This amount must therefore be estimated and subtracted from the figures available on both the *total* interest payments of the Treasury and on its borrowing from the Bank of Italy. Salvemini and Salvemini (1987) contains useful institutional and statistical information on the Treasury's indebtedness with the Bank of Italy, the interest payments to which the Bank should be entitled, and the portion of them that is rebated to the government.

Table 1. Italy: Breakdown of Growth Rate of Real
Value of Public Debt Held Outside the Central Bank, 1976–87

(Average yearly rates in percent)

Years	Growth Rate of Real Debt	=	Contribution of:		
			Deficit Net of Interest	+ Real Interest Rate on Debt	− Treasury's Seigniorage
1976–81	8.8		17.0	−3.5	4.7
1982–87	12.2		10.8	4.0	2.6
1976–87	10.4		13.5	0.3	3.4
1984–87	10.7		8.3	5.3	2.9

Note: See equation (1) in the Appendix. Calculations are based on Bank of Italy data and official forecasts. The decomposition for 1987 has been partially estimated by the authors; it is not exact, and small errors of approximation have been distributed proportionally for rounding-off purposes.

parts of the base (issued or destroyed as a counterpart to changes in official reserves and/or in the central bank's credit to the private sector) decrease or become proportionally smaller. Table 3 evaluates the contribution of these three causes of the "seigniorage tax" collected by the Treasury, subtracting the negative contribution of the Treasury's interest payments to the central bank. The tax can be expressed as the product of a tax rate and a tax base,[3] and the latter can be related to the stock of nonmonetary debt or to GDP. (See Appendix for a formal derivation of the analytical division.)

Table 1 shows that in the post-1982 years the real debt growth rate was much higher than in the previous six-year period, in spite of the much smaller contribution of the accumulation of deficits net of interest expenses. This rise in the growth of debt is mainly explained by the huge increase in the real interest rate paid on the debt, although the more moderate resort to the seigniorage tax was also partly responsible. If one focuses on the last four years, the increase in the interest component is even more impressive.

---

[3]Seigniorage is also collected on the portion of the monetary base issued through channels other than the financing of the Treasury. It will accrue to a consolidated public sector that includes the central bank. To the extent that this portion of the base has nonindexed financial assets as a counterpart on the asset side of the central bank's balance sheet, the proceeds of the inflation tax may be retransferred to the issuers of those assets (foreign central banks or domestic commercial banks). To the extent that the central bank keeps the proceeds of seigniorage, they can be transferred in one way or another to the Treasury, net of the cost of running the bank and issuing the base. But if this happens, they will decrease the total deficit instead of increasing the portion of the deficit that is considered to be financed with direct Treasury seigniorage. To calculate the latter, only the Treasury's monetary base should be taken into account.

Table 2. Italy: Breakdown of Change in Ratio of Nonmonetary Public Debt to GDP

Years	Average Yearly Change in GDP Ratio (in percent)	=	Real Interest Rate on Debt Less Real Growth of GDP (in percent)	×	Debt/GDP Ratio	+	Deficit Net of Interest (in percent of GDP)	−	Treasury's Seigniorage (in percent of GDP)
					Contribution of:				
1976–81	1.6		−6.9		0.42		6.6		2.1
1982–87	5.4		1.7		0.62		6.1		1.7
1976–87	3.3		−2.4		0.51		6.4		1.9
1984–87	4.3		2.2		0.70		4.9		2.1

Note: See equation (2) in the Appendix and Note to Table 1.

Table 3. Breakdown of Italian Treasury's Seigniorage, 1976–87

(Average yearly rates, in percent except where otherwise noted)

Years	Inflation (1)	Change in Real Stock of Total Monetary Base			Change in Treasury Base/ Monetary Base Ratio (5)	Avg. Interest Rate on Treasury Monetary Base (6)	Total (1)+(4)+(5)–(6) (7)	Seigniorage Tax Base (monetary base of the Treasury)		Total Seigniorage	
		Real GDP Growth (2)	Velocity (3)	Total (2)–(3) (4)				(percent of debt*) (8)	(percent of GDP) (9)	(7)x(8) (percent of debt**) (10)	(7)x(9) (percent of GDP) (11)
1976–81	16.6	3.4	3.0	0.4	–1.8	4.1	11.1	0.42	0.19	4.7	2.1
1982–87	10.1	2.2	–0.7	2.9	1.4	3.2	11.2	0.23	0.15	2.6	1.7
1976–87	13.4	2.8	1.2	1.6	–0.2	3.6	11.2	0.30	0.17	3.4	1.9
1984–87	7.5	3.1	–1.8	4.9	4.2	3.3	13.3	0.22	0.16	2.9	2.1

Note: See equation (1) in the Appendix and Note to Table 1. The average interest rate on the monetary base has been estimated by setting the rate on the overdraft account of the Treasury with the Bank of Italy at 1 percent, and the rate on Treasury notes and bonds held by the Bank at 5.5 percent.

*Public debt held by the private sector.

The picture looks the same in Table 2, which shows a breakdown in the increase in the debt-to-income ratio. The third column of the Table makes it clear that besides the increase in the real rate of interest, which in the last few years has been significantly higher than GDP growth (as shown in the second column), the explosion of interest expenses was caused by the higher debt-to-income ratio accumulated over time.

When seigniorage is measured as a percent of GDP, as in Table 2, its reduction during the 1980s does not appear so strong; to be sure, in the four years 1984–87, the weight of Treasury seigniorage returned to its average level during the high-inflation period of 1976–81,[4] and constituted a high percentage of total explicit tax revenues.[5] This development makes the recent strength of debt growth more worrisome, because it can hardly be considered the result of a more prudent resort to monetary financing. It also makes clear that seigniorage does not coincide with the inflation tax.

We can now consider Table 3, which is a breakdown of seigniorage. Columns 8 and 9 show a definite decrease in the seigniorage tax base, even if, when expressed in proportion to GDP, the trend appears somewhat weak and has not continued in more recent years. The stock of Treasury indebtedness with the central bank remains high and constitutes a robust base from which seigniorage can be extracted in favor of the Treasury. Nevertheless, the decrease in that stock (in proportion to total debt and GDP) is the only cause of the lower weight of tax seigniorage in the post-1982 period, because, as shown in column 7, the tax rate has remained constant in the two periods of the past 12 years (1976–81 and 1982–87), but has clearly increased in the years 1984–87.

How could this happen with a sharply decreasing inflation rate? The answer can be found in columns 4 and 5 of Table 3. In the last four to five years, the real demand for total monetary base has been rising rapidly because of a pronounced decrease in its velocity of circulation (see column 3); at the same time, a higher

---

[4]Also from the calculations performed in a recent paper, Buiter (1987) concludes that "seigniorage seems to have disappeared as a serious source of government revenue in the main industrial countries (*except for Italy*)," p. 74 (emphasis added). Giavazzi (1987) estimates seigniorage in European Economic Community countries, taking into account the total creation of monetary base: in proportion to GDP, Italy comes third, after Portugal and Greece, with 2.3 percent in the 1979–86 period (3.4 percent in 1971–78); the percentage for Spain is only 1.8; and for France and the Federal Republic of Germany, 0.6 percent and 0.3 percent, respectively.

[5]The percentage is above 6 percent, and among European countries only Portugal and Greece have a higher percentage; it is slightly lower in Spain, about 1 percent in France, and below 1 percent elsewhere. See Giavazzi (1987) Table 1, p. 42. Does this mean that in an optimal taxation framework, explicit taxes should substitute for seigniorage in Italy? See Phelps (1973) and Mankiw (1987). The question is not easy to answer, because one has to consider that the collection of taxes has different social costs and produces different distortions, depending on the structure of the economy.

proportion of its supply has been provided through the Treasury's financing.[6] Had the ratio of GDP to monetary base, and the proportion of the monetary base issued in favor of the Treasury, been stable since 1984, the same seigniorage could have been collected by the Treasury, other things being equal, if the yearly inflation rate had been only 6 percentage points (1.8 percent + 4.2 percent) higher; that is, if prices had increased at about the same rate as in 1983.

The increase in the base's velocity is in part a consequence of the behavior of money velocity, an international phenomenon that is not easily explained but that is definitely related to the decrease in interest rates and inflation. However, as we argue in Section IV, the higher demand for monetary base has also been caused by a compulsory reserve regulation imposed on banks, which has functioned as a taxing device to collect seigniorage. The increase in the Treasury's monetary base in relation to the total monetary base cannot be attributed entirely to a strategy directed toward collecting seigniorage; it is rather the indirect result of exchange rate policy and the destruction of the monetary base through the balance of payments.

It is fairly unlikely that both velocity and the Treasury share of high-powered money will be able to change in the same direction and at the same speed in the near future. This will complicate the problem of stabilizing the rate of growth of public debt in the coming years. If the real rate of interest, the rate of inflation, and the rate of growth of GDP stay at present levels, the reduction in the deficit net of interest will have to be very strong and fast, in order to make up for a probable decrease in the collection of seigniorage.

To better understand the past dynamics of the various components of Italian public debt growth and the current and future problem of fiscal adjustment, *administrative controls* on financial markets have to be taken into consideration. We can think of them as a form of *implicit taxation*, which can in part substitute and/or complement Treasury seigniorage, even if, unlike Treasury seigniorage, they do not have a universally acknowledged fiscal dimension. We shall try to show how the "tax-from-controls" concept can be especially helpful in a discussion of the behavior of the interest component of debt accumulation; it can also be

---

[6]To be sure, the average value of the velocity of circulation of monetary base with respect to GDP (GDP/M) was somewhat higher in the 1982–87 period than the average of the preceding six years. This fact, together with a stable value of the average ratio of Treasury's to total high-powered money (MT/M), led to the noted decrease in the seigniorage tax base (MT/GDP). But within the last period, and specifically from 1984 on, there has been a sharp decrease in velocity, corresponding to a sharp rise in the real stock of monetary base (more than 20 percent in four years), and accompanied by a strong increase in the ratio of Treasury's to total base (approximately 18 percent, or 4.2 percent a year, as reported in Table 3), which at the end of 1983 was much lower than in the middle of the 1970s. In the calculation of the seigniorage tax rate, what matters are the changes within the period.

used to help explain the working of the seigniorage-inflation tax mechanism and the reaction of the noninterest deficit to monetary stabilization.

II. Controls Sustaining Demand for Public Bonds

Administrative controls on domestic and international financial flows can have the indirect effect of artificially sustaining the private sector's demand for public bonds for any given level of their interest yield by lowering the interest rate required to finance a given public deficit through the issue of bonds. The decrease in the interest cost of public sector borrowing that is obtained in this way can be considered an implicit tax collected by the Treasury.

The presence of a substantial tax of this kind is undoubtedly the explanation for the significant negative differential between the real interest cost of Italian public debt and the international real interest rate that obtained during the 1976–81 period.[7] Conversely, the removal of an important set of financial controls is certainly one of the main reasons for the huge increase of the interest cost that took place, as mentioned above, after 1982. A reintroduction of controls might therefore be considered one of the instruments required to bring about fiscal adjustment by slowing down the rate of growth of public debt. However, the negative effects and distortions caused by this solution should be stressed. Controls diffuse the pressures that would otherwise force the authorities to make the political decision to tackle the first-best solution—that is, to reduce the basic deficit, net of interest, and to rationalize the structure of taxes and public expenditure so as to enhance the productivity of the public (and private) sector. In what follows, we shall comment on both the distortions and on the decrease of fiscal discipline that we think result from financial protectionism.

The characteristics and time profile of the main administrative controls that have been phased in and out of the Italian financial system during the 1970s and the 1980s are summarized in Table 4, which shows the evolution of the most important controls on both domestic financial markets and on international capital flows. Many of these controls were considered short-term measures, designed to enhance the authorities' ability to influence aggregate demand and external accounts. In fact, the controls have played an important structural role in sustaining the demand for public bonds, even if this objective was achieved in an indirect way and without explicit declaration by the authorities.

Among the domestic controls, the most significant were the administrative constraints placed on bank assets. These constraints did not directly force the

---

[7]"In the [1970s], the system of foreign exchange controls in Italy has been directed to hinder capital outflows, allowing the maintenance of a lower level of interest rates than the one prevailing on international markets" Bank of Italy (1987), p. 161 (authors' translation). See also Palmisani and Rossi (1987), p. 11.

banking system to hold government securities; rather, this objective was accomplished indirectly through a *ceiling on bank loans* that imposed severe limits on the growth of private sector credit. The ceiling was introduced for the first time as an emergency measure in July 1973. Although it was only supposed to be in effect for eight months, it was subsequently renewed on several occasions, and, with the exception of the period March 1975–October 1976, it remained in force until June 1983.

The ceiling increased the placement of public bonds with the banking system; by the end of the 1970s, their share in total public debt, which was 15 percent in 1973, had more than doubled (Table 5). The ceiling also reduced the availability of credit to the private sector and increased its cost, while at the same time it created many distortions in financial markets, among the most important of which was a reduction in competition in the market for bank loans.[8]

In July 1973 another administrative constraint on bank assets was imposed with the introduction of a *portfolio requirement*, by which banks were committed to buy bonds issued by special credit institutions. These institutions extended long-term loans, and at the beginning of the 1970s had been experiencing serious problems in their financing because of the high liquidity preference of Italian savers. The requirement, which obliged the banks to give to the credit institutions the funds they were not able to secure on the market, was initially stringent (40 percent of the increase in banks' deposits in the first half of the 1970s), but was relaxed subsequently.

The portfolio requirement also had an effect on the market for public bonds for at least two reasons. The yields on bonds issued by the special institutions were kept below the market levels, thus dampening the competitive pressure they would otherwise have exerted on public bonds. It should also be remembered that during the 1970s, special institutions had extended many subsidized loans; the portfolio requirement, by allowing a reduction of the public sector expenditure on those subsidies, helped to reduce the public deficit.

Foreign exchange regulation has also had an important effect on the effort to sustain the demand for public bonds. Until the beginning of the 1970s, Italian foreign exchange policy was directed at achieving a progressive financial integration. But in 1972–73 the policy stance was reversed and was replaced by a policy characterized by increasing financial protectionism—the acquisition of financial assets abroad by the economy was severely restricted, and the raising of funds on international financial markets was stimulated.

---

[8]An empirical analysis of the effects of the ceiling is presented in Cottarelli and others (1987).

Table 4. Controls Sustaining Demand for Public Bonds: Main Measures, 1970–87

Control	1970–79	1980–87
Domestic Controls		
Ceiling on bank loans	*July 1973.* First introduction (renewed on several occasions). *March 1975.* Suspension. *October 1976.* Reintroduction, confirmed by subsequent measures.	*March 1980.* Strengthened by introduction of penalty on overdrafts. *June 1983.* Suspension. *January 1986.* Reintroduction for six months. *September 1987.* Reintroduction for six months.
Portfolio requirement (to buy bonds issued by special credit institutions)	*June 1973.* First introduction.	*January 1987.* Suspension.
Controls on International Capital Flows		
Capital outflows	*June 1972.* Suspension of external convertibility of Italian banknotes. *June 1973.* Introduction of 50 percent zero-interest deposit on investment abroad.	*November 1984.* Reduction of compulsory deposit to 40 percent (30 percent for EEC securities). *October 1985.* Reduction of deposit to 25 percent. *August 1986.* Reduction of deposit to 15 percent. *May 1987.* Abolition of deposit.

Foreign trade financing	Measures directed at: —discouraging deferred settlements of exports and advanced settlements of imports; —imposing foreign currency financing requirements. Many policy measures; their stance has changed according to evolution of foreign accounts. Controls favored sizable expansion of foreign liabilities.	No radical changes in objectives. Recent increases in terms of settlements and attempts to reduce foreign currency financing requirements.
Regulation of external position of banks	*June 1972.* Banks authorized to assume position of net external indebtedness and forbidden to assume a creditor position. *July 1974.* Imposition of ceiling on net external indebtedness. *July 1975.* Ceiling lifted on net external indebtedness.	*July 1984.* Imposition of ceiling on net external indebtedness. *December 1985.* Ceiling lifted on net external indebtedness. *March 1987.* Introduction of reserve requirement on net external indebtedness. *September 1987.* Abolition of reserve requirement on net external indebtedness.

Table 5. Italy: Public Debt, 1970–86

(In percent)

Source	1970	1971	1972	1973	1974	1975	1976	1977	1978	1979	1980	1981	1982	1983	1984	1985	1986
Borrowing from the																	
Bank of Italy	25.6	24.0	23.3	28.0	31.7	36.7	40.0	30.7	27.3	22.7	23.2	23.5	21.8	17.5	16.6	17.6	16.5
Postal deposits	21.1	20.5	20.7	19.5	17.3	16.0	15.6	15.5	15.2	16.2	14.5	12.6	10.9	9.7	8.9	8.7	8.9
Borrowing from credit																	
institutions	30.9	35.1	36.3	34.5	33.8	37.0	33.9	40.9	40.9	40.0	37.0	31.8	35.4	35.5	32.0	27.9	24.8
Bills and securities	13.6	17.0	17.2	15.0	14.9	20.1	17.5	29.4	32.0	31.2	29.3	25.3	28.9	29.1	25.2	22.6	20.1
Loans	17.3	18.1	19.1	1.95	18.9	16.9	16.4	11.5	8.9	8.8	7.7	6.5	6.5	6.4	6.8	5.3	4.7
Bills and securities																	
placed with economy	17.6	16.2	16.3	14.9	14.3	7.9	8.0	10.7	14.5	19.1	23.1	29.2	28.7	34.1	39.2	42.7	47.2
Other debts	2.1	1.9	1.6	1.4	1.3	1.1	1.0	0.9	0.9	0.8	0.7	0.6	0.5	0.5	0.4	0.4	0.3
Foreign debt	2.2	2.3	1.8	1.7	1.6	1.3	1.5	1.3	1.3	1.2	1.5	2.3	2.7	2.7	2.9	2.7	2.2

The measures taken fall into the three broad categories shown in Table 4:[9] (1) controls on capital outflows; (2) controls on terms and conditions of foreign trade financing; and (3) regulation of the external position of banks.

The most important among the measures designed to control capital outflows was the imposition in June 1973 of a compulsory zero-interest deposit on property and portfolio investment abroad. This measure affected the assets side of the process of financial integration, leading to a drastic reduction of the share of external financial assets held domestically, particularly by the household sector. By preventing the legal acquisition of foreign bonds, the compulsory deposit forced Italian savers to increase their demand for domestic assets, thus helping to sustain the demand for public bonds.

The primary aim of the measures designed to control the terms and conditions of foreign trade financing, on the one hand, was to prevent speculative capital movements connected with foreign trade. Their principal effect was to increase the demand for foreign currency loans from the banks. The regulation of the external position of banks, on the other hand, was intended to increase the supply of foreign loans by the banking system. On the whole, these measures encouraged the banks to borrow abroad, thereby enabling them to meet the domestic demand for foreign currency loans. In fact, the regulations prevented the banks from assuming a net creditor external position and permitted them to maintain an unlimited net debtor position, except for short periods. These two different categories of controls were complementary and were used intensively during foreign exchange crises to keep official reserves above their equilibrium levels. By stimulating the growth of foreign liabilities, they also achieved the objective of dampening the demand by enterprises for domestic financing, thereby creating conditions for a more favorable placement of public bonds in the domestic markets. Foreign exchange regulations also helped to keep Italian real rates of interest at levels lower than those prevailing in other countries (see Tables 6 and 7).[10]

During the 1980s there has been a reduction in the recourse to administrative constraints. The deregulation began first in the domestic markets and has subsequently been extended to international capital flows.

The ceiling on bank loans was suspended in June 1983. Its abolition was prefaced by radical changes in the conduct of monetary policy, which, beginning with the end of the 1970s, was increasingly directed at raising the amount of public bonds placed on the market. As shown in Table 5, when the ceiling was removed in 1983, the share of credit institutions in total public debt was already

---

[9]For a more detailed analysis of Italian foreign exchange policy, see Micossi and Rossi (1986), and Palmisani and Rossi (1987).

[10]The effects of controls on capital flows on the interest rate differential are discussed in Giavazzi and Pagano (1985).

Table 6. Interest Rates: Italy and Other Industrial Countries
(Real short-term rates in percent)

Country	1981	1982	1983	1984	1985	1986
United States	6.62	7.03	4.20	5.99	4.42	3.75
Japan	4.48	4.76	4.22	4.34	5.04	5.83
Federal Republic of Germany	6.28	4.90	2.92	3.68	4.72	5.12
France	1.96	5.64	3.91	5.41	6.45	4.50
United Kingdom	3.18	7.39	5.06	4.54	7.36	7.04
Italy	3.87	3.85	6.14	6.96	6.45	7.69
Canada	7.26	6.72	4.38	7.54	5.39	5.18

declining from a peak of about 40 percent reached in the second half of the 1970s. Following the removal of the ceiling, that share continued to decrease, falling to 24.8 percent at end-1986. The portfolio requirement, which had become progressively less stringent since its introduction, was also abolished in January 1987.

It must be noted that during 1986 and 1987 there was an interruption and a reversal of the deregulation process. On two occasions (January 1986 and September 1987) the authorities were compelled to reintroduce the ceiling for a six-month period. In both cases, the ceiling was used as an emergency measure to counter a worsening of the balance of payments. But there is no doubt that the recourse to the ceiling was also necessitated by the high level of public debt that continues to prevent the authorities from confronting foreign exchange crises with interest rate increases only, since this expedient by itself would have too strong an effect on the interest expenditure of the public sector.

Starting in 1984, foreign exchange policy underwent a gradual deregulation, beginning with the progressive reduction and eventual removal in May 1987 of

Table 7. Interest Rate Differentials:
United States and Federal Republic of Germany

Differential	January 1977–March 1979	April 1979–March 1983	April 1983–July 1987
Real differential[1]	−2.73	−3.84	+0.95
Nominal covered differential[2]	−1.89	−2.45	+0.80

Note: Average of the differentials with respect to the United States and the Federal Republic of Germany calculated using monthly data on short-term (three months) interest rates.
[1]Deflated with the consumption price index.
[2]Forward discount of the lira (monthly averages).

the compulsory deposit on portfolio investment abroad.[11] In September 1986, the Italian Parliament passed a foreign exchange reform law empowering the government to overhaul the present regulation. The bill laid the foundations for a complete recasting of the regulatory framework and overrode the principle underlying the former system, replacing it with the principle that "everything is allowed except what is explicitly forbidden."

A gradual liberalization has also been undertaken of the terms and conditions of foreign trade financing. However, this process has proven to be quite difficult; in May 1987 some constraints on foreign exchange financing were relaxed, but the authorities were compelled to reintroduce them a few months later.

III. Controls Sustaining Treasury's Seigniorage

Seigniorage is determined by the supply of the monetary base created by the Treasury's borrowings from the central bank, but it is also determined by the demand for monetary base by the private sector—that is, the quantity of real balances that the private sector absorbs in its portfolio. Seigniorage is influenced by regulation in two ways: by controls relating to the financing of the Treasury in the monetary base, which act on the relative supply of the Treasury's base; and by controls relating to banks' reserve requirements, which influence the demand for monetary base by the banking system. Table 8 summarizes the evolution of these regulations during the 1970s and 1980s.

In Italy, the financing of the Treasury in monetary base takes place in two ways: either through the Treasury's use of its current account with the Bank of Italy, or by the Treasury's placement of its securities with the Bank of Italy. The financing of the Treasury in the monetary account allows it to draw on this account up to 14 percent of its planned expenditure at a very low interest cost (1 percent). This regulation has been in force, more or less unchanged, since 1948; in recent years, however, it has been the subject of discussion on several occasions because of the severe limitations it imposes on the autonomy of the Bank of Italy in the creation of the monetary base.[12]

The creation of monetary base through the placement of government securities with the central bank has also been regulated for many years by rules that also greatly restrict the autonomy of the central bank. This was particularly true after February 1975, when the Bank of Italy was committed to intervene in Treasury bill auctions and to buy all the bills not absorbed by the market. The commitment implied substantial purchases of bills by the central bank that were

---

[11]A description and evaluation of recent developments in Italian foreign exchange policy can be found in Ministero del Tesoro (1987), Chap. 3.

[12]The limits of this autonomy and the need for a change in regulation were discussed by the Governor of the Bank of Italy in the 1984 Annual Report. See Bank of Italy (1985), p. 295.

Table 8. Controls Sustaining Treasury's Seigniorage: Main Measures, 1970–87

Control	1970–79	1980–87
Treasury Financing in Monetary Base		
Treasury account with Bank of Italy	Regulation (from 1948) authorized Treasury to draw on its current account up to 14 percent of its planned expenditure.	No changes in regulation.
Placement of government bonds with Bank of Italy	*February 1975.* Bank of Italy committed to intervene at Treasury bill auctions, buying bills not placed on the market.	*July 1981.* Commitment to intervene in Treasury bill auctions suspended.
Reserve Requirements		
Required reserves coefficient	*January 1975.* Marginal coefficient made uniform at 15 percent for all categories of banks. *February 1976.* Marginal coefficient increased to 15.75 percent.	*March 1981.* Marginal coefficient increased to 20 percent. *December 1982.* Marginal coefficient increased to 25 percent.
Remuneration on required reserves	*October 1970.* Rate paid on reserves, which previously moved according to the official discount rate, fixed at 5.5 percent.	*December 1982.* Rate raised to 9.5 percent for reserves against certificates of deposit only.

not always easy to neutralize with subsequent open market sales; furthermore, the confidence in central bank support created by this rule induced the Treasury to offer lower rates on its bills than would otherwise have been required by the market. In July 1981 this commitment was suspended by the so-called divorce between the Bank of Italy and the Treasury, and regulations concerning the creation of monetary base since then have tended to increase the autonomy of monetary policy.

It should be noted, however, that the reduction in borrowing from the central bank by the Treasury started well before 1981. As Table 5 shows, such borrowing reached its peak in 1976 (40 percent of total public sector debt) and declined thereafter, falling to 16.5 percent in 1986. This decreased reliance on borrowing from the central bank was achieved by means of heavily increased sales of public sector securities on the market. As has already been noted (see Section I and Tables 2 and 3), notwithstanding the reduction in the share of debt financed with monetary base, the monetary base of the Treasury has declined only slightly in proportion to GDP, and its seigniorage relative to GDP has returned in recent years to its 1976–81 level.

The stock of monetary base in Italy is still much higher than in other countries. Table 9 compares the Italian monetary base as a percentage of GDP with that of other industrial countries at end-1986; from the table it can be seen that the value for Italy is more than twice the average of the other countries. The data shown in the table refer to total monetary base, to which the Treasury contributes a much higher proportion in Italy than in other countries. If the comparisons had been based on the Treasury's contribution alone, the ratio to GDP would be even higher for Italy.

Table 9 also shows that the ratio of currency to GDP in Italy is only slightly above the average of the other industrial countries. In contrast, the ratio of

Table 9. Monetary Base/GDP Ratio at End-1986: An International Comparison

Country	Monetary Base (total)	Bank Reserves	Currency
Italy	15.5	10.1	5.4
United States	5.7	1.3	4.4
Japan[1]	8.4	1.8	6.6
United Kingdom	4.1	0.5	3.6
Federal Republic of Germany	9.3	3.7	5.6
France	6.5	1.9	4.6

[1]End-1985.

bank reserves to GDP is particularly high, relative to the other countries. This difference may be partly explained by the greater degree of banking intermediation in Italy than in the other countries, but this intermediation has been declining rapidly in recent years. *Reserve requirements* provide a more probable explanation for the larger ratio of bank reserves to GDP. These requirements can be viewed as regulations that have substantially increased the demand for monetary base by the Italian banking system.

As shown in Table 8, during the 1970s and 1980s the reserve coefficient was increased many times. The upward trend began with the reform of January 1975, which imposed a uniform (15 percent) marginal coefficient in place of the previous system whereby the reserve requirements differed appreciably according to the type of deposit and category of bank. The reserve coefficient was progressively increased, reaching, with the measures taken by the authorities in December 1982, its present value of 25 percent. [13]

The influence of the reserve requirements may be seen both on the tax rate and on the tax base (see Appendix for the simple algebra used to calculate seigniorage). The reserve coefficient requires that during each quarter a substantial increase be made in the stock of monetary base held by the banking system; in this respect, the coefficient is analogous to a tax rate and its effect is captured mainly by changes in velocity. The rise in the reserve coefficient in recent years has led to a decrease in velocity, which has been stronger than that shown in Table 3, if one considers that the decrease in velocity caused by the reserve regulation has been partly offset by an increase in velocity in the portion of monetary base held in the form of free bank reserves and currency. [14] By requiring substantial additions to reserves in each period, the regulation also had the effect of preventing a reduction of the tax base over time, which would have been prompted by the decline in the share of bank deposits in GDP.

To assess the implicit fiscality of the reserve requirements, one must also consider the provisions concerning the remuneration paid by the central bank on required reserves. Until 1970, the rate of remuneration moved according to the official discount rate. Thereafter, except for the portion of reserves pertaining to certificates of deposit, which was made subject to a rate of 9.5 percent at

---

[13]The coefficient of 25 percent has to be applied to the increases in bank deposits until the ratio of stocks of required reserves and deposits reaches 22.5 percent (subsequently, the marginal coefficient will decrease to 22.5 percent). For many banks the ratio is well below this value, and the marginal coefficient will therefore stay at 25 percent for some time. The measures of December 1982 further strengthened reserve requirements by specifying that in case of a decrease in deposits, reserves had to be decumulated by the application of a lower coefficient (20 percent).

[14]One must, of course, take into account other factors that have influenced velocity in recent years, among which declines in nominal interest rates and inflationary expectations have played a significant role.

end-1982, the remuneration has remained fixed at 5.5 percent. The higher rate on certificates of deposit has so far made little difference to the average return on reserves because of their limited share in total reserves.

The fixed rate of 5.5 percent paid on reserves substantially increased the burden of the reserve requirements on the banking system during a period in which interest rates moved to levels much higher than those prevailing at the beginning of the 1970s.[15] The fixed rate also allowed the central bank to pay back to the Treasury the interest (as perceived by the central bank) on the securities it was holding in its portfolio.

IV. Tax from Controls and Inflation Tax

In the previous sections, we have argued that administrative controls on domestic financial flows and international capital movements can help finance the public deficit in two ways: by lowering the real cost of interest-bearing public debt independently of the prevailing rate of inflation; and by raising the real demand for monetary base, which allows the collection of seigniorage. We will now briefly discuss the relation between these effects and the well-known operation of the "inflation tax."

One connection is that higher inflation can increase the taxing power of a given set of controls. In more precise terms, a given set of direct controls on nominal interest rates becomes more binding when inflation increases. With higher inflation, controls on nominal rates have more pervasive distortionary consequences on credit and financial markets, but since they usually constrain the remuneration of bank deposits, a larger amount of seigniorage is also indirectly collected by the public sector.[16]

This type of connection between higher inflation and the effect of controls was widely recognized as obtaining in the United States during the 1970s.[17] And it has often been stated that strong inflation stimulates financial deregulation by magnifying the disturbing consequences of fixed nominal rates.[18] In the Italian

---

[15]For an evaluation of the burden placed by reserve requirements on the Italian banking system and for an analysis of the effects of the fixed remuneration on the efficacy of monetary policy, see Porta (1984) and Bruni (1982).

[16]For a theoretical discussion of the collection of seigniorage through the banking system see, for instance, Siegel (1981).

[17]"The incentives to elude regulatory constraints intensified during the 1970s as inflation increased significantly. *Interest rate limitation became binding*, the opportunity cost of holding reserve balances and below-market interest-bearing assets rose sharply. . ." (Evanoff (1985), p. 3, emphasis added).

[18]"[F]inancial institutions were trying to circumvent regulatory constraints. . . . The introduction of new money substitutes and a shrinking reserve base caused the central bank to seek legislative changes. . ." (Evanoff (1985), p. 3). For a discussion of the origins of the Depository Institutions Deregulation Act of 1980, see also West (1982). On inflation as a cause of financial innovation in the United States, see Silber (1983), Table 1, p. 91.

case, however, explicit controls on nominal rates have never played an important role; consequently, the crucial connection between inflation and controls is of a different kind.[19]

In fact, there is a second type of relation, which moves in the opposite direction: namely, the imposition of controls can increase the amount of the implicit tax collected through a given rate of inflation. This is obvious when controls, such as compulsory reserve requirements, increase the real demand for high-powered money, because that money is also the base for the inflation tax. The effect on the bond market is similar.

With no controls, only unexpected inflation can levy a tax on bondholders. The anticipated component of inflation, via the Fisher effect,[20] will be incorporated in the nominal yield and will leave real returns unchanged. We argue that administrative controls can interfere with the working of the Fisher effect, by decreasing the substitutability among the various assets in the portfolio of the private sector. In particular, if it is relatively more difficult to substitute away from government bonds, the Treasury will collect a tax from expected inflation and from an expected acceleration in inflation.[21] If purchasing power parity holds, for instance, exchange controls can decrease the availability of assets hedged against inflation, and it will be easier for anticipated domestic price increases to

---

[19]The only exception is the fixed interest rate paid on banks' compulsory reserves, which was discussed in the previous session; the implicit tax associated with the reserve requirement increases with the level of market nominal interest rates and inflation.

[20]Disregarding the effects described by Mundell (1963) and Tobin (1969). We also disregard the possible effect of a close substitutability between money and bonds, which could turn out to play an important role in the case of Italian public debt instruments. See, for instance, Fried and Howitt (1983), and Placone and Wallace (1987). Standard theoretical effects of expected inflation on real rates are commonly recognized to be quantitatively small; but Boschen and Newman (1987) have recently presented evidence pointing to a substantial impact in Argentina.

[21]See Bruni and Porta (1981), pp. 29-48. Let b be the proportion of interest-bearing to total public debt, i and r the nominal and real ex-ante equilibrium interest rates, respectively, and u and e the unexpected and expected components, respectively, of the rate of inflation; the average real cost of one unit of public debt will be

$$
\begin{aligned}
c &= (i - e - u)b - (e + u)(1 - b) \\
&= (r + e - e - u)b - (e + u)(1 - b) \\
&= rb - u - e(1 - b).
\end{aligned}
$$

The taxing power of unexpected inflation can then be expressed as $dc/du = 1$. If controls produce a negative correlation between r and e seigniorage from anticipated inflation will be

$$
-dc/dc = -b(dr/d) + (1 - b).
$$

transfer wealth from creditors to debtors. If internal controls favor the holding of government debt, the public sector will be a privileged collector of that transfer. It is worth noting that this taxing mechanism (which more or less works in all countries) can rely upon a large variety of controls and on all the regulations and imperfections that hinder portfolio adjustments and asset or liability substitution. Controls that are not used for stabilization purposes— for instance, limits to entry in the banking industry, or protection of banks from the competition of nonbanks in the collection of savings or obstacles to securitization—these can work to lower the real cost of debt as expected inflation increases, and vice versa.[22]

From this point of view, the introduction of real-indexed bonds works in the opposite direction (provided they are not forced into the system at lower-than-equilibrium real rates).[23] Not only do these bonds increase the supply of assets that are protected from inflation surprises, but they also prompt substitution away from bonds when inflation is expected, thus decreasing the collection of implicit taxes via anticipated price increase.[24]

During the last two to three years, the ex-post average real interest rate on short-term government bonds (see Table 1) has been nearly 10 percentage points above its average level at the end of the 1970s. Such a large increase cannot be explained entirely by a decrease in both unanticipated inflation and administrative controls; nor can it be the effect of other often cited causes. Some liberalization has taken place, and this has allowed an upward movement of real rates, which have also been pushed up by the prevailing international fiscal-monetary policy mix; inflation risk-premium and some expected real devaluation of the lira are other probable causes. However, the increase in the real cost of public debt still appears too high. Therefore, the rise in interest rates must also be a result of the substantial inverse correlation between expected inflation and

---

[22]Consider a numerical example. Suppose that with no controls and zero-expected inflation, the nominal interest rate on government bonds was 5 percent, and with no controls and 10 percent expected inflation, it would rise to 15 percent; suppose also that the presence of controls would lower the nominal rate prevailing with zero-expected inflation to 2 percent, collecting a 3 percent implicit tax. We are arguing that with the same set of controls and 10 percent expected inflation, the nominal rate would be lower than 12 percent (say, 10 percent), because inflation, even if expected, would have the power to increase the implicit tax (from, say, 3 percent to 5 percent).

[23]A limited amount of public real-indexed bonds was issued in Italy in August 1983. The introduction of real bonds had been proposed by a Commission chaired by Paolo Baffi, which had been entrusted by the Treasury with the task of writing a report on how to protect financial saving from inflation. See Ministero del Tesoro (1981) and Monti (1982).

[24]Real-indexed bonds also provide protection from the effects, described by Mundell (1963), of expected inflation on real rates of interest.

ex-ante real rates of interest that is generated by regulations and imperfections in the financial system. Even at the present, reduced level of administrative controls, an anticipated increase in inflation would exert some downward pressure on real rates of interest.

Inflation and administrative financial controls can thus be said to reinforce each other in lowering the real cost of public debt and in collecting seigniorage for the Treasury. To some extent, they can be substitutable sources of implicit taxes for a highly indebted government. If the adjustment of the Italian basic deficit is insufficient and inflation is kept low, it is highly probable that financial deregulation will be interrupted and/or new controls will be imposed. (Are the developments of fall 1987 a start in this direction?) In contrast, further liberalization could necessitate higher inflation.[25]

But the substitution between the two implicit taxes cannot be pushed too far. An overdose of controls, besides giving rise to tremendous distortions, becomes ineffective as a consequence of all sorts of regulation-avoiding innovations. An overdose of inflation decreases the real demand for money, thus eroding the base of its taxing power and moving to the "unpleasant side of the seigniorage Laffer curve."[26]

V. Implicit Taxes, Capital Controls, and the Equity Market: The Issue of Crowding-Out

As documented in previous sections, the Italian Government has relied on administrative controls to collect implicit taxes. Although the money, credit, and foreign exchange markets have borne the brunt of the distorting effects of the controls, all financial markets have been affected by them. In this section, we focus on the indirect effects of across-the-board capital controls on the stock market and, consequently, on the cost of equity.

Until May 1987, Italian portfolio investments abroad were severely restricted. A liberalization process is now taking place, but many restrictions still remain in effect. By limiting the menu of assets available for domestic savers with capital controls, the authorities have reduced the interest rate on government debt because they have artificially increased the demand for it. Controls thus imply a subsidy for the government. But have other borrowers benefited from the same subsidy? The answer may be negative, because the controls may

---

[25]McKinnon and Mathieson (1981) show how the rate of inflation required to finance public expenditure can increase following a deregulation in a financially repressed country. But higher inflation and freedom of capital movements can be incompatible for a country participating in a fixed but adjustable exchange rate system like the European Monetary System. See Giavazzi and Pagano (1985).

[26]Buiter (1987), p. 74.

have raised the cost of equity—thus crowding out investment projects—even though the "risk-free" rate—the interest rate paid by the government on its debt—has been maintained below its equilibrium level.

The cost of equity for a company depends on the risk premium that investors demand in order to hold its stock. Stocks are viewed as riskier than fixed-income government debt because—apart from default risk—their prices are more volatile than bond prices, so that their returns are more uncertain. Consequently, investors must expect to receive a higher return from the share components of their portfolio to be compensated for the higher risk.

Stock prices tend to move together in the various capital markets. This empirical regularity has led to the conjecture that there is a common source of share price fluctuations, which is the risky factor. Because risk-averse investors dislike risk, demand will be high for those stocks that have a low correlation with all other stocks—and therefore, low correlation with the risky factor—whereas demand will be low for those stocks highly correlated with the rest of the market. In equilibrium, the first group of stocks will clearly demand a lower risk premium than the second.

When investors in a country are prohibited from investing abroad, they cannot reduce the variability of their portfolios by adding foreign stocks. Their portfolios will then be composed entirely of domestic stocks—and will necessarily be riskier than an internationally diversified portfolio. They will then demand a higher risk premium for holding the domestic stocks than they would have in a regime with free capital movements.

By segmenting the domestic capital market, a government may reduce the cost of funding its own debt but, at the same time, may increase the riskiness of domestic equities for domestic investors, thereby raising the cost of funding capital expansions for the corporate sector—in other words, the crowding-out effect. An interesting empirical question is whether the long history of capital controls has effectively raised the cost of equity financing for the Italian corporate sector. To examine this issue, we adopt a few simple international capital asset-pricing models in order to assess whether a "super-risk" premium characterized the Italian market during the last eight years.

In principle, if foreign investors were free to invest in the domestic market—and to repatriate profits—there would be no crowding-out because they would immediately reap the super-risk premium that would emerge in that market.[27] A premium found in the Italian data would be a "political-risk" premium—that is, foreigners are reluctant to invest in Italy because of institutional uncertainties, market illiquidity, and lack of information.[28]

---

[27]See Errunza and Losq (1985).

[28]See Frankel and MacArthur (1987).

We begin our empirical investigation with the establishment of the European Monetary System (EMS). This monetary union amounted to a switch in regime that added credibility to Italian economic policies and presumably reduced foreign investors' risk-perception of the country. Because we are testing for market segmentation, we have excluded the pre-EMS years from the sample to avoid spurious results due to the lack of homogeneous periods. We have ended the sample period in June 1987, when portfolio investments abroad were liberalized.

Any implementation of a capital asset-pricing model requires a measure of the risky factor for equity prices. A well-known approach uses the return on the "market portfolio" as the single measure of risk. In a world of perfect capital mobility, the world equity market is the appropriate market portfolio—a weighted index of the various national stock markets. In our study we consider ten countries—the United States, the United Kingdom, France, Canada, Sweden, Switzerland, Germany, Japan, the Netherlands, and Italy—which together account for 98 percent of the capitalization of world stock markets.

For each market we present both the average monthly real rate of return and the real return in excess to the risk-free rate, which was approximated by the rate on three-month government debt in every country. We computed real returns by taking the monthly percentage changes of the various stock indexes deflated by domestic consumption price indexes (we did not take into account reinvestment of dividends). Different indexes were needed because consumption baskets differ across countries and because purchasing power parity does not hold. Figure 1 shows that the Italian stock market provided the highest monthly real rate of return among the industrial countries with a rate of 1.5 percent, and was second only to Japan in terms of real excess return. The picture is even more clear-cut if we consider the last three years when the Italian stock market developed very rapidly following the introduction of mutual funds.

To compare returns among different countries, we have to adjust returns for their risk. As explained above, we initially used the world market portfolio as the source of risk and measured riskiness by regressing the real returns of the various stock indexes on the real return of the world market portfolio. The cross section of the average returns in the different stock markets was then regressed on the estimated *betas* to obtain what is known as the security market line. This line gives the empirical equilibrium trade-off between real return and systematic risk in the international capital market. If a country is above the line, an international investor could have increased the return on his portfolio, without increasing risk, by investing more in that country. In Figure 2, we show the security market line for the period 1984–88; the same picture would emerge if we looked at the full sample period, which is not shown here.

**Figure 1. Real Rates of Return on
Stock Indexes, January 1979–June 1987**

(In percent)

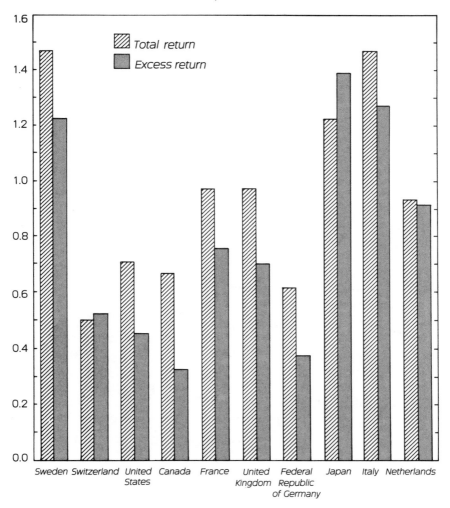

Italy and Japan appear to have generated returns that were way above those prevailing in the other markets, even when they are adjusted for systematic risk. For example, an investor would have greatly enhanced the return on his portfolio per unit of risk by moving out of the U.S., U.K., and Dutch markets and investing in the Italian market.

Figure 2. Portfolio Model: Risk-Return
Relation, January 1984–June 1987

(In percent)

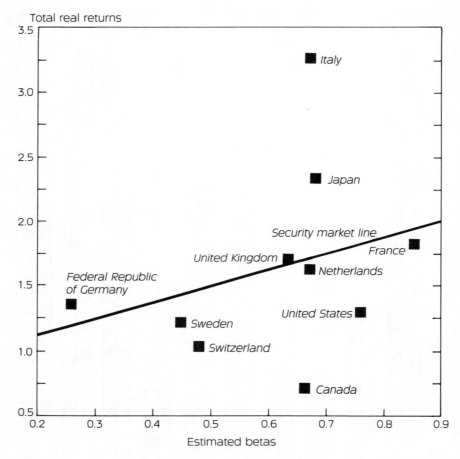

The world market portfolio is not the only way to measure the source of risk. It has been shown that this measure is correct only for the truly "international investor," whose consumption preferences are not biased toward goods of one country and therefore does not want to hedge against the losses of purchasing power of the currency in which the price of these goods is expressed.[29] An alternative way to measure risk is to note that risk-averse individuals accumulate

---

[29]See Adler and Dumas (1983).

wealth to smooth consumption, even if their incomes fluctuate widely. To those investors, assets that have high returns when consumption is low are more valuable than assets with rates of return highly correlated with consumption. Risk can then be measured by consumption *betas*—namely, the empirical correlation between real asset returns and real consumption changes. The relevant consumption concept for the measurement of risk is world real consumption, because in equilibrium—and with perfect capital mobility—this is the only risk that is systematic to all stocks in the world and consequently cannot be diversified away by trading with foreigners.[30]

In practice, we measured world real consumption by creating a gross national product (GNP)-weighted index of consumption at constant prices for eight countries with quarterly data—the same cross section of countries used before, with the exclusion of France and Switzerland for which data were unavailable. We used the same sample period 1979–87. The consumption *betas* and the average total real returns were then used to calculate the security market line, which is shown in Figure 3. The results are similar to those found with the market portfolio model. The rate of return per unit of risk in the Italian equity market exceeded the international norm as measured by the security market line.

No firm conclusion can be made based on the empirical evidence presented in the paper because of the limited sample size and the inevitable shortcomings of the pricing models used. However, one can point to the high real return per unit of risk, relative to the rest of the world, which Italian corporations appear to have paid to investors. One possible explanation for this phenomenon—although not the only one—is that domestic investors, not being allowed to diversify internationally, demanded an extra-risk premium to hold the existing stock of Italian equities. If this is the case, the liberalization process now undertaken by the government should gradually reduce the cost of equity financing and, therefore, bring the expected rates of return in the Italian stock market more in line with international markets.

VI. Concluding Remarks

As shown at the beginning of the paper, the growth of the real stock of Italian interest-bearing public debt has accelerated in recent years, in spite of some reduction in the basic deficit and notwithstanding a sustained collection of seigniorage by the Treasury. We have argued that inflation and financial controls are two sources of implicit taxes that reinforce each other. When inflation was high, even if anticipated, it could not be entirely incorporated in nominal interest rates because of controls and imperfections in capital markets. On the contrary,

---

[30]See Stulz (1981).

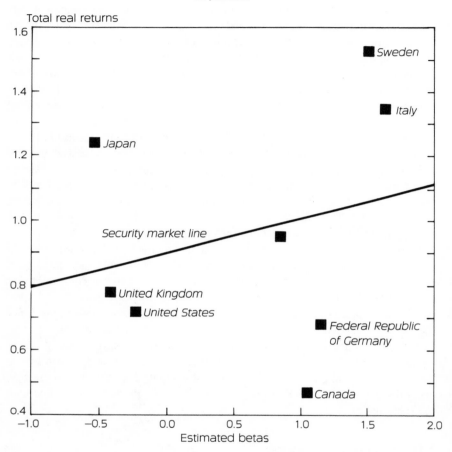

**Figure 3. Consumption Beta Model: Risk-Return
Relation, March 1979–June 1987**

(In percent)

the decrease in inflation has been among the main causes of the higher levels of real rates.

When implicit taxes decrease the cost of public debt, they do not necessarily also lower the cost of capital for private firms. To be sure, controls on the allocation of credit and capital flows can be organized to obtain the opposite result,[31] by placing part of the burden of implicit taxation on private debtors (thus

---

[31]See McKinnon and Mathieson (1981), p. 16.

relieving the burden on savers) and obtaining a crowding-out of private spending in spite of the lower rates paid by the Treasury. We have studied a particular effect of this kind—that is, the positive impact of foreign exchange controls on the risk premium built into the cost of equity capital. The Italian stock exchange commands a higher premium than that of other countries' capital markets, which could be lowered by liberalization, thus compensating for a higher risk-free rate and limiting the possible crowding-out effect of deregulation.

But the problem remains. Can the financial situation of the Italian sector stand the real interest rates that are determined on free financial markets? Or will the authorities be compelled to choose a mix of stronger controls and higher inflation? We are convinced that this choice can still be avoided, and that fiscal adjustment can take place through a sufficient reduction of the basic deficit. To support this conviction, we make three final points, which have often been raised in the research conducted and proposals made by the Centre for Monetary Research and Financial Economics of Università Bocconi.

First, the *qualitative composition of public debt* must be carefully engineered. An efficient diversification of the various debt instruments can help reduce the Treasury's interest expenses. In this respect, we think that in a period when inflation is low but inflation expectations are uncertain, issuing a substantial amount of real-indexed bonds could decrease the risk premium on real interest rates.[32]

Second, liberalization must be balanced between domestic and international flows. If it proceeds too rapidly or too slowly on one front, the steps on the other front can become more difficult and more costly and less effective. Even with financial deregulation, there is an *order-of-liberalization problem*, not unlike the one encountered in less-developed countries when the removal of real trade and financial protectionism needs to be measured out in appropriate doses.[33]

Finally, we think that political decisions that determine the basic deficit, net of interest expenses, are not independent from *financial discipline* nor from the level of real interest rates, and cannot be considered exogenous when the issue of deregulation is being confronted. Stronger administrative controls can certainly decrease the real interest component of public debt growth and/or sustain seigniorage; but they will probably also remove some of the pressure on the authorities to adjust noninterest expenses and explicit taxes. There are signs that some "disciplinary effect" of financial liberalization is already influencing

---

[32]The proposal (see footnote 23) was recently renewed, stressing the risk-premium motive, in a recent report of the Treasury's Study Commission. See Ministero del Tesoro (1987), p. 114.

[33]The relation between internal and external financial liberalization is discussed in Bruni and Monti (1986), pp. 94–99; on the trade versus financial order-of-liberalization problem, see, for instance, Khan and Zahler (1985) and the literature they cite.

Italian fiscal policy. From this point of view, the international financial community and institutions perform a valuable role when they push for liberalization of international capital movements, thus raising the political cost of financial protectionism, stimulating the country's financial discipline, and indirectly promoting fiscal adjustment.[34]

Appendix

Analytical Decomposition of the Growth of Public Debt in Real Terms and as a Share of Gross Domestic Product

Let B be the nominal stock of public debt held by the private sector, i the interest rate paid on it, MT the debt held by the central bank (that is, the Treasury's monetary base), i_M the interest rate paid on MT, and F the public sector deficit net of interest expenses. We can thus write:

$$dB = iB + F - dMT + i_M MT = iB + F - (dMT/MT - i_M)MT$$

and, dividing by B:

$$dB/B = i + F/B - (dMT/MT - i_M)MT/B.$$

Now let M be the total monetary base and $p = dP/P$ be the rate of inflation of the price index P. Since

$$MT = (M/P)P(MT/M)$$

we can approximate dMT/MT with

$$\frac{d(M/P)}{M/P} + p + \frac{d(MT/M)}{MT/M},$$

and the rate of change of the real value of B with

$$\frac{d(B/P)}{B/P} \approx \frac{dB}{B} - p = r + \frac{F}{B}$$

$$- \left[p + \frac{d(M/P)}{M/P} + \frac{d(MT/M)}{MT/M} - i_M \right] \frac{MT}{B}, \tag{1}$$

---

[34]On the disciplinary effect of financial liberalization on public finance, see Bruni and Monti (1986), p. 97, and Bruni (1988), Section III. Section 3 in Bruni and Giavazzi (1987) contains a formalization of this effect in a simple model where both public deficit and the level of financial protectionism are endogenous.

where $r = i - p$ is the approximately calculated ex-post real rate. Equation (1) is the breakdown of the growth rate of B/P estimated in Tables 1 and 3 in the text. The term in parentheses is the seigniorage tax rate (let us call it t); MT/B is the seigniorage tax base; and $t(MT/B)$ is total seigniorage in proportion to privately held debt. Now let Y be nominal gross domestic product (GDP), and then let $g = dY/Y - p$, the approximately calculated real growth rate of Y. We can write

$$d(B/Y) = \frac{d(B/Y)}{B/Y} \frac{B}{Y} \approx \left[\frac{dB}{B} - \frac{dY}{Y}\right]\frac{B}{Y}$$

$$= \left[\frac{dB}{B} - (p + g)\right]\frac{B}{Y}$$

and, using equation (1):

$$d(B/Y) = \left[r + \frac{F}{B} - \frac{tMT}{B} - g\right]\frac{B}{Y} \qquad (2)$$

$$= (r - g)\frac{B}{Y} + \frac{F}{Y} - \frac{tMT}{Y},$$

which is the breakdown estimated in Table 2 and a well-known differential equation often used in the literature to study the stability conditions of the debt-to-income ratio (tMT/Y is total seigniorage to GDP).

References

Adler, Michael, and Bernard Dumas, "International Portfolio Choice and Corporation Finance: A Synthesis," *Journal of Finance* (New York), Vol. 38 (June 1983), pp. 925–84.

Bank of Italy, *Assemblea Generale Ordinaria dei Partecipanti*, May 31, 1985, Annual Report 1984 (Rome: Bank of Italy, 1985).

_____, *Assemblea Generale Ordinaria dei Partecipanti*, May 30, 1987, Annual Report 1986 (Rome: Bank of Italy, 1987).

Boschen, John F., and John L. Newman, "The Effects of Expected Inflation on Real Returns in the Argentine Indexed Bond Market," *Economics Letters* (Amsterdam), Vol. 25, No. 2 (1987), pp. 137–42.

Bruni, Franco, "L' 'imposta implicita' sulla riserva obbligatoria delle banche e l'efficacia della politica monetaria," *Rassegna Economica* (Napoli), Vol. 46 (March–April 1982), pp. 325–35.

—————, "Costs and Benefits of Capital Flows: Some Theoretical and Policy Issues with Special Reference to the Italian Case," in *International Monetary and Financial Integration: the European Dimension*, ed. by D. E. Fair and C. de Boissieu (Boston: Kluwer Academic Publishers, 1988), pp. 223–37.

—————, and Francesco Giavazzi, "Debito pubblico, debito estero e protezionismo valutario," in *Debito pubblico e politica economica in Italia*, ed. by Franco Bruni (Rome: SIPI, 1987), pp. 135–62.

—————, and Mario Monti, "Protezionismo valutario e integrazione internatazionale," Chap. 6 in *Il sistema dei cambi, oggi*, ed. by Tommaso Padoa-Schioppa (Bologna: il Mulino, 1986).

—————, and Angelo Porta, "Allocazione delle risorse e inflazione: il caso dei mercati finanziari," *Economia Internazionale* (Genova), Vol. 34 (May/November 1981), pp. 261–321.

Buiter, Willem H., "A Guide to Public Sector Debt and Deficits," *Economic Policy: A European Forum* (London), Vol. 1 (November 1985), pp. 13–79.

—————, "The Current Global Economic Situation, Outlook and Policy Options, with Special Emphasis on Fiscal Policy Issues," Discussion Paper Series No. 210 (London: Centre for Economic Policy Research, November 1987).

Cividini A., G. Galli, and R. Masera, "Vincolo di bilancio e sostenibilita' del debito: analisi e prospettive," in *Debito pubblico e politica economica in Italia*, ed. by Franco Bruni (Roma: SIPI), 1987, pp. 12–64.

Cottarelli, C., and others, "Il massimale sui prestiti bancari: aspetti teorici e verifiche empiriche," in *Richerche quantitative e basi statistiche per la politica economica* (Rome: Bank of Italy, 1987), pp. 911–73.

Errunza, Vihang, and Etienne Losq, "International Asset Pricing Under Mild Segmentation: Theory and Test," *Journal of Finance* (New York), Vol. 40 (March 1985), pp. 105–24.

Evanoff, Douglas, D., "Financial Industry Deregulation in the 1980s," *Economic Perspectives*, Federal Reserve Bank of Chicago, Vol. 9 (September/October 1985), pp. 3–5.

Frankel, Jeffrey A., and Alan T. MacArthur, "Political vs. Currency Premia in International Real Interest Differentials: A Study of Forward Rates for 24 Countries," NBER Working Paper 2309 (Cambridge, Massachusetts: National Bureau of Economic Research, July 1987).

Fried, Joel, and Peter Howitt, "The Effects of Inflation on Real Interest Rates," *American Economic Review* (Nashville, Tennessee), Vol. 73 (December 1983), pp. 968–80.

Galli, G., "Tasso reale, crescita e sostenibilita' del debito pubblico," in *Contributi all'analisi economica*, Bank d'Italia, del Servizio studi, (Rome), No. 1 (December 1985), pp. 101–36.

Giavazzi, Francesco, "The Exchange-Rate Question in Europe," (mimeographed, Brussels: Centre for European Policy Studies, November 1987).

_____, and M. Pagano, "Capital Controls and the European Monetary System," in *Capital Controls and Foreign Exchange Legislation*, Euromobiliare Occasional Paper (Milan: Euromobiliare, 1985), pp. 19–38.

Khan, Mohsin S., and Roberto Zahler, "Trade and Financial Liberalization Given External Shocks and Inconsistent Domestic Policies," *Staff Papers*, International Monetary Fund (Washington), Vol. 32 (March 1985), pp. 22–55.

Mankiw, Gregory N., "Optimal Collection of Seigniorage: Theory and Evidence," *Journal of Monetary Economics* (Amsterdam), Vol. 20 (September 1987), pp. 327–41.

McKinnon, Ronald I., and Donald J. Mathieson, *How to Manage a Repressed Economy*, Essays in International Finance, No. 145, Princeton University (Princeton, New Jersey: Princeton University Press, 1981).

Micossi, Stephano, and Salvatore Rossi, "Controlli sui movimenti di capitale: il caso italiano," *Giornale degli Economisti e Annali di Economia* (Milano), Vol. 45 (January–February 1986), pp. 17–53.

Ministero del Tesoro, *La difesa del risparmio finanziario dall' inflazione* (Roma: Istituto Poligrafico e Zecca dello Stato, 1981).

_____, *Ricchezza financiaria, debito pubblico e politica monetaria nella prospettiva dell'integrazione internazionale* (Roma: Istituto Poligrafico e Zecca dello Stato, 1987).

Monti, Mario, "Indicizzazione e politica del debito pubblico: Una nota sui Buoni del Tesoro Reali," in *Scritti in onore di Innocenzo Gasparini* (Milan: A. Giuffr'e, 1982).

Mundell, Robert, "Inflation and the Real Interest," *Journal of Political Economy* (Chicago), Vol. 71 (June 1963), pp. 280–83.

Palmisani, F., and Salvatore Rossi, "Aspetti macroeconomici dei controlli valutari: il caso italiano" (mimeographed, Rome: Bank of Italy, September 1987).

Phelps, Edmund S., "Inflation in the Theory of Public Finance," *Swedish Journal of Economics* (Stockholm), Vol. 75 (March 1973), pp. 67–82.

Placone, Dennis, and Myles S. Wallace, "Monetary Deregulation and Inverting the Inverted Fisher Effect," *Economics Letters* (Amsterdam), Vol. 24, No. 4 (1987), pp. 335–38.

Porta, Angelo, "L' 'imposta implicita' sulla riserva obbligatoria e il suo gettito per lo Stato: alcune riflessioni sul caso italiano," *Bancaria* (Rome), Vol. 40 (July 1984), pp. 652–60.

Salvemini, G., and M.T. Salvemini, "Il credito automatico del Tesoro presso la banca centrale" (mimeographed, Rome: Consiglio Nazionale delle Richerche, August 1987).

Siegel, Jeremy J., "Inflation, Bank Profits, and Government Seigniorage," *American Economic Review, Papers and Proceedings of the Ninety-Third Annual Meeting of the American Economic Association* (Nashville, Tennessee), Vol. 71 (May 1981), pp. 352–55.

Silber, William L., "The Process of Financial Innovation," *American Economic Review, Papers and Proceedings of the Ninety-Fifth Annual Meeting of the American Economic Association* (Nashville, Tennessee), Vol. 73 (May 1983), pp. 89–100.

Spaventa, Luigi, "La crescita del debito pubblico in Italia: evoluzione, prospettive e problemi di politica economica," *Banca Nazionale del Lavoro, Moneta e Credito* (Rome), Vol. 37 (September 1984), pp. 251–84.

_____(1987a), "The Growth of Public Debt: Sustainability, Fiscal Rules, and Monetary Rules," *Staff Papers*, International Monetary Fund (Washington), Vol. 34 (June 1987), pp. 374–99.

_____(1987b), "Commento" (to Cividini, Galli, and Masera), in *Debito pubblico e politica economica in Italia*, ed. by Franco Bruni (Rome: SIPI), pp. 65–77.

Stulz, Rene M., "A Model of International Asset Pricing," *Journal of Financial Economics* (Amsterdam), Vol. 9 (December 1981), pp. 383–406.

Tobin, James, "A General Equilibrium Approach to Monetary Theory," *Journal of Money, Credit, and Banking* (Columbus, Ohio), Vol. 1 (February 1969), pp. 15–29.

West, Robert Craig, "Depository Institutions Deregulation Act of 1980: A Historical Perspective," *Economic Review*, Federal Reserve Bank of Kansas City (February 1982), pp. 3–13.

Comment

*Nicholas C. Garganas**

The paper by Bruni, Penati, and Porta deals with the consequences of controls on financial markets in Italy and their possible impact on public sector deficits and on the burden of the public debt. The paper contains a number of interesting and useful findings and draws a number of conclusions with important policy implications.

The paper begins with a decomposition of the change in the ratio of nonmonetary debt to gross domestic product (GDP) in Italy since 1976. The results of this accounting exercise (see Tables 1 and 2, pp. 199, 200) bring out neatly the familiar fact that the very rapid growth of the public debt as a ratio of GDP since the beginning of the 1980s reflected the escalation of interest payments over the period. The real interest burden has grown for two main reasons: first, the increase in the outstanding debt inevitably contributed to higher interest payments; and, second, real interest rates rose steeply in excess of real output growth from 1980-81 on.

A remarkable feature of this period, brought out by the results presented in Table 2, is the high level of revenue from seigniorage as a proportion of GDP. A natural question, which the authors also pose, is why a lower inflation rate, especially after 1981, has not been accompanied by an equivalent lower rate of money creation? The reasons the authors suggest, after presenting data on the decomposition of the Treasury's seigniorage (see Table 3, p. 201), are mainly the steep fall in the velocity relating the monetary base to nominal GDP, and the increased monetary base of the Treasury. In their discussion of the fiscal implications of quantitative credit controls (see Section IV, pp. 215–18), the authors argue that the main factor that lies behind the decline in money base velocity is the use of higher reserve requirements on the banking system. By increasing the demand for money per unit of output and sustaining the seigniorage tax base (see column 9 in Table 3), the reserve requirement system maintained the weight of seigniorage revenue at a time when inflation was falling. The analysis here is straightforward and uncontroversial. But the results of the

---

*The views expressed here are the author's and are not necessarily those of the Bank of Greece.

calculations presented in Tables 2 and 3 in the paper cover only seigniorage revenue collected through money-base financing of the Treasury. For a better approximation of the amount of financial resources that the government managed to appropriate through the introduction of administrative controls, account must also be taken of the remaining part of the monetary base.

The authors rightly note that the reliance on direct regulatory measures, such as higher reserve requirements and portfolio coefficients on the banking system, or on the use of the Treasury's line of credit with the central bank to ensure an adequate level of revenue from seigniorage, is becoming increasingly difficult to sustain over the medium term. The fact that seigniorage cannot be sustained over the longer term by a step-up in administrative controls leads the authors to conclude that, on current assumptions about the growth of GDP, inflation, and real interest rates, fiscal correction will have to be relatively larger and faster to secure a sustainable position in the public finances. But it is not clear from the paper whether the authors would favor such a policy stance or would prefer the use of higher reserve requirements and portfolio coefficients, if such measures could be implemented, or of increasing recourse to central bank credit for the financing of the Treasury deficit to ensure adequate seigniorage revenue over the longer term.

It seems to me continued reliance on regulatory measures to secure additional government revenue by money-base creation is becoming an increasingly costly way of reducing the public debt burden. A sustained expansion of the monetary base is bound to lead, sooner or later, to more inflation and would therefore be inconsistent with a stance of monetary policy aimed at narrowing Italy's inflation differential with its main trading partners. There is also the growing concern regarding the distortions engendered by the prolonged resort to direct regulatory measures, particularly the consequences for the operating conditions and efficiency of the financial system in collecting and allocating resources. Curbing tax evasion and broadening the tax base, raising explicit taxes, and cutting public spending are perhaps less costly ways of easing the twin constraints of a big deficit and a high level of public debt in Italy.

The authors next make the point that recourse to quantitative statutory controls on domestic and external financial flows, particularly ceilings on bank credit, minimum security holding requirements for banks, and controls on outward capital movements over the period 1976–81, helped to sustain private sector demand for public bonds, thus keeping real interest rates and the cost of servicing the public debt artificially low; and they rightly argue that this can be thought of as an implicit tax collected by the Treasury. The analysis here is a little imprecise, based on intuition rather than on the use of a well-defined model, and the assertion that such controls were actually effective in holding down interest rates in 1976–81 is in no way substantiated.

The authors then go on to argue that the gradual lifting of these controls after 1982 was one of the main reasons for the sharp increase in real interest rates, which, in turn, have boosted the cost of servicing the public debt.

To the extent that such controls helped to maintain low real rates for most of the 1970s, the move toward increased reliance on indirect, market-oriented mechanisms of monetary control, which began in the early 1980s, may well have been in itself an important factor behind the steep rise in real interest rates since that time. But this is only one possible explanation. There were several other contributory factors: first, the increase in world interest rates; second, the persistence of a positive inflation differential between Italy and its partners in the European Monetary System (EMS), which forced the authorities to maintain a positive real interest rate differential to relieve pressure on the exchange rate; and third, the inflation expectations of buyers of securities that were built into interest rates and had probably been reinforced by the persistence of a large public sector borrowing requirement and the fear that the government might be prompted to resort to higher taxation. The discussion here, and in the concluding section, is somewhat obscure, in that Bruni, Penati, and Porta do not come up with a clear view on whether a policy aimed at holding down interest rates on the public debt through administrative controls is an acceptable choice or not, thus leaving the reader in search of a clear-cut message. This is a central issue of the whole analysis and deserves to receive some attention.

Given the high debt service burden—and the desire to encourage the growth of investment—one can understand the concern expressed by the authors regarding the rise in real rates. But this trend reflected the constraints on the authorities in their conduct of interest rate policy. On the one hand, anti-inflation policy, the fragile external position, and the need to ensure the absorption of very large amounts of government debt in the public's portfolios required high and generally rising real interest rates. On the other, this interest rate policy has had the effect of increasing the debt service burden and, hence, the general government borrowing requirement. This is apparently the reason why the authorities in 1986 and 1987 chose temporarily to resort once again to statutory controls. Such measures cannot, however, bring about a lasting reduction of the burden of the public debt.

There is a risk that such policies may jeopardize the disinflationary process and the external position through an excessive expansion of the monetary base. Italy's present policy is conducted within the EMS framework. There would thus seem to be very little leeway for any substantial lowering of real rates in view of the need to make further progress on the inflation front, so as to achieve a measure of convergence in Italy's performance with those of its EMS partners and generate sufficient financial savings to cover the borrowing requirement of the public sector. A reduction both in inflation and the government borrowing requirement, implying discretionary fiscal correction, appears to be the only way to break loose from the current policy dilemma.

Comment

Jorge Braga de Macedo

Three authors for an economics paper may seem a large number, but Franco Bruni, Alessandro Penati, and Angelo Porta suggest that, in their case, it is a small number. Because they are bringing together research in the areas of debt management, banking, and international finance conducted at the Centre for Monetary and Financial Economics of Università Commerciale Luigi Bocconi (UCLB), this work represents the views of yet more authors on Italy's financial integration and monetary and financial policy. Claiming that economic survival with a high public debt will involve a mix of higher implicit taxes, stronger administrative controls, and faster inflation, Bruni, Penati, and Porta argue for fiscal adjustment by pushing for the liberalization of international capital movements. Borrowing from the title of a paperback about another successful business school, I will refer to these proposals as "the gospel according to UCLB."

In this comment, I will briefly characterize the accounting framework used by the authors, and then describe the various solutions to the Italian public debt problem and their links to the literature. I will then show that the framework is useful for analyzing other public debt problems and, drawing on Macedo and Sebastião (1989), refer to the recent experience of Portugal. My conclusion is that the UCLB gospel travels well, to the extent that it requires a careful analysis of the specific conditions of each high public debt country.

The analysis of Bruni, Penati, and Porta begins with a standard decomposition of the debt-accumulation equation, whereby the increase in privately held public debt equals the primary deficit plus the interest account minus seigniorage. This framework is used to uncover the various implicit taxes implied by the structure of the public sector. Seeing controls as sources of revenue makes it easier to understand the difficulties of fiscal adjustment and the dangers of financial deregulation in Italy. The collaboration with the International Monetary Fund (IMF) is thus welcome; the recent Occasional Paper No. 55 (IMF (1987)) still touches all too briefly on the link between financial programming and fiscal policy.

To understand the link, it is necessary to identify the various ways in which the public sector deals with financial intermediaries, a major undertaking begun by Bruni, Monti, and Porta (1982). A shortcut is to focus on the borrowing of the

Treasury from the central bank, analyzed in great detail by Salvemini and Salvemini (1987). Here, the UCLB gospel asserts the rights of the lender and turns the subordination of the central bank to the Treasury on its head. The refusal to buy more public debt, rather than being "an act of rebellion" (as the 1973 Report of the Bank of Italy calls this possibility), may then be in accordance with the practices of the international financial community and institutions.

The 1981 "divorce" between the Bank and the Treasury was an incomplete and easily reversible liberating experience. There are still hidden taxes and controls that delay fiscal adjustment, and the change in operating procedures has not been ratified by a legislative act of Parliament, as emphasized by Tabellini (1988). The opening of the Italian capital market that is required by the objective of a single European market in 1992, by imposing financial discipline, is the only credible measure to end the direct financing of the Treasury by the central bank. The current system is unsustainable, and the alternatives, according to the gospel, involve a closing of the Italian market, perhaps sharing McKinnon-type "financial repression" with other soft currencies in the European Economic Community.

Because of the emphasis on the role of the central bank, the UCLB gospel departs from the fully consolidated view of the public sector. In such a view, shown for the closed economy in Buiter (1985), the change in the monetary base would be treated like any other source of government revenue. Instead, Bruni, Penati, and Porta prefer to focus on the public debt held by the central bank, which they call the Treasury monetary base. Other central bank assets, especially claims on foreign monetary authorities, may change the profit and loss account, but they are considered as lowering the deficit rather than financing it. The same may be said, incidentally, of foreign-held public debt, which turns out to be low in Italy but is of course high in many Latin countries involved in financial programming exercises with the IMF.

This accounting framework shows that the Italian Treasury has adjusted to high real interest rates by maintaining a sizable source of revenue from the central bank, not so much in the form of currency but rather bank reserves and controls, which increase the demand for public debt on the part of the banking system. Concentrating on the public debt held by the central bank at below market interest rates, the authors record roughly 2 percent of gross domestic product (GDP) from this type of seigniorage from 1976 to 1987—about the same as the total seigniorage reported by Giavazzi (1989). More interesting perhaps, Treasury seigniorage remained constant, while real interest rates net of growth rose from –7 percent in 1976–81 to 2 percent in 1984–87, and the primary deficit fell from 7 percent to 5 percent. This decline was due to an increase in the tax rate from 11 percent to 13 percent, since the base actually fell from 19 percent to 16 percent.

Aside from the Treasury seigniorage and the inflation tax, administrative controls help to finance the deficit because they enhance the demand for public debt relative to private domestic and foreign instruments. This is evident in a positive real interest rate differential relative to the United States and the Federal Republic of Germany, which was close to 1 percent in the period 1983–87. Actually, the higher cost of equity more than compensates for the lower real cost of issuing public debt, thus inducing international investors to require a premium to hold stock in Italian firms. A higher degree of capital mobility, by breaking this financial protectionism, may thus require a lower public debt to be credible. The trade-off is, once again, between a closed system with more inflation and controls and an open system with less government spending and less "disguised fiscal policy."

Three closing points made by the authors illustrate the links of the UCLB gospel to other strands of the literature. First, the structure of the public sector matters, and, in particular, more attention should be paid to the qualitative composition of public debt. This point is indisputable and has a broad significance. Once again, in the Italian context it has often been seen in terms of marriages and divorces between *Banca* and *Tesoro*, but the broad implication is for the careful study of the variety of roles the public sector takes with respect to banks, as suggested in Bruni, Monti, and Porta (1982).

This particular aspect of the gospel is also documented by Tabellini (1988) and other contributors to Giavazzi and Spaventa (1988). Alesina (1988) and Salvemini and Salvemini (1987), moreover, show how this approach touches upon recent advances in the strategic analysis of government behavior and raises the issue of the independence of the central bank. The specific implication of this point, brought out in this paper, is to have more real-indexed bonds. Nevertheless, without a regime change, more Baffi bonds may induce more spending, as Morcaldo warns in his comment (see p. 246). In effect, the independence of the central bank cannot be advocated in a vacuum, it must be seen in the framework of the monetary constitution, so dear to the members of the public-choice school (see Brennan and Buchanan (1981)).

A second tenet of the UCLB gospel—that domestic and external financial liberalization must be balanced—touches upon an entirely different strand of literature, which has a flavor of Latin America rather than of Lombardy. The insight, both theoretical and empirical, about the order in which real trade and financial protectionism must be removed is of relevance here. Sometimes shown by the so-called Arriazu box, the preferred order seems to be real first and financial second (see Edwards (1984)). If domestic also precedes external, we see that the removal of financial protectionism in Italy requires domestic financial liberalization—namely, the end of the implicit taxes and administrative controls designed to favor borrowing by the Treasury. Skepticism about the ability to bring about an irreversible monetary reform without external pressure is another feature of the gospel. In light of the establishment of the single European market in 1992, however, one wonders whether expected external financial liberalization could validate a change in the domestic financial regime.

The importance of uncovering implicit taxes and disguised fiscal policy is that, once again, it shows the political element behind the financial discipline. The idea that external financial liberalization may be a way of neutralizing the domestic lobbying efforts for deficit financing is once again reminiscent of some of the development literature focusing on rent-seeking. It is also found, of course, in the game-theoretic approach of Alesina (1988) and has been used by economic historians.

We could even rationalize the super-risk premium on Italian equity discussed in the last section of the paper as a kind of "lira problem," familiar to students in Chicago of the forward market for Mexican pesos and relate it to the degree of capital mobility. The approach of Frankel (1988) or Frankel and MacArthur (1988) is to take the real-interest differentials as measures of capital mobility. The figures in the paper suggest that both the real and nominal interest rate differential between the lira and the dollar turned from negative to positive after the 1983 realignment. We can see this change in the covered differential, which is a measure of political risk, as a move from restrictions on capital outflows to restrictions on capital inflows. The decrease in the magnitude of the spread, however, suggests that there is some expectation of liberalization but that the lira problem can be seen as a risk of future controls on outflows. Indeed, the most recent data suggest that the domestic return may have become lower once again. This approach is of course consistent with the finance literature summarized by Adler and Dumas (1983), which Bruni, Penati, and Porta use in their analysis.

Rather than pursuing this route, I will show how the gospel can be useful in an explanation of the Portuguese experience. Figure 1 shows the Portuguese public debt as a proportion of GDP from 1970 to 1987, as well as its decomposition between debt held privately—that is to say, mostly by commercial banks—and debt held by the central bank. The latter component began to rise after the 1974 Revolution, in the wake of which the domestic banking system was nationalized without compensation. There was a drop in 1980, offsetting the capital gain due to the revaluation of the gold reserves. The accumulation of both components of public debt accelerated subsequently, but after the stabilization program agreed on with the IMF in 1983–84, the central bank component began to decline. The external surplus of 1986/87 was a factor in the decline of the Treasury monetary base, but there is also increasing awareness that the "high public debt" (70 percent of GDP as seen in Chart 1, plus all the guaranteed debt) may reverse the anti-inflationary program initiated in late 1985, which managed to cut the rate of increase of the output deflator from 20 percent in 1985 to 11 percent in 1987,

Figure 1. Portugal: Public Debt, 1970–85

(In percent of GDP)

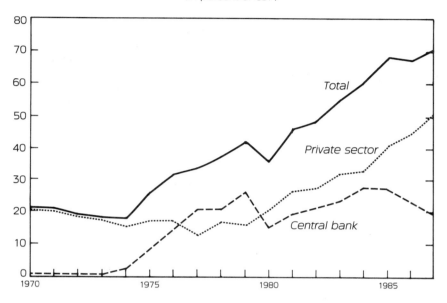

Source: Data from Macedo and Sebastião (1989)

thus bringing ex-post real interest rates up from –11 percent to –1 percent. Meanwhile, the primary government budget deficit fell from 4 percent to 2 percent of output over the same period.

Reproducing the decomposition used by Bruni, Penati, and Porta for Portugal requires some adaptations, mostly because the official budget figures (even "adjusted" like the ones on the primary deficit just cited) cannot be used in the debt-accumulation equation, due to accounting deficiencies. An "implied deficit" obtained as a residual is thus presented after the real interest payments and seigniorage are accounted for. As explained in Macedo and Sebastião (1989), it matters whether we use total or domestic debt, and whether the interest payments of the Treasury to the central bank are net of central bank payments to the commercial banks due to the interest subsidies and the interbank market. With total debt and the gross interest figures, the implied nominal rate on privately held debt rises from 9 percent to 10 percent between 1985 and 1987, whereas the one paid on the public debt held by the central bank falls from 19 percent to 15 percent, implying that the contribution of seigniorage as a proportion of output fell from 3 percent in 1985 to –17 percent in 1987. The implied deficit

in turn, fell from 38 percent to 13 percent of output, the difference from the
actual figures being due to external borrowing and adjustments.

These figures underestimate seigniorage however, since the interest revenue
of the central bank is spent compensating the banking system for the low
profitability of its operations due to the system of credit ceilings. Taking these
into account, the implied effective interest falls from 2 percent to –3 percent, and
the contribution of seigniorage as a proportion of output falls from 14 percent to
zero, whereas the implied deficit falls from 50 percent to 20 percent of output.

Tables 1–3, using the same format as Bruni, Penati, and Porta, are based on
total debt and the net interest payments. The period averages since 1976 have a

Table 1. Portugal: Breakdown of the Growth Rate of the Real Value of Public Debt Held Outside the Central Bank

(Average yearly rates in percent)

				Contribution of:		
Years	Growth Rate of Real Debt	=	Deficit Net of Interest	+	Real Interest Rate on Debt –	Treasury's Seigniorage
1976–79	3.0		64.0		–11.0	50.0
1980	31.0		0.0		–7.0	–36.0
1981–84	12.0		41.0		–8.0	22.0
1985–87	19.0		31.0		–6.0	6.0

Source: Data from Macedo and Sebastião (1989).

rough correspondence with governments, including the odd year of 1980 (see
details in Macedo and Sebastião (1989)). Overall, the tables show a situation that
appears more distorted than the situation in Italy before the 1981 divorce, with
highly negative real interest rates, high primary deficits, and high seigniorage.
Despite the fall in the seigniorage tax rate from 28 percent in 1981/84 to 8 percent in 1985/87, the base remains high and is seen to be rising from 22 percent to
25 percent. This has kept total seigniorage at 2 percent of output. Although this
is the same share as in Italy, the difference between the two situations is what the
UCLB gospel—and these tables—bring out.

Table 2. Portugal: Breakdown of Change in Ratio of Nonmonetary Public Debt to GDP

Years	Average Yearly Change in GDP Ratio	=	Real Interest Rate on Debt Less Real Growth of GDP	×	Debt/GDP Ratio	+	Deficit Net of Interest	−	Treasury's Seigniorage
	(in percent)								*(in percent of GDP)*
1976–79	0.0		−16.0		16.0		10.0		8.0
1980	5.0		−11.0		19.0		0.0		−7.0
1981–84	3.0		−8.0		29.0		12.0		6.0
1985–87	6.0		−10.0		43.0		13.0		2.0

Contribution of:

Source: Data from Macedo and Sebastião (1989).

Table 3. Breakdown of Portuguese Treasury's Seigniorage, 1976–87

(Average yearly rates, in percent except where otherwise noted)

Years	Seigniorage Tax Rate							Seigniorage Tax Base (monetary base of the Treasury)		Total Seigniorage	
		Change in Real Stock of Total Monetary Base			Change in Treasury Base/ Monetary Base Ratio	Avg. Interest Rate on Treasury Monetary Base	Total			(7)x(8)	(7)x(9)
	Inflation	Real GDP Growth	Velocity	Total (2)–(3)			(1)+(4)+(5)–(6)	(percent of debt*)	(percent of GDP)	(percent of debt**)	(percent of GDP)
	(1)	(2)	(3)	(4)	(5)	(6)	(7)	(8)	(9)	(10)	(11)
1976–79	19.0	5.0	12.0	–7.0	38.0	5.0	44.0	12.0	19.0	49.0	8.0
1980	18.0	4.0	2.0	2.0	–52.0	1.0	–33.0	10.8	20.0	36.0	–7.0
1981–84	20.0	0.0	3.0	–3.0	18.0	7.0	28.0	7.6	22.0	21.0	6.0
1985–87	16.0	4.4	9.0	–5.0	–4.0	0.0	8.0	5.8	25.0	6.0	2.0

Note: Data from Macedo and Sebastião (1989).
*Public debt held by the private sector.

References

Adler, Michael, and Bernard Dumas, "International Portfolio Choice and Corporation Finance: A Synthesis," *Journal of Finance* (New York), Vol. 38 (June 1983), pp. 925–84.

Alesina, Alberto, "The End of Large Public Debts," in *High Public Debt: The Italian Experience*, ed. by Francesco Giavazzi and Luigi Spaventa (Cambridge: Cambridge University Press, 1988).

Brennan, Geoffrey, and James Buchanan, "Revenue Implications of Money Creation Under Leviathan," *American Economic Review, Papers and Proceedings of the Ninety-Third Annual Meeting of the American Economic Association*, Vol. 71 (May 1981), pp. 347–51.

Bruni, Franco, Mario Monti, and Angelo Porta, "Bank Lending to the Public Sector: Determinants, Implications and Outlook," Chap. 10 in *Bank Management in a Changing Domestic and International Environment: The Challenges of the Eighties*, ed. by Donald E. Fair and Francois Léonard de Juvigny (Boston: Martinus Nijhoff, 1982).

Buiter, Willem H., "A Guide to Public Sector Debt and Deficits," *Economic Policy: A European Forum* (London), Vol. 1 (November 1985), pp. 13–79.

Edwards, Sebastian, *The Order of Liberalization of the External Sector in Developing Countries*, Essays in International Finance, No. 156, Princeton University (Princeton, New Jersey: Princeton University Press, 1984).

Frankel, Jeffrey, "Quantifying International Capital Mobility," NBER Working Paper 2856 (Cambridge, Massachusetts: National Bureau of Economic Research, February 1988).

————, and Alan MacArthur, "Political vs. Currency Premia in International Real Interest Differentials: A Study of Forward Rates in 24 countries," *European Economic Review* (Amsterdam), Vol. 32 (June 1988), pp. 1083–1114.

Giavazzi, Francesco, "The Exchange-Rate Question in Europe," Discussion Paper Series No. 298 (London: Centre for Economic Policy Research, January 1989).

————, and Luigi Spaventa, eds., *High Public Debt: The Italian Experience* (Cambridge: Cambridge University Press, 1988).

International Monetary Fund, *Theoretical Aspects of the Design of Fund-Supported Adjustment Programs*, Occasional Paper No. 55 (Washington: International Monetary Fund, 1987).

Macedo, Jorge Braga de, and Manuel Sebastião, "Implicit Taxes and Public Debt: The Portuguese Experience," *European Economic Review* (Amsterdam), Vol. 33 (March 1989), pp. 573–79.

Salvemini, G., and M.T. Salvemini, "Il credito automatico del Tesoro presso la banca centrale" (mimeographed, Rome: Consiglio Nazionale delle Richereche, August 1987).

Tabellini, Guido, "Monetary and Fiscal Policy Coordination With a *High Public Debt*," in *High Public Debt: The Italian Experience*, ed. by Francesco Giavazzi and Luigi Spaventa (Cambridge: Cambridge University Press, 1988), pp. 90–126.

Comment

Giancarlo Morcaldo*

The topics examined in this paper should be viewed within the framework of problems arising from the large structural deficit of the public budget in our country. In the long run, the sharp rise of the public debt outlined by Bruni, Penati, and Porta, is not compatible with internal and external stability. The structural deficit of the public budget, in the absence of an accommodating monetary policy, would require a continuous increase in the absorption of public bonds by the market; in this situation, a larger and larger share of gross domestic product (GDP) would be distributed to public-debt holders.

To ensure placement of these bonds, it would be necessary to modify those factors on which formation of saving and its allocation depend. There are only three alternatives: 1) an increase in the total propensity to save; 2) an increase in the propensity to save through financial saving; and 3) a crowding-out of other financial assets by public bonds.

With market instruments, the above alternatives would require an increase in interest rates in real terms and, in particular, in interest rates paid on public bonds. On the basis of past experience, high and rising interest rates should be able, in the short and medium term, to raise the propensity to save through financial saving and, in some measure, total propensity to save. In the long run, however, this effect could be counterbalanced by other factors; the substitution between financial and real assets also depends, for instance, on the expected rate of inflation, which may be influenced by the continuous accumulation of public debt.

Within this framework, the paper under examination points out that a large contribution to the financing of the public budget deficit can be ascribed to administrative regulations. These institutional factors and the limitations imposed on the activity of the private sector have increased the share of the public deficit that is financed with monetary-base creation and have ensured the absorption of large quantities of public bonds by the market, at an interest rate lower than otherwise would have prevailed.

---

*The views expressed here are the author's and are not necessarily those of the Bank of Italy.

The possibility of the Treasury's being able to draw from the current account with the Bank of Italy (even if limited) and (until 1981) the obligation for the latter to buy Treasury bills not placed in auctions increased the monetary base supply; this increase was met by a rise in demand, which was caused by the changes in the reserve coefficient on bank deposits.

At the same time, administrative controls imposed on both domestic and international flows of funds allowed the placement of large amounts of public bonds, thereby depressing the level of interest rates. In the 1980s, partly as result of the gradual slackening of administrative controls, interest rates rose sharply.

Institutional factors and administrative controls can be regarded as implicit taxes, as has been correctly pointed out in this paper. Inflation produces similar effects by increasing the seigniorage represented by monetary-base creation; it has also the effect of increasing implicit taxes resulting from administrative regulations.

The effects of inflation described in this paper are strengthened by their influence on the public budget. An acceleration in prices causes a reduction of the ratio between the public deficit corrected for inflation and GDP (given constant interest rates in real terms); proportionally, the increase in tax receipts is larger than that in expenditures. This is mainly due to the progressivity of personal income tax (corrections of fiscal drag are usually partial and not timely); the disproportionately sharp increase in the tax on interest paid on bank deposits; and other factors, such as effects on the pension system (in terms of percent, the increase in social security contributions is larger than that in new pensions whose amount is linked to the inflation of the preceding five years, excluding the most recent).

I agree with the authors that the effect of capital controls on interest rates is limited by other factors (for example, limitations on the use of savings can give rise to a portfolio composition that is less diversified and consequently riskier). In this regard, it should be pointed out that other kinds of administrative controls, like ceilings on increases in bank loans, may reduce interest rates on these loans, because the ceilings enable the banks to choose loans with relatively less risk. Nevertheless, crowding-out might be lessened if the reduction in interest rates as a result of capital controls extended to other kinds of financial assets.

The problems outlined here give some indications of economic policy options available in our country. The evolution of tax revenues, expenditures, and deficits observed in the last few years confirms the conclusions that the budget deficit corrected for inflation is not a good measure of the structural deficit—that is, the deficit that would prevail if inflation declined. The fall in inflation, the growth of the economy, and the corrective actions taken have not been sufficient to bring about a substantial reduction in the public deficit in nominal terms.

In the long term, administrative controls cannot ensure a large increase in the absorption of public bonds without the serious consequences to the efficiency of the productive system outlined in the paper by Bruni, Penati, and Porta. In this context, it should be noted that the contribution to the financing of the public deficit coming from the regulation of bank assets would not be substantial, because the public deficit is far larger than the flows of banks' new assets.

However, a continuous increase in interest rates required by the market to absorb large quantities of public bonds cannot be sustained in the long run; the increase in the revenue of public-debt holders coming from the sharp increases in interest payments could have destabilizing effects; as already noted, substitution between financial and real assets depends on other important factors.

In the presence of a large structural deficit, monetary policy loses its effectiveness; in the long run, new placements of public bonds in the market caused by rising interest rates would be largely matched by a rise in interest payments, not only because of the size of the public debt, but also because of the size of the share that is financially indexed. The increase in interest rates, even if sustainable, would negatively affect private investment and economic growth. The failure of policies aimed at absorbing the overall financial requirements of the public sector could, as the authors point out, result in the strengthening of administrative controls or an increase in the rate of inflation.

In the last few years, some success has been achieved in controlling the public deficit; but it has to be said that part of the improvement can be ascribed to interventions whose effects decrease with time.

Because the problem persists, I agree with the conclusions reached by Bruni, Penati, and Porta. The actions already introduced directed at gradually absorbing the public deficit net of interest payments have to be continued and strengthened; at the same time, the types of public bonds supplied to the market need to be diversified, in order to reduce interest rates to a minimum level. The absorption of the public deficit has to be conducted strictly in accordance with economic activity considerations, so as to ensure that the conditions the economy needs for stable and durable growth are maintained.

The corrective action should be directed mainly toward the control of public expenditure. Waste and inefficiency need to be limited in order to minimize negative effects on the level of economic activity. On the revenue side, the ratio of fiscal receipts to GDP needs to be increased through reductions in tax evasion and a reversal in the erosion of the tax base. The lag between the ratio of receipts to GDP in Italy and those prevailing in other major industrial countries depends more on these factors than on lower tax rates.

Real-indexed bonds would be helpful in the financing of the overall borrowing requirements of he public sector. However, a large increase in these bonds would probably postpone service on the debt, thereby leaving room for other expenditure programs. For this reason, it is necessary to proceed with caution.

Panel Discussion

Paolo Baffi
Chairman

This panel discussion is more or less independent of the proceedings of the previous two days of this conference. I think we are free to refer to all the papers presented and perhaps elaborate on some of the points over which there were differences of opinion. I have especially in mind the different notes which Tanzi and Makin struck, in my view, about the possibility for international cooperation. Tanzi seems to think that the process of decision making, starting with the legislative procedure, is so drawn out that the decisions take effect beyond the time horizon for which reasonable forecasts can be made; so it is better to give up all ideas of coordination, except perhaps in the structure of taxation, where reforms could be directed toward rational allocation of resources and efficiency.

Makin strikes a more hopeful note; he speaks, for instance, of a slight expansion in the Federal Republic of Germany and Japan to generate a more balanced equilibrium vis-à-vis the United States. Tanzi seems to think that such an approach would merely lead to an increase in interest rates and so to an increased burden for servicing the public debt of the United States. If the discussion addresses these sorts of questions, I think it could be very profitable for all concerned.

Now, apart from international coordination, there is the problem of domestic coordination between different tools of policy and, maybe, between fiscal and monetary policy, not to speak of other tools like incomes policy. Now, I remember that in the famous article that was published in 1981 in the *Minneapolis Federal Bank Review*,[1] Sargent and Wallace examine Friedman's thesis that monetary policy does not have the capacity to change the rate of growth of employment. But Friedman conceded that monetary policy might have a positive effect in the fight against inflation. The two authors go beyond Friedman in a negative sense, because they argue that if monetary policy is dominant, in the sense that in the scheme of coordination between fiscal and monetary policy fiscal policy plays a dominant role, fiscal policy itself may be conducted in such a

---

[1]Thomas J. Sargent and Neil Wallace, "Some Unpleasant Monetarist Arithmetic," *Federal Bank of Minneapolis Quarterly Review* (Minneapolis, Minnesota), Vol. 5 (Fall 1981), pp. 1–17.

way as to nullify any attempt by the central bank to control inflation. And, in fact, a strict monetary policy will advance the day of reckoning when monetary control will have to be abandoned—the day of surrender to inflation. I think that Mr. Spaventa might elaborate on this point very well, and, of course, our friend Mr. Arriazu, because the political process in Argentina seems closer to what happens in Italy than in Germany. And there must be structural reasons for this. Once there was an Argentinian Governor of the Central Bank—a very decent fellow—who came to explain to all the central bankers who convened every month in Basle at the Bank for International Settlements that he had attained great success, because from whatever peak, which I do not remember, the rate of inflation had been brought down to about 100 percent a year. I do not know what the inflation rate is now, but Mr. Arriazu can tell us what lies behind that and what is the relation between monetary policy and fiscal policy in Argentina.

Mr. Haller could probably address some points of comparison between Italy and Germany. I wonder, for example, what are the natural differences that let Germany stay in a position of a roughly balanced budget.

As regards Italy, we know that it is largely misaligned, compared with other countries in terms of the ratio of its budget deficit to gross national product (GNP). In fact, if you have a look at Table 6 in Tanzi's paper (p. 28), you can see that for Italy, this ratio is twice as much as for Canada and five times as much as that for the other countries. But to be quite fair to the Italian government and the public sector in general, I must say that part of this deficit is also due to larger transfers that the government makes to the private sector—and not only to households, but also to businesses in the form of fiscalization of social security payments, incentives of various kinds, and of course, the losses of public sector groups. If this unnatural and, in the long run, unsustainable situation is to be redressed, some considerable pruning in the budget must be done, and must also be accepted by Italian businesses.

Moreover, I should say that the ratio of the deficit is too high because this expense does not reflect goods and services only, but interest payments as well. So it is a process that feeds upon itself and will ultimately end in crisis unless we intervene.

The last point I would make is that we are not in such a desperate situation as the United States, because the United States combines a large public sector deficit with low saving propensity on the part of households. I think that in the case of Italy, at least some fraction of the transfers that are made to households increases their propensity to save and is translated in a roundabout way through the capital market into investment. And perhaps, through this process, we have performed this conjurer's trick—which the United States has not—of being able to combine a tremendous deficit with an equilibrium in the balance of payments.

John Vanderveken

Mr. Chairman, fellow participants, let me start by thanking the International Monetary Fund (IMF) and the Università Bocconi for inviting me to join this panel for a discussion of fiscal policy adjustment and economic agents. I am the General Secretary of the International Confederation of Free Trade Unions (ICFTU). For those of you unfamiliar with our organization, it is a worldwide confederation of trade unions. We have 143 affiliates in 97 countries, with a total membership of 87 million unionists. Our affiliates are national centers, such as the American Federation of Labor-Congress of Industrial Organizations (AFL-CIO) in the United States; the Confederación General del Trabajo (CGT) in Argentina; and the Confederazione Italiana Sindacati Lavoratori (CISL) and the Unione Italiana del Lavoro (UIL) in Italy. Our role on their behalf is to develop policies on a wide range of issues of common concern; the protection and promotion of trade union rights and economic and social questions are two of the most important areas of our work. In recent years the issue of economic adjustment in both developing and industrial countries has been one of our major concerns.

As I understand the concept of adjustment, it is the process of adapting the economy to produce competitively a different range of goods and services. That easy phrase describes a difficult and challenging task affecting all workers. Some people may find it novel that trade unions wish to have a say in structural adjustment. However, the process is of such importance to the creation of jobs and the improvement of living standards that unions cannot simply sit back and criticize the failures of others. Furthermore, one of the key elements of a successful adjustment or transformation is, in my view, the cooperation and active involvement of workers in the process. Commitment, participation, and cooperation do not come automatically at the push of a button. They must be built up through discussion, exchange of information, and agreement both in the workplace and at the national and international policymaking level. My contribution to this morning's discussion will be to argue that for a variety of economic, social, and political reasons, a great deal more needs to be done to ensure the involvement of trade unions and, by inference, other major groups, such as employers, in the development and application of adjustment policies and, in particular, fiscal policies.

As trade unionists, we have as a priority the protection and enhancement of the conditions of work and life of our members. More jobs, better wages and working conditions, pensions, and holidays are what members expect from their unions. Of course, behind these daily preoccupations are wider and deeper issues—dignity, justice, freedom—which decades of struggle have proven can

only be gained and preserved by working people through trade union organizations. Most politicians and bankers—but not all—would admit that trade unions
have a legitimate right to talk about wages and conditions. However, they are less
willing to admit that we must also express our views about the running of the
national and, indeed, world economy.

For many years now the ICFTU, the Trade Union Advisory Committee to the
Organization for Economic Cooperation and Development (OECD), and our
national affiliates have presented policy statements to governments and the
international agencies. I think we have gained some respect for the seriousness
of our approach, but I have to say that our members and working people generally
do not see much return for our efforts.

Most developing country workers are no better placed now than they were six
years ago. Many, in fact, have lost their jobs or found that inflation has cut into
their wage packets. Poverty and hunger in both city and countryside are rising in
most nations. Indicators of health problems among children are rising. The
much-heralded recovery has just not arrived for millions of ordinary hard-
working people. In industrial countries many groups of workers have not benefited from the slow growth since 1983, and many have experienced periods of
unemployment devastating to their lives and savings.

Whenever I read or hear the economists or bankers say the worst of the world
economic crisis is past, I point out that for the majority of working people in the
developing world, the crisis continues and, for many, worsens. In the industrial
countries there is considerable concern about job security in the private sector
and wage squeezes in the public sector.

Is there a light at the end of the tunnel? Will these sacrifices result in improved
economic performance, more jobs, and rising living standards next year, or the
year after? I fear that my reading of the economic forecasts of the major
international organizations leads me to say no. Each new forecast merely seems
to explain why the last was overoptimistic, but that things should improve soon.
But I do not see it. The United States and Japan are not growing at a sufficient
pace to generate a worldwide fall in unemployment. A European recovery seems
far away, and the greater part of the developing world is locked into tough
programs of adjustment.

It is our strong view that economic policies must respond to the needs of the
working people if they are to stand a chance of success. Free trade unions are
ready to join with governments and industry, at both the national and international levels, to help define and implement the immediate and long-term objectives and policies needed to sustain, spread, and strengthen the process of
economic revival and to overcome the urgent problems of unemployment and
poverty.

Our conviction is that increased coordination of policies could yield benefits for all and would certainly help to reduce the risks of a pronounced downturn. We are looking for relatively modest first steps, but steps that would send a message that the major democratic economic powers are giving some degree of direction to a confused and worried world.

We believe that one important and necessary way to reduce uncertainty and inconsistent expectations is improved coordination nationally and internationally among policymakers, among whom I include ourselves. The first area is exchange rates and interest rates, which, of necessity, will also lead to some degree of fiscal coordination.

A reform of tax systems to spread the base of revenue raising, to improve the efficiency of collection, and to ensure a progressive sharing of the burden of government expenditure is important in most countries. Decisions about public expenditure, especially on issues such as health, education, housing, social security, and other essential aspects of the social and economic infrastructure, can help to reduce unemployment and provide efficient services. And as trade unionists, we accept that efficiency in public expenditure is as important as its level and rate of growth.

Mr. Chairman, trade unions are prepared to play their part in the promotion and implementation of national and international development policies that meet the difficult challenges of restoring growth, correcting trade imbalances, increasing employment, and tackling poverty. Dialogue between governments, industry, and unions is essential to increase economic efficiency and social justice. Fiscal policy is probably the most important area to tackle because of its linkages to the international scene through financial markets. The trade union movement is eager to participate fully in these processes, but on the clear understanding that progress cannot be achieved by creating more insecurity for large sections of the population. If we don't start a serious and much broader debate on the current realities, we may all be facing a much more unpleasant world economic situation fairly soon.

Mr. Chairman, the painfully slow process of re-examination of current economic problems that is now underway will, we are convinced, eventually lead governments back to the realization that full employment, low inflation, a stable foreign trade balance, and steady growth in living standards can only be achieved simultaneously on the basis of a wider policy consensus arrived at through tripartite consultations and constructive international cooperation.

In this regard I was much encouraged by the outcome of the recent International Labor Organization's (ILO) high-level meeting on Employment and Structural Adjustment, which set out a constructive program for that organization's role in international development and cooperation—a role, incidentally, that I believe that the IMF and the World Bank will welcome.

I was also encouraged by some high-level meetings the ICFTU had in Washington in July last year with the IMF and the World Bank. The top officials recognized the value of considering social issues with economic policies. We believe that adjustment through growth makes it possible for socially necessary policies to be worked out that focus on employment and poverty alleviation and are economically efficient.

Effective tripartism can create widespread support for agreed policies of national development that address the urgent needs of working people and establish a sound economic structure for the future. This is where the ILO comes in. It can help to broaden the base for action by involving employers' and workers' organizations in the formulation of policy and its implementation.

In conclusion, let me make a couple of political points. Although many speeches by trade unionists are critical of the IMF, we are prepared to admit that if the Fund didn't exist, we would have to invent it. And furthermore, it would be much harder in 1988 than it was in 1944 to establish a body with the necessary authority to oversee international monetary matters. However, the IMF needs support from its member governments, and if those governments do not in turn have support from public opinion for international cooperation through the IMF and other institutions, they will not be interested in associating themselves with internationalist solutions.

In addition, I think we are all concerned to see the deepening and strengthening of democracy. We must not get ourselves into a position where somehow obligations under international adjustment programs are in conflict with democratic institutions, and I count free trade unions as among the most fundamental. The Fund and its members must be responsive to the calls for wider participation in policymaking; this is not just a matter of attitude, it is a question of establishing mechanisms for discussion that can survive periodic disagreements. It is also not simply a political matter, because as I stressed earlier, in our view, adjustment is likely to work best on the basis of a broad national and international consensus derived from wide participation in the formulation of policies.

Ricardo Arriazu

I would like first to refer to some conceptual aspects of inflation. Economists do not all give the same explanation of inflation. If you are a monetarist you will say that inflation is the result of a disequilibrium in the monetary market; if you are a structuralist you will say that inflation is a reflection of a fight among sectors for the biggest increase in their respective shares of income. I am much more simple than that. I think that inflation is a fraud. The word in Spanish is *estafa*. I was looking for the word in Italian and was told that it is *truffa*. Actually, what it means is that the government has borrowed from the private sector and has promised to return real resources, paying back less than what it promised. If this were the only problem, what would happen is exactly the same as what happens in the private sector. If somebody does not fulfill his obligations, then people will stop lending to him, and he will be forced to go to the money market sharks—to the *usureros*, as we say in Spanish—and pay higher interest rates.

But the problem is that the government is making an *estafa* with an instrument that is the unit of account of the system. This has much wider implications than you might expect. Suppose, for example, that the government was borrowing a certain amount of wheat measured in tons and that it decided to change the unit of measurement of the system; say, it decided the kilo equaled only 900 grams, or only 700 grams. Of course, it would pay less. But if the unit of account "tons of wheat" is used by the rest of the system as the unit of account of economic flows (wages, prices, etc.), when the government cheats on its own debt, it produces tremendous transfers of real resources among other sectors in the economy. We economists tend to forget that money is used as a unit of account. Therefore, when a country is using inflation as a means to obtain financing and, as a consequence, uses "cheating" as a source of funds, the private sector abandons the unit of account of the government and also abandons the use of national currency as a way of making deals. For example, in Argentina most of the big transactions are not denominated in national currency.

How do you get to high inflation? It is very simple. I can assure you that with persistence, patience, and the right policy, you could all arrive at high inflation. You start with a fiscal deficit and then you persist with it. At the beginning, you obtain large inflationary tax revenues because the tax base is large, so that the tax rate needed (inflation) is low. Then when people start to fly out of the currency and the inflationary tax base starts to be reduced, you need a higher inflationary tax to finance the same deficit.

To give you an idea of what this means, consider the case of Argentina. In 1945 total national-denominated financial assets of the private sector were equivalent to 67 percent of gross domestic product (GDP). Now, they represent only 10 percent of GDP. The non-interest-bearing monetary base used to be equivalent to 25 percent of GDP. Now it is equivalent to only 2.5 percent of GDP. Private sector sight deposits used to be 20 percent of GDP; now they are 1 percent of GDP! The internal private debt used to be very high. Now it is only 7 percent of GDP and is mostly in the form of mandatory minimum reserve requirements, which means that capital markets have disappeared. A large part of this is used to finance the public deficit.

Most of these numbers are fictitious. The fact is that when you have inflation, most of your assets and savings are not held in the form of national currency instruments but rather in the form of foreign currency instruments. More than two thirds of our financial wealth is definitely held abroad; we have almost $30 billion abroad, and less than $10 billion inside the country.

However, the main problem with inflation is not financial but moral. The government starts with a deficit and is very happy with imposing an inflationary tax, because it is a simple way of getting real resources; what the government forgets is that the ones who pay the inflationary tax are normally the least informed segment of the population—the workers. When people start to learn, they begin to fly out of the national currency and to buy dollars, therefore eroding the inflationary tax base, so the government says, "We have a capital outflow problem," and imposes controls on capital movements. Those people who are taking the money out are supposed to be unpatriotic. But actually, the only thing they are doing is protecting themselves against cheating by the government. We all know that our grandparents have lost all their savings because of inflation. But the government likes this form of taxation, and the public is forced to make a decision: either to buy dollars to protect themselves, which is illegal; or to stay and be cheated by the government. The public finally reacts, saying, "If I buy dollars it is not immoral, even if it is illegal; what the government is doing is immoral." And for the first time, we start breaking up the relationship between morality and legality, which is the base of any organized society. Once I sunder the relationship between morality and legality, then nothing is an impediment to my going further.

The same thing happens with taxation. What the government normally does is to increase unproductive public expenditures—in doing this, it is increasing taxes only partially to pay for them, which reduces productivity and increases the deficit. Since the tax system is normally inefficient in the face of inflation, people can ask themselves how much tax they want to pay. But if I pay taxes for the government to spend the money in a really inefficient way, then I can ask myself: is it moral or immoral not to pay unproductive taxes? In a context such as the one described here, the public tends to decide how much taxes they wish to pay, and not paying taxes is no longer considered immoral.

Of course, in a context of excessive expenditures, countries will tend to, and most tend to, apply protectionist policies. Protective policies will never solve a balance of payments problem. It is always a question of one sector of the economy against another sector of the economy. But protective policies are widely applied to solve balance of payments difficulties. For example, in Argentina it is forbidden to buy, among other things, computers. We have factories that import all of their parts and sell their computers at prices three times higher than the international price. The question is, should I be noncompetitive, or should I get the computer in any way I can? And, of course, smuggling becomes a way of getting the computer. Again, the public is forced to break the law, because protectionism makes it impossible to become competitive.

Once people start to judge the rightness of certain legislation, where do they finish? What is the definition of morality? Each of us has his own definition of morality, and once I have severed the relationship between morality and legality, I can continue unchecked. In this context, for example, stealing can be moral. After these awful examples, I hope it should be quite clear why inflation is not only an economic problem but a political and a moral problem as well.

Let us go now to the final question, which is how you manage monetary policy in an inflationary environment. The answer is that you do not manage monetary policy; it is monetary policy that manages you. We do not have a capital market, since there is no way of introducing bonds into the system because nobody wants to hold a national-denominated debt instrument. To cover the fiscal deficit you have to print money. But if the non-interest-bearing monetary base is equivalent to just 2.5 percentage points of GDP, a deficit of similar magnitude will produce a 100 percent increase in the monetary base. If we had the Italian fiscal deficit in Argentina—which at this moment we do not have—the inflation rate would be in the range of thousands of percent. Since inflation itself tends to increase the budget deficit, once you are in this situation there is no alternative but to reduce the fiscal deficit practically to zero because you cannot make monetary policy.

How do we change it? Consider the accounting identity, which says that the current account of the balance of payments is equal to the sum of the public sector budget plus the private sector budget. Let us take the case of Argentina last year. We had a consolidated public sector budget deficit of approximately $6 billion. Assume that we could get external financing for only $2 billion as voluntary lending, and that, internally, nobody was willing to lend even 1 percent to the government in real terms. This leaves us three alternatives. Either we get more resources from abroad—voluntarily or mandatorily. Mandatorily means that if we have to pay interest of $4 billion, we do not pay it; so we get $4 billion worth of financing. The other possibility is to get $4 billion internally. But if the total deposit in the system is $10 billion, and we do not have any way of getting more financing internally, the only remaining recourse that we have is forced financing. And forced financing means increasing the minimal reserve requirements. But nonremunerated reserve requirements are an *estafa*. Perhaps it is possible to get $1 billion in that way—and we are left again with the problem of how to finance the rest of the fiscal deficit. Since I am using dollars as the unit of account, the way to reduce the fiscal deficit in terms of dollars is by inflation. And the way that we produce inflation is by devaluation. Devaluation is in substance a mechanism to obtain inflationary tax. You need to estimate how much you have to devalue in order to get an inflationary tax to reduce your budget in terms of dollars to something approaching equilibrium. Now, the calculus is not simple because the budget itself is related to inflation, so you have to know how much the deficit will increase when you are increasing inflation.

As I mentioned yesterday, there is some point at which the net inflationary tax becomes negative, when it does not produce any real resource transfer to the government. Then you are forced either to get the resources from abroad or to get them from inside the country, because the inflationary tax produces nothing. When this happens and you cannot get resources from abroad or within the country, you are close to hyperinflation. And in Argentina at this moment, what we have is a situation with no internal financing, no external financing, and no way of getting net resource transfers from the inflationary tax.

Therefore, we are very close to hyperinflation.

Luigi Spaventa

Since several references have been made in this seminar to the situation of Italian public finance, let me begin by briefly recalling some aspects of the debate on the control of public expenditure that has taken place in Italy and elsewhere—namely, the new legislation and stricter monetary policy.

Let me start with a few data. The development of the primary deficit goes back to the end of the 1960s and continued in the 1970s; therefore, it is by no means a recent phenomenon. The decisions made by both the Parliament and, no less frequently, by the Government, were made without any regard to their future consequences. The major examples are the legislation on social transfers and pensions, which in Italy are managed in a way that is both inequitable and expensive. When this legislation was passed, no prior thought had been given to demographic developments or the need to cover future expenditures with future revenues. This is particularly true in the case of the civil service—specifically, the measures relating to early retirement, salary increases, and creation of new employment.

It should be clear that in Italy there has never been any Keynesian "fine-tuning." Expenditure decisions have not been inspired by any Keynesian philosophy. Some form of fine-tuning was attempted on occasion, but it was always ineffective. The response to the short-lived recessions of the 1960s was the decision to increase investment expenditures; but these sums were never used for investment and were gradually appropriated for current expenditures. So there was nothing Keynesian about the policy.

This practice led to debt accumulation; if we look at the profile of the accumulation of nonmonetary debt, we can distinguish two periods. In the early 1970s total debt accumulated, but nonmonetary debt did not because of the high degree of monetary financing by the Treasury. Nonmonetary debt began to accumulate in 1977, continuing until 1979, and then again after 1981. As was pointed out in the paper by Bruni, Penati, and Porta, we passed from a situation in which the main factor in debt accumulation was the primary deficit to one in which the main factor was the self-generating aspect. The change was due to the fall in the growth rate and the increases in the interest rate and the stock of accumulated debt. The primary public sector borrowing requirement (PSBR) was around 6 percent until 1984–85. It has been halved since, although debt accumulation continues at a rate of 4 percentage points a year.

In the wake of these developments, there has been a growing awareness of the need to control expenditure. Now, what are the possible and conceivable ways to control expenditure? Here, the Italian debate has something in common with the American debate. First, there has been lot of talk about constitutional provisions or law enforcement along the lines of the the Gramm-Rudman-Hollings Act. We have, of course, an article in our Constitution that limits expenditure—Article 91, paragraph 4—which, in principle, should ensure the financing of additional expenditure by means of higher revenues.

My problem with new laws restraining legislative power or constitutional provisions is that governments and parliaments are normally very good at circumventing these restrictions. They are very good at underestimating future expenditures and overestimating revenues that should offset future expenditures. They are very good at window dressing. As has recently been pointed out, the U.S. Senate has learned the Italian lesson very well; consider, for example, the extent of window-dressing evident in recent provisions for cutting the budget. The Italian experience does not instill much confidence in these kinds of remedies, even though I think things could be improved, and there actually has been some improvement. I do not want to go into the details here, but we do have a law that could work more effectively and could restrain the legislative power a bit more.

Another possibility that has been debated is an increase of controls. By this I mean external auditing of expenditure bills. The dream of the good Italian parliamentarians who worry about the growth of expenditure is the creation of an entity equivalent to the U.S. Congressional Budget Office—that is, some kind of independent body that audits bills, in the sense of determining that there is no overestimation or underestimation of revenues or expenditures. This would help, of course. But I do not think it would be enough, because the worst part of the story in Parliament does not always happen with the bills, but with the amendments, which are approved on the spot. It is extremely difficult to have an auditing of amendments that are proposed at the last minute, either by the Government, or by the members of the Parliament.

Another topic that has caused serious debate is the possibility for a change in parliamentary procedures. Here I think something could be done. One of the major causes of the uncontrolled increasing expenditure in Italy has been the fact that expenditure bills can often be approved at the committee stage, without going to the floor of the House. At the committee stage, it is extremely easy to find compromises among various parties and to have a sort of club-sandwich bill, in which if I like the ham there is the ham, and if somebody likes the omelet, there is the omelet as well. I think that if the Parliament were to agree that expenditure bills should go directly to the floor of the House, these compromises would become more difficult to effect, and some element of restraint could be introduced. Another method would be to set a limit on the possibility of amending expenditure bills.

The third hotly debated issue at the moment is whether a secret vote should be allowed on expenditure laws and expenditure bills. In the Italian Parliament almost everything is voted on by secret ballot, so that the majority can easily become a minority, especially on matters concerning the budget.

All of these measures, or some combination of them, may be useful. But I have never been able to understand why people worry so much about inventing ways to constrain their own behavior, instead of behaving virtuously; I mean, if you want to be virtuous, all right, be virtuous, instead of going through a whole process of legislation to invent a constraint on your own behavior. The real point, I think, is the political will to do something; you can invent a number of ways to proceed, but there will always be some lack of effectiveness unless there is a political will to act.

The Italian case is complicated by two other difficulties, which are perhaps more substantial. The first one is the political system. As you well know, we have the most stable political system in the whole Western world. It does not matter if governments change every six months, or every two months. At the same time, this is a nonpolarized system, in the sense that all parties fish in the same large pool.

What we really have in the Parliament is a coalition. We do not have a great coalition government in the sense that it includes all parties. The parties in the government have always been the same: there is a kind of implicit understanding that there is at least one party that will never go into the government in the foreseeable future and another party that will always stay in the government in the foreseeable future. However, when I speak of parliamentary coalitions, I mean there can be a convergence of interests in legislating, which very often results in larger public expenditure.

The other difficulty arises from the employment situation, regional inequalities, and insufficient growth.

What I want to point out is that often we remain at the surface of the problem; we simply consider external ways of controlling expenditures, while the deeper troubles and deeper causes are not sufficiently considered. This is a very important issue and there is much good literature on the subject. It is often maintained that nonpermissive, tougher monetary policy would compel the

Treasury and the legislature to face their problems; whereas if they are always helped out of trouble, they will never face the stark reality, and they will never try to stick to the straight and narrow path. This view has much dignity and good theoretical support.[1] There are however some counterindications, concerning economic analysis or, if you wish, political theory.

One is the Sargent and Wallace story: the danger that if fiscal policy does not react in the expected way, you may end up in trouble. And you may end up in trouble in two cases: 1) if there is a limit to the amount of bonds agents are ready to hold, as in the Sargent-Wallace story; and 2) if there is a maximum accepted level of taxation, which is the Keynes story in his "Tract on Monetary Reform," where he talks about France.

The second possible objection is that the effectiveness of this prescription depends on the arguments of the loss function of the political agents. I really think that this point should be investigated a bit more carefully. In the theoretical literature, there is a central bank that only cares about inflation, and a government that cares little about inflation and much about employment. That is a very simplified story. I would surmise that since the 1970s, control of inflation has become dramatically important in the loss function of governments. The most valuable feather in a government's cap today is the claim: "I have brought down inflation." So if this is the case, I think governments could be perfectly happy with a tough central bank that shielded them from inflationary dangers even though the cost of this protection might be debt accumulation. They can go to the electorate and say: "When we came to power, inflation was 12 percent; now it is 5 percent." Debt accumulation has not been very important in the loss function of our politicians. It is a problem for the future. Probably they will not be in power when something happens. At the same time, everybody is happy with disposable income because of the interest paid on the public bonds. Those who maintain that tougher monetary policy and capital liberalization are good ways to provide an indirect incentive for controlling public expenditure should perhaps formalize their argument and try to model this issue with a different loss function from the one normally used in the theoretical literature, where this aspect of the problem is usually neglected.

However, the prescription I have discussed may be effective if tight monetary policy, capital liberalization, and other similar measures eventually precipitate a financial crisis, which may be the only way to force adjustment and may, thus, be a blessing in disguise.

Having begun with the Italian case, I shall end with it. As I said, in my view there has been some improvement. We have had a decline on the order of 2–3

---

[1]See Guido Tabellini, "Monetary and Fiscal Policy Coordination With a High Public Debt," in *High Public Debt: The Italian Experience*, ed. by Francesco Giavazzi and Luigi Spaventa (Cambridge: Cambridge University Press, 1988), pp. 90–126.

percentage points in our primary deficit. And if we look at the future, we can see that not much effort is really needed to stabilize debt growth. There is a large literature on tax smoothing that maintains that the level of debt is irrelevant, provided you stabilize it, wherever it is. This argument has some merits, although it neglects distributional aspects. In our case, to stabilize the debt ratio in a few years, given a difference between the interest rate and the growth rate of 2 percentage points, we need to achieve a primary surplus of some 1 percent of GDP, with a turnaround of 3–4 percentage points—not a terribly demanding task. However, the fact is that our expenditure structure is very rigid. Our primary expenditure/GDP ratio has remained steady at 44 percent, no matter what has been done: if some items have been reduced, others have grown—because of demographic factors in the case of pensions, as well as for a number of other reasons.

Therefore, I am not terribly optimistic about the possibility of reducing expenditure, even though our chairman here, Professor Baffi, is a member of the commission that is supposed to propose means to this end. I would surmise that of this turnaround of 3–4 percentage points, not more than 1 percentage point can be obtained through expenditure reduction; the rest will have to come from an increase in the fiscal burden. Here I think our governments are behaving very rashly, because they keep promising that the fiscal burden will remain unchanged; with our debt situation, this is impossible. Their political business should be to increase the fiscal burden not only by increasing tax rates, but also by enlarging the tax base. This is not only a technical problem but a political one. At this stage the effort is still possible and feasible. But let another three or four years elapse and we might find ourselves in serious trouble.

Gert Haller

I would like to return to the question of international coordination. I was expecting Professor Spaventa to give me some powerful arguments that would force me to defend the German position. Now he has left me rather alone, and I will have to try to start from a different point. I took part in this conference, and I listened very carefully to what was said by other participants. One point that I found puzzling, not only in this conference but also in other discussions, is the idea some people have of the Federal Republic of Germany as a strange country, a country where people do not want any growth, where people sitting at home watching television do not need anything else. I do not know anybody in Germany who does not want more goods, more services, and let's say, simply a better life.

This brings me to another point. If one discusses problems of growth in economic contexts and in conferences like this, one can gain the impression that the whole discussion focuses only on demand-management problems, in the sense that if Germany were to step up public spending or pursue an easier monetary policy and, by this means, increase total demand, everything would be fine. This is certainly a misleading point of view. Even if one approaches the question of faster growth from the supply-side view, it would still be only half of the truth, because supply-side economics implies that the government is able to remove obstacles. I think that is a half-truth, because growth is more than just having the management that helps us to reach aims. Growth is something that is in the mind of the people. Growth means being prepared to make a greater effort, to take risks and to be mobile, for example. And if, let's say, German steel-workers decide to reduce their working time from 40 hours a week to 35 hours and this is done through a democratic process, it has to be accepted, by Germany as well as by other countries, even if it leads to lower growth.

I'd like now to move closer to the field of economics. I tried to explain yesterday how far the economic adjustment process has come in Germany in the past few years. I tried to give figures on that and on the development of the current balance in real terms. The current balance has gone from a surplus of DM 82.5 billion in 1985 to about DM 36.5 billion in 1988. In relation to gross national product (GNP), this means a reduction in the current balance from 5.2 percent to 2.2 percent at a rate of 1 percentage point a year. This is quite a bit and should be taken into account if one talks about an adjustment process, especially focusing on Germany. I also said that a further reduction of the foreign surplus in the years through 1990–91 by 1 percent or 1.5 percent would mean that the internal demand had to rise by about 3.5 percent a year. I'm pretty sure that this cannot be achieved. It would imply growth beyond our present capacity and could easily lead to the danger of rekindling inflation. Moreover, if one asks Germany to increase internal demand in order to help the process of international adjustment, one has to refer to the instruments that could make this possible. In principle, on a macroeconomic level there are two instruments: monetary policy and fiscal policy.

As regards monetary policy—and this is an issue I face not as an economist but as an administrator in the government—far-ranging discussions have been, and still are, taking place in the board of the Bundesbank on whether monetary policy is already too expansionary in Germany. I personally have the impression that the present monetary situation in Germany could be described as a kind of liquidity trap, in the classical sense. Money demand in Germany is highly elastic; all the additional money is easily absorbed by individuals and enterprises. And in the present situation, it seems that long-term interest rates cannot be brought down appreciably below 6 percent in Germany—a limit that long-term interest rates have fallen short of only in a few periods. During the 1950s and the 1960s, when long-term interest rates were somewhere around 6 percent, people bought long-term government bonds. At the end of the 1970s, the long-term interest rates rose enormously, and people consequently lost part of their wealth.

Another consideration that points in this direction is that the interest curve is very steep in Germany. Money market rates are very low and the long-term rate does not go down. This is also normally an indicator for the expansionary stance of monetary policy. Of course, one can discuss the whole question in the framework of real interest rates, and the real interest rate in Germany, compared to the very low rate of inflation, is relatively high. This indicator would probably give another impression. In my opinion, it is a question of whether or not one talks about a liquidity trap or about which additional criteria have to be found to evaluate monetary policy in Germany.

The second important point is fiscal policy. It is probably well known that the budget deficit in Germany will rise sharply to about DM 40 billion this year, which is DM 10 billion more than originally planned. Of course, it is due to the fact that the Bundesbank profit will be zero this year, but it is also due to other factors. What is more important, and was stressed in Vito Tanzi's paper, is the question of the future burden that will fall on the public, since the German population is aging rapidly. This means a big burden for our social security system and for public finances.

The only question about expanding fiscal policy that could be discussed in Germany is whether it would or could be useful to bring the tax reform, which is planned for 1990, forward to 1989. You probably know that a part of this tax reform has already been brought forward to 1988 and has been added to the tax relief that had been decided for 1988. The amount has been raised from about DM 9 billion to about DM 14 billion. However, to answer the question, one has to know the German tax system, which is different from that of many other countries.

The Federal Republic of Germany is a federal state with strong individual states, each of which has extensive duties as far as education and public investment are concerned. Nearly half of public expenditure is effected by the states, whereas the tax system is nearly completely centralized. This means that all decisions on taxes are made by the central government, with far-reaching repercussions for the states. In the German tax system, the central government gives some amount of total tax revenues (income tax as well as value-added tax) to the states. But nearly every tax measure has to be agreed to by the states in the second house of parliament. This means that the Minister of Finance has to convince his colleagues from the states, which presents a lot of problems for the Federal Minister of Finance.

This point should be kept in mind when tax policy in Germany is being discussed.

Lord Roll of Ipsden

As you have suggested, Mr. Chairman, I have been on both sides of the barricades. At the moment I am on the same side as the so-called economic agents. So I will begin by speaking as an economic agent, particularly as one active in financial markets and in the financial services industry, but with an occasional glance across the barricade where I was some years ago. If you will turn a moment from the broad macroeconomic issues you have been considering for the past two days, I would like to emphasize that what concerns those in finance most as far as fiscal policy is concerned—and what, more than anything else, influences their day-to-day behavior—is the microeconomic aspect, the minutiae of fiscal policy.

Generally speaking, if you talk to someone in investment or commercial banking or securities and try to direct his attention to the raging debate on whether deficits do or do not matter, and whether deficits are responsible for crowding out or for high interest rates, you may hold his attention for 10 or 20 minutes, but he will soon move on to other concerns. For instance, he may ask you how the tax treatment of provisions for certain debts differs in different countries, or even in the same country—a subject that has become extremely important lately because of the enormous burden of sovereign debt and the involvement of commercial banks in it.

Another issue that directly concerns investment bankers is the question of capital ratios, about which there is increasing debate—again arising, at least in part, out of the growing concern over sovereign debt—and the attempt to coordinate differing national capital ratio systems and different types of banking.

Then there is the question of the tax treatment of exchange rate fluctuations. For example, in the United Kingdom, we treat losses on outward exchange rate transactions considerably differently from losses on inward transactions. And the repatriation of revenues derived from exchange rate transactions is often treated differently from the repatriation of profits from the same transactions. Another basic concern involves capital gains and corporation tax—two measures that were introduced by the Labour Government between 1963 and 1966. You may have read in the press that there has been great rejoicing in commodity trader circles in Paris, because the capital gains tax treatment of commodity trade was recently brought into line with that of other capital gains; hitherto, the treatment of commodity trade was much more severe and had caused a tremendous fall in such trade in Paris, compared to Tokyo, New York, and London.

All these examples are intended to make you aware that the economic agents—at any rate, those that I am familiar with—are much concerned with the minutiae of fiscal policy in its execution, whatever the broader concerns may be. However, having said that, I do not mean to ignore the other aspects of fiscal policy. It is quite clear that fiscal policy in its broadest application is perhaps the most potent instrument for affecting aggregate economic activity and growth and is thus of great concern to the operators in financial markets. And here I will turn to the still unresolved debate about the extent to which budget deficits do or do not matter and the perception of these problems in the minds of the economic agents, particularly in the financial services industries.

This question was at the center of an interesting debate in the columns of the *Financial Times* soon after "Black Monday"—the stock exchange crash on October 19, 1987—particularly in regard to the United States. One of the protagonists in that debate argued that it was really quite absurd to ascribe such importance to the U.S. budget deficit, when, as he put it, in relation to national income, it was similar in scale to the deficits of France and the United Kingdom, one half of that of Canada, and one quarter of that of Italy. I do not want to go into the intricacies of this argument (for example, whether these comparisons of ratios to national income really matter), but I can assure you that financial agents in the markets do not spend their days trying to discover whether the U.S. budget deficit has risen in relation to national income compared with that of Italy. What they are concerned about is the idea that has been drummed into them by some economic analysts—that the U.S. budget deficit does matter in one way or another; this explains why the haggling between the U.S. Executive and the Congress is followed with such interest in the financial markets. Thus, on days when there appears to be an optimistic view of the outcome, the market breathes a sign of relief; whereas, the next day if the view is pessimistic, the market will go down.

This seems to me to be something that economic analysis has not been, and perhaps never will be, able to cope with, but it does not exempt economic analysts from some responsibility. You remember Keynes's famous dictum: "The practical men who ignore theory are very often the victims of some defunct scribbler." Well, often they are also the victims of some very much alive scribbler, and therefore I think you should remember that what concerns them is the perception operators have of what analysts are trying to say.

Another participant in the debate in the *Financial Times* agreed that the attention paid to the budget deficit had been greatly exaggerated, but ended his article by saying, "But, of course, the perception of the markets is not unimportant." Indeed so! Let me just say that the concerns that are very properly expressed here (and I still remember enough about economics to share some of them) are not necessarily those that have the most influence on the behavior of markets.

There is a large area between the minutiae of tax treatment, on the one side, and the broader aspects, on the other; and that is the way economic analysis is reproduced in the minds of bankers, securities traders, brokers, investment bankers, and so on. This large area is much more difficult to analyze. For one thing, it contains the results of the mix of government policies at any one time, particularly fiscal and monetary policies. For instance, when I served in the first Wilson government—as an official, of course, not as a politician—we conducted a series of fiscal policy experiments, both microeconomic (the introduction of the capital gains tax and the corporation tax) and macroeconomic (an increase in personal income taxation, both on average and at the top end). I have not yet seen a totally satisfactory analysis of the macroeconomic policies of those years. I think that such an analysis would encounter some difficulty for two reasons. First, during those years, the mix of fiscal and monetary policy was very obscure, because at that time a major struggle was going on over which entity was the guardian of the monetary conscience, the Bank of England, on the one hand, or the government (that is, the Treasury), on the other. The composition of the mix that resulted from that continuing struggle between monetary and fiscal policy fluctuated throughout the period.

Second—and you referred briefly to this, Mr. Chairman—was that other important policy instruments were used that analytical economists regard as dubious, but which, unfortunately, politicians do from time to time resort to. These included incomes policy and what was called in those days "regional and industrial policy," which was in a curious way a Labour version of supply-side policy. It was really an attempt to influence the supply side of the economy, but with a much larger degree of government intervention and participation— ranging from providing subsidies to directing the location of industries—than would be tolerated or even dreamed of by our present government and many other governments. As a result, you did not get—and this, notoriously, is nearly always the case in our discipline—a controlled experiment. It was quite impossible to isolate the consequences of fiscal policy—at least in the medium and short term—from all the other things that were happening at the same time.

I offer you an example. One fiscal policy measure was introduced with the definite intention, backed by intensive economic analysis, of influencing growth and the engines of growth in the economy. This was the selective employment tax, which was a re-emphasis of the Verdoorn law—that manufacturing industry was really the engine of economic growth. Now, how do you change the balance between manufacturing industry and services? You put a selective employment tax on services. And that is what happened. As I said at the time, it shows how dangerous economics can really be when applied to policy, because what happened—and this was all that happened—was that the next day your haircut cost more.

One final word about financial operators as economic agents. The important factor in this relationship is the way in which fiscal and monetary policy interact. The fluctuating relationship between the fiscal and monetary policy instruments makes itself felt in the stock and foreign exchange markets and all markets connected with investment banking through interest rates and exchange rates. I leave it to the distinguished economists here to trace the path by which fiscal and monetary policy influence these two important rates. But this is really what the operator in the market is primarily concerned with.

A study by the Sanford Bernstein Institute in New York, which came out toward the end of 1987, correlates fluctuations in interest rates with fluctuations in the revenues and net profits of various investment banks. The study showed that there was some correlation, as you would expect, because a large part of investment banking's profits, or at any rate revenues, is dependent on the margin between different kinds of interest rates. But the correlation is sometimes difficult to identify; first of all, because there is always a time lag, and you can never be quite sure what kind of time lag to build into the correlation. Second, banks' revenues, particularly those of investment banks, come from many different sources, some of which are not directly, and perhaps not at all, dependent on interest rates—for example, advisory functions, mergers, and acquisitions.

These activities of banks that are not directly related to interest rate differentials, particularly mergers and acquisitions, deserve considerable further study. The growth in these activities is important not only for the investment banks themselves, but because of the way this growth has been brought about through changes in regulations, the liberalization of markets, the tremendous amount of liquidity that is being generated in international financial markets, and the ability now, thanks to globalization and securitization, to raise funds in a variety of ways that were never thought of five, let alone ten, years ago. This availability of finance and the different methods of financing mergers and acquisitions are extremely important new features in financial markets, and beyond that, in the flow of investment.

In your earlier sessions, you appear to have spent a good deal of time debating the pros and cons of Japanese acquisition of U.S. industry, which recalls to my mind a similar debate about the acquisition of European industry by the Americans in the earlier part of the postwar period. This new development, which I think is going to change the location of industry, the location of investment, the direction and volume of capital flows, and all the rest of it, has been brought about by some of the broader fiscal and monetary policy developments that you have been discussing for the last two days. But I do not think that the path these changes will follow is clear yet. I would suggest to you that another conference might well concern itself with this question: what are the ways in which the adoption by governments and central banks of these new concepts of fiscal and monetary policy—changes in regulation, deregulation, reregulation, new institutions, and eventually, liquidity and methods of financing—will affect such activities as mergers and acquisitions and the flow of capital and investment across international boundaries.

Concluding Remarks

Mario Monti

During these two-and-a-half days, our minds have been processing very remarkable material, in terms of both quantity and quality. We have heard addresses by the President of the Italian Senate and the Treasury Minister. Six papers have been presented. We have had 17 official discussions, numerous interventions in the debate, plus, this morning, an extremely stimulating panel discussion, steered by the masterly hands of Paolo Baffi. As moderator of the conference, I will confine myself to a few concluding reflections.

My main reaction is one of interest in the way in which the discussion deepened distinctively along two axes: (1) the interrelations among the three terms in the title of the conference—that is, *fiscal policy, economic adjustment,* and *financial markets*; and (2) issues relevant to *economic analysis, economic policy,* and *political economy*.

* * *

As was to be expected, an intensive discussion developed on the role and problems of *fiscal policy*. The discussion encompassed three interrelated topics:

1. *Fiscal policy at the domestic level.* (Of course, each of the papers in this category exhibited full awareness of the external influences.) This part of the analysis was organized around four carefully selected case studies: the United States (John Makin); Denmark (Claus Vastrup); Greece (J. Dutta and H.M. Polemarchakis); and Italy (Franco Bruni, Alessandro Penati, and Angelo Porta).

2. *Fiscal policy in the context of countries assisted by International Monetary Fund programs.* In this category, the issue of *conditionality* played a key role (Manuel Guitián).

3. *Fiscal policy in the context of international coordination* (Vito Tanzi).

The debate on coordination raised a number of issues, which in some cases flowed back into the discussion of the first two topics. Is coordination needed at all? What are its difficulties? What is the role of fiscal policy coordination versus monetary policy coordination and exchange rate coordination? What is the specific role of each combination of the three forms of coordination, at the domestic as well as at the international level? What should be the time frame for implementing coordination? What degree of activism is desirable? Should there be an explicit or implicit trigger mechanism to identify those conditions that alone justify the efforts and risks of coordination?

Some participants thought that coordination was both desirable and feasible only when economic activity was confronted with a serious crisis—as was the case in 1982—and not under more ordinary conditions.

Another question, following from the above discussion, was what part or dimension of fiscal policy should be coordinated—demand management or tax structure? The lengthy discussion on these issues led to a consideration of two subjects that went beyond the explicitly stated concerns of the conference— namely, economic integration in Europe, and the role of the Federal Republic of Germany. On the first topic, the issue of coordinating tax structures was raised in connection with the outcome of the internal market unification in the European Economic Community after 1992. On the role of Germany, some participants thought that that country's contribution to greater macroeconomic expansion should come more from structural adjustments, including changes in the tax system, than through adherence to external pressures for more courageous demand management through fiscal and monetary policies.

In the course of the discussions, the other two concerns of the conference— *economic adjustment* and *financial markets*—were taken into account. I found two developments particularly interesting. First, the concept of *fiscal policy* was enlarged to include inflation tax and implicit taxation through direct financial controls. Second, considerable attention was paid to the increasing importance of the interaction between *fiscal policy* and *financial markets*. Financial markets were not only considered to be the arena where ordinary debt-management policies work themselves out—with the classical conflicts between fiscal and monetary policies and between public and private users of finance—but they were also viewed as possibly the main vehicle for the working out of nonexplicit fiscal policies through the inflation tax and taxes from controls.

* * *

This brings me to the second axis—that is, the movement from *economic analysis* to *economic policies* (which I have already touched on), and from there to *political economy*.

The issues raised in the discussions on *economic analysis* can be grouped into at least five distinct groups of questions.

1. Do certain supposed phenomena *exist* at all? Discussion on this question centered on how the "inflationary fog" should or could be cleared from national and financial accounting. Not only the size, but, on occasion, the very existence of certain imbalances depends crucially on what procedure is followed.

2. What are the appropriate *concepts* and *measures*? A number of measures were discussed for correcting public sector imbalances, including the "zero-

inflation budget." Several measures for dealing with external imbalances were also discussed.

3. Are certain problems *really* problems? These discussions not only addressed peripheral problems, but others usually considered to be key problems. For example, more than one participant remarked that we may not be sure, after all, that current-account deficits, even ones that persist over several years, are necessarily a problem, unless they are associated with fiscal imbalances of some kind. Other participants clearly disagreed with this position.

4. Is the aspect that *really* matters the one that is normally *thought* to matter? For instance, some fiscal rules may comply with the intertemporal budget constraint and yet may not be sustainable. Conversely, some fiscal rules may be sustainable and yet violate the intertemporal constraint.

5. Are the phenomena in certain cases *qualitatively* different from the way we normally define them? A question raised in this context was whether certain uses of financial markets made by the authorities, as already hinted above, cannot or should not be considered a component of *fiscal*, rather than *financial*, policies.

The third topic along our second axis, *political economy*, received considerable attention. Public-choice arguments were explicitly taken up in some papers and discussions. There was not enough discussion of this, in my view, but there was much more than is usual in discussions about fiscal policy among general macroeconomists.

Public-choice arguments were considered on two levels—international coordination and the behavior of domestic public and private agents. Even constitutional themes crept into the debate and into the panel discussion—rightly so, in my view.

Another political economy issue raised was: Should "financial crises" be avoided at all costs, or should the emergence of a crisis be considered partly desirable if and when the underlying conditions that might generate a financial crisis can be perceived clearly by public opinion and policymakers? Elements of a potential theory of "repressed versus visible crises" could be discerned in the discussion of this question.

One interesting aspect of the discussions on political economy was the attempt on the part of several authors and participants to disentangle fiscal policy from monetary-financial policy. Most of the discussion centered on the case of Italy, but other countries and circumstances were also considered.

This problem of disentangling fiscal policies from monetary policies has institutional, if not constitutional, implications. For example—these are personal remarks, not intended to be a summary of the proceedings—it is not clear to me what the rationale is for requiring a finance minister to go to parliament to have explicit taxes approved, whereas a treasury minister or a central bank governor can levy implicit taxes on the economy by a simple decree or by a circular letter to the banks introducing portfolio constraints.

Of course, these issues, which pertain to the interrelationships between fiscal policy and financial markets, do have institutional implications. I dare take up just one of them in the presence of Governor Baffi. If one were to follow the line of reasoning that postulates a clearer separation between fiscal policy and monetary policy, as well as between the respective authorities, one could argue that a central bank should be given the powers (more fully and extensively than is presently the case, for example, in Italy) that are necessary for the conduct of monetary policy through indirect market-oriented methods. For example, the central bank should have the power not only to propose, but to set, the discount rate and to decide, based on its own judgment, the extent to which it is prepared to finance the Treasury. At the same time, however, and still following this line of reasoning, one could argue strongly for a reduction of certain other central bank powers: for example, in the case of Italy, the power to levy implicit taxes on economic agents through direct controls. A different view would be possible only if one believed that direct controls were strictly necessary for the conduct of monetary policy, and that the principle of "no taxation without representation" was perfectly implemented through representation by a central bank, rather than by an elected parliament.

A final issue in the political economy of financial markets and their relation to the budget process is the fundamental question of whether or not we want the financial markets to function better. In fact, if one were to take seriously the notion that what the public sector needs is more financial friction and less financial accommodation, one extreme implication would be that the worse the markets function in their handling of public debt, the greater the pressure on the public sector to contain its deficit.

I would not take that extreme view, but I think the discussion was certainly stimulated by the suggestion of one of the participants that we should inquire more deeply into the economics of transforming *thin* markets into *thick* markets. One other participant is presently actively engaged in improving the functioning of the secondary market for Treasury bonds in Italy. And references were made to the need to improve the functioning of the secondary market for bonds or other instruments representing the external debt of the developing countries. Now, I do not think there is any inconsistency between advocating an improvement in the functioning of markets for Treasury issues and calling for greater skill in the choice of appropriate types of Treasury securities, on the one hand, and supporting a substantial reduction in compulsory measures aimed at making financing of the Treasury easier, on the other.

Even normative issues were raised in the context of political economy: namely, should seigniorage be contained? should the inflation tax be given up?

should the hidden taxes from financial constraints be given up? My own impression is that, ultimately, these issues deal with what the role of economists should be. Should economists assist governments in devising new ways to maximize the amount of nonvisible taxation extracted from the economy, on the grounds that these forms of taxation are less painful? Or should economists help the public see what used to be invisible, to perceive what used not to be perceived?

I tend to share the latter view, and because the tradition of Italian public finance scholars was alluded to yesterday, I would like to quote from Amilcare Puviani's book of 1903, *Theory of Financial Illusion*. In an appendix entitled "Of Financial Disillusion," he compares direct and indirect taxes. His indirect taxes are very similar in nature to our hidden or implicit taxes. Puviani quotes a passage from Dupont de Nemours' *Cahier* presented to the *Etats Généraux*: "'The treacherous resource of indirect taxation must be avoided, it must be rejected as the greatest of evils; only through it can nations be eventually ruined . . . . Direct [that is, explicit] taxation makes most noise and irritates most. Precisely for this reason it is to be feared less and it is more consistent with freedom. It makes itself heard and generates complaints.' "[1]

I shall not comment specifically on the panel discussion held this morning. I would indeed be unable to add anything to Professor Baffi's remarks. May I simply express the view that from this discussion we have gained a deeper and more articulate perception of the difficulties, incentives, costs, and benefits— political as well as economic—through which fiscal policies have to make their way, and in which they may well be trapped from time to time. May I suggest that this more articulate perception is not usually supplied by many academic conferences on fiscal policy.

As a final reflection, I think an observation applies to this conference that was made in our Aula Magna in October 1977 by Professor Baffi in his intervention at the "Raffaele Mattioli Lecture" given by Professor Franco Modigliani. According to the record of the proceedings, Baffi, who was then the Governor of Banca d'Italia, "stressed that he wanted to address himself to points of analysis, rather than policy. This should not surprise the audience since, as academics rightly tried to draw conclusions from their analyses in terms of rules for economic policy, he, as a policy maker, was trying with equal validity, he thought, to discover the analytical roots of his actions."[2]

---

[1]Amilcare Puviani, *La teoria dell'illusione finanziaria* (Palermo: Sandron, 1903). Reprinted in *Teoria della illusione finanziaria*, ed. by Franco Volpi (Milan: ISEDI, 1973), p. 247 (English translation by the author).

[2]Franco Modigliani, *The Debate Over Stabilization Policy* (Cambridge: Cambridge University Press, 1986), p. 178.

May I conclude by saying that this theme has to some extent also characterized our own discussions during this conference. It would not be inappropriate to say that we have had a seminar in political economy, with some shifting of roles between the analysts and the policymakers.

Biographical Sketches
of Participants

Mario Arcelli
Professor of Economic Policy, director of the Institute of Economics, and member of the Board of Directors of the University of Padua. Also holds the chair of Monetary Economics at the University of Rome. Served in various public administrative capacities, including economic adviser to two Italian Prime Ministers and member of the Italian Delegation at Group of Seven summits.

Ricardo Arriazu
Consultant to the United Nations, Organization of American States, Economic Commission for Latin America and the Caribbean, the World Bank, and several financial institutions. Previously an Alternate Executive Director at the International Monetary Fund (1968–74); Deputy to the Committee for the Reform of the International Monetary System and the Group of Twenty and the Group of Twenty-Four.

Giorgio Basevi
Professor of International Economics at the University of Bologna. Previously an economist with the Commission of the European Communities; Professor at the Université Catholique de Louvain, Belgium; Visiting Professor at the University of Chicago, Université de Montréal, The Johns Hopkins University, and Brown University. Member of the editorial board of several journals, including *European Economic Review, Empirical Economics*, and *Politica Economica*.

Charles Bean
Reader in Economics at the London School of Economics and Political Science, Research Fellow at the Centre for Economic Policy Research in London, and Managing Editor of *Review of Economic Studies*. Undergraduate degree from Cambridge University, and doctorate from Massachusetts Institute of Technology.

Franco Bruni
Professor of Economic and Financial Policy at the University of Brescia; and Professor of International Monetary Theory and Policy at the Universitá Commerciale Luigi Bocconi and Director of the Master's Program in International Economics and Management. Participant in government-appointed commissions

to study the Italian credit and financial systems and author of several publications on macroeconomics, banking, and monetary economics.

Christian de Boissieu
Professor at the University of Paris-I (Panthéon-Sorbonne), consultant to the World Bank and the European Commission, and economic adviser to the Paris Chamber of Commerce and Industry. Previously visiting scholar at the University of Minnesota and the Board of Governors of the Federal Reserve System in Washington, D.C. Author and editor of several publications on monetary analysis and policy.

Rudiger Dornbusch
Professor at the Massachusetts Institute of Technology since 1977. Has also taught at the University of Chicago and the University of Rochester and was Visiting Professor at the Fundacão, Getulio Vargas in Rio de Janeiro.

J. Dutta
Teaches at Barnard College, Columbia University, New York. Received her Ph.D. in Economics from the Delhi School of Economics.

Nicholas C. Garganas
Director and Adviser of the Economic Research Department, Bank of Greece. Previously Chief Economic Adviser, Ministry of National Economy; member of the Monetary Committee of the European Communities; Head of the Research Department, Agricultural Bank of Greece; and joint managing editor of the *Greek Economic Review*.

Augusto Graziani
Professor of Economic Policy at the University of Naples, consulting editor of the *Journal of Economic Literature*, editor of *Studi economici*, and member of "Accademia Nazionale dei Lincei." Previously vice-president of the Italian Economic Society; and Visiting Professor at the University of Birmingham (United Kingdom), University of Michigan (United States), and Université de Dijon (France).

Manuel Guitián
Deputy Director in the European Department and previously in the Exchange and Trade Relations Department of the International Monetary Fund. Author of a variety of articles on monetary and international economics as well as on Fund policies. Holds a Ph.D. in Economics from the University of Chicago.

Gert Haller
Deputy department head, Fiscal Policy Department at the German Federal Ministry of Finance, Federal Republic of Germany.

Jorge Braga de Macedo

Professor of Economics at New University of Lisbon. Currently with Commission of the European Communities, Directorate-General for Economic and Financial Affairs.

John H. Makin

Directs fiscal policy studies at the American Enterprise Institute, Washington, D.C. Also co-manages an investment advisory service. Served as consultant to the U.S. Treasury, the Federal Reserve Board, the International Monetary Fund, the U.S. Congressional Budget Office, and the Bank of Japan. Writes frequently for major newspapers, including the *Wall Street Journal* and the *Financial Times*. Holds M.A. and Ph.D. degrees in Economics from the University of Chicago.

Patrick Minford

Edward Gonner Professor of Applied Economics at the University of Liverpool. Previously Economic Adviser, Ministry of Finance, Malawi; Economic Adviser, Ministry of Overseas Development; Economic Adviser to H.M. Treasury's External Division; and editor, *Review of National Institute for Economic and Social Research*. Author of several publications on monetary economics and the international economy.

Giancarlo Morcaldo

Director of Public Finance Section in the Research Department, Bank of Italy. Author of several papers on public expenditure and debt, focusing on crowding-out and forecasting models for the budget deficit and pension schemes. Member of various advisory committees to the Italian Government in the area of public finance.

Antonio Pedone

Professor of Public Finance at the University of Rome and Economic Adviser to the Minister of the Treasury. Previously Economic Adviser to the Italian Prime Minister and an economist in the Fiscal Affairs Department of the International Monetary Fund. Author of several publications on the economics of taxation, public expenditure, and macroeconomic policy.

Alessandro Penati

Head of Research at Akros Finanziaria, Milan, and Adjunct Professor at Università Commerciale Luigi Bocconi. Previously an economist in the Research Department of the International Monetary Fund and Assistant Professor of Finance at the Wharton School of the University of Pennsylvania. Author of several publications on international monetary and financial economics.

H.M. Polemarchakis
Teaches at the Graduate School of Business, Columbia University, New York. Previously Director of the Center of Planning and Economic Research, Athens. Received his Ph.D. in Economics from Harvard University.

Angelo Porta
Professor of Economics at the University of Genoa and Universitá Commerciale Luigi Bocconi and Deputy Director of the Centro di Economia monetaria e finanziaria. Previously Associate Professor at the University of Trento and author of several publications on monetary theory and policy and macroeconomics.

Richard Portes
Director of the Centre for Economic Policy Research, London; Professor of Economics at Birkbeck College, University of London; and Director d'Etudes Associé at the Ecole des Hautes Etudes en Sciences Sociales, Paris. Previously taught at Princeton University and Harvard University. Has written on sovereign borrowing and debt, central planning, and East-West economic relations. Co-chairman of the Board and a senior editor of *Economic Policy*.

Carlo Santini
Head of the Research Department, Bank of Italy since 1985. Previously head of the Foreign Department, Bank of Italy. Graduated from University of Naples.

Claus Vastrup
Professor at the University of Aarhus, Denmark, and Chairman of the Economic Council. Previously economist at the Central Bank of Denmark. Holds degrees in Economics from the University of Copenhagen.

Vito Tanzi
Director of the Fiscal Affairs Department at the International Monetary Fund. Previously a consultant for the World Bank, the United Nations, the Organization of American States, and the Stanford Research Institute. Has published widely in the field of public finance, monetary theory, and macroeconomics, and, more recently, the underground economy, fiscal deficits, the determination of interest rates, and economic coordination.

Charles Wyplosz
Professor of Economics at INSEAD, Fountainbleau, and at the Ecole des Hautes Etudes en Sciences Sociales, Paris. Managing Editor of *Economic Policy* and Research Fellow of the Centre for Economic Policy Research, London. Serves on the Board of Editors of the *European Economic Review* and the *Annales d'Economie et de Statistique*.

Salvatore Zecchini
Special Counselor for Economic Affairs at the Organization for Economic Cooperation and Development. Previously Executive Director at the International Monetary Fund (1984–89); Director of the Research Department, Bank of Italy; economic adviser to the Italian Prime Minister and the Minister of the Treasury, Minister for Agriculture, and Minister for Coordination of European Community Policies. Author of several publications on economic and financial subjects.

List of Participants and Observers

Moderator

Mario Monti
Centro di Economia monetaria e finanziaria,
Università Commerciale Luigi Bocconi

Authors

Franco Bruni
Centro di Economia monetaria e finanziaria,
Università Commerciale Luigi Bocconi
J. Dutta
Columbia University
Manuel Guitián
International Monetary Fund
John H. Makin
American Enterprise Institute
Alessandro Penati
Centro di Economia monetaria e finanziaria,
Università Commerciale Luigi Bocconi
H.M. Polemarchakis
Columbia University
Angelo Porta
Centro di Economia monetaria e finanziaria,
Università Commerciale Luigi Bocconi
Vito Tanzi
International Monetary Fund
Claus Vastrup
Aarhus University

Discussants

Mario Arcelli
University of Rome

Ricardo Arriazu
Consultant, various financial institutions
Giorgio Basevi
Università degli Studi
Charles Bean
London School of Economics
Christian de Boissieu
Université de Paris-I (Panthéon-Sorbonne)
Rudiger Dornbusch
Massachusetts Institute of Technology
Nicholas C. Garganas
Bank of Greece
Augusto Graziani
University of Naples
Gert Haller
German Federal Ministry of Finance
Jorge Braga de Macedo
Commission of the European Communities
and New University of Lisbon
Patrick Minford
University of Liverpool
Giancarlo Morcaldo
Bank of Italy
Antonio Pedone
University of Rome
Richard Portes
Centre for Economic Policy Research
Carlo Santini
Bank of Italy
Charles Wyplosz
European Institute for Business Administration
Salvatore Zecchini
Organization for Economic Cooperation and Development

Panelists

Paolo Baffi, Chairman
Honorary Governor of the Bank of Italy
Ricardo Arriazu
Consultant, various financial institutions

Gert Haller
  German Federal Ministry of Finance
Lord Roll of Ipsden
  S.G. Warburg and Group plc
Luigi Spaventa
  University of Rome
John Vanderveken
  International Confederation of Free Trade Unions

Observers

Samuel Brittan
  Financial Times
Ottorino Beltrami
  Associazione Industriale Lombarda
Innocenzo Cipolletta
  Confindustria
Fabrizio Galimberti
  Il Sole-24 Ore
Reinhold Gemperle
  Neue Zuercher Zeitung
Carl Gewirtz
  International Herald Tribune
Felice Gianani
  Associazone Bancaria Italiana
Francesco Giavazzi
  University of Bologna
Luigi Guatri
  Università Commerciale Luigi Bocconi
Elmar Kowalski
  Süddeutsche Zeitung
Riccardo Franco Levi
  Il Corriere della Sera
Dimitris Maroulis
  Center for Planning and Economic Research
Elena Polidori
  La Repubblica
Stephen Pursey
  International Confederation of Free Trade Unions
Riccardo Rovelli
  Centro di Economia monetaria e finanziaria,
  Università Commerciale Luigi Bocconi

Emilio Sacerdoti
 International Monetary Fund
Hans-Eckart Scharrer
 HWWA-Institut für Wirtschaftsforschung
Giacomo Vaciago
 University of Ancona

Conference Coordinator

Hellmut Hartmann
 International Monetary Fund

Fiscal Policy, Economic Adjustment, and Financial Markets

Designed and composed by the Composition Unit of the International Monetary Fund.

The text was set using Linotype Century Old Style and tabular matter was set in Oliver Light.

Cover design by Sanaa Elaroussi.
The cover type is Revue and Lucida.

Printed and bound by Kirby Lithographic Company in Arlington, Virginia, U.S.A.